KU-112-736

THE BIBLE

OLD TESTAMENT

God the Father Enthroned from the Polyptych of the Apocalypse *by Jacopo Alberequo*

THE BIBLE

OLD TESTAMENT

ILLUSTRATED SELECTIONS

EBURY PRESS

First published 1994

1 3 5 7 9 10 8 6 4 2

Selected and edited by Joanne Cracknell
Designed by David Fordham
Picture research by Philippa Lewis

First published in the United Kingdom in 1994 by
Ebury Press Limited
Random House, 20 Vauxhall Bridge Road, London SW1V 2SA

Random House Australia (Pty) Limited
20 Alfred Street, Milsons Point, Sydney,
New South Wales 2061, Australia

Random House New Zealand Limited
18 Poland Road, Glenfield
Auckland 10, New Zealand

Random House South Africa (Pty) Limited
PO Box 337, Bergvlei, South Africa

Random House UK Limited Reg. No 954009

A CIP catalogue record for this book
is available from the British Library

ISBN 0 09 178364 X
Printed in Singapore by Tien Wah Press

THE BIBLE

OLD TESTAMENT

Contents

Acknowledgements

Archiv für Kunst und Geschichte 14 (Prado), 15 (Gemaldegalerie, Dresden)
Bridgeman Art Library 23, 28 (Kunsthistorisches Museum, Vienna), 29, 58 (Fitzwilliam Museum, Cambridge), 70 (St. Peter's Leuven), 98 (The British Library), 119 (York City Art Gallery), 146 (National Gallery of Art, Washington), 157 (Kunsthistorisches Museum, Vienna), 174 (Uffizi), 195 (St. Peter's Leuven), 203, 207, 223 (Gemaldegalerie, Berlin), 247 (Hôtel Dieu, Beaune), 250, 251 (Gemaldegalerie, Kassel), 259, 274 (Museo di San Marco, Florence), 286 (The British Library), 295 (Hôtel Dieu, Beaune), 311 (Fitzwilliam Museum, Cambridge), 314 (Galleria dell'Accademia, Florence), 319 (Musées Royaux des Beaux-Arts, Brussels), 326 (Prado), 331 (Tate Gallery), 347 (Uffizi)
Christie's Images 17, 19, 26, 38, 50, 143, 148, 182, 279, 298, 334
E. T. Archive 10 (Sucevita Monastery), 150 (Brera, Milan)
Fine Art Museum, Ghent 290
Frans Hals Museum, Haarlem 271
Getty Museum, Malibu 131
Giraudon 32 (Musée d'Art and d'Histoire, St. Germain-en-Laye), 35 (The Hermitage), 42 (Musée des Beaux-Arts, Orléans), 102 (Musée des Beaux-Arts, Nîmes), 134 (Musée des Beaux-Arts, Rouen), 138 (Louvre), 142 (Musée des Beaux Arts, Dunkirk), 160 (Musée Cluny, Paris), 167 (Museo Correr, Venice), 179 (Musée Condé, Chantilly), 187 (Ecole des Beaux-Arts, Paris), 214, 231 (Galleria dell'Accademia,

Florence), 234 (Musée des Augustins, Toulouse), 238 (Musée Condé, Chantilly), 338 (Musée Condé, Chantilly).

Giraudon/Bridgeman Art Library 24 (Musée des Beaux-Arts, Valenciennes), 43 (Musée des Beaux-Arts, Rouen), 46 (Musée des Beaux-Arts, Nancy), 62 (National Gallery of Art, Washington), 63 (Musée Nationale, Compiègne), 107 (Bibliothèque Nationale, Paris), 171 (Musée des Beaux-Arts, Quimper), 254 (Musée des Beaux-Arts, Nantes), 283 (Musee Condé, Chantilly), 303 (Musée des Beaux-Arts, Nantes).

Kunsthistorische Museum, Vienna 123

Museo Civico, Bassano del Grappa 331

National Gallery, London 67

National Gallery of Art, Washington 202

North Carolina Museum of Art, Raleigh 114

Her Majesty The Queen 191

Rijksmuseum, Amsterdam 156, 203

Scala 11 (Vatican Museums), 21 (Vatican Museums), 30 (Vatican Museums), 66 (Uffizi), 78 (Vatican Museums), 83 (Vatican Museums), 86 (Vatican Museums), 91 (Vatican Museums), 94 (Vatican Museums), 111 (Vatican Museums), 114 (Vatican Museums), 186 (Vatican Museums), 151 (Vatican Museums), 155 (Louvre), 163 (Vatican Museums), 219, 263 (Vatican Museums), 307 (Vatican Museums).

Wallraf-Richarz Museum, Cologne 242

Chapters & Verses FROM THE FIRST BOOK OF MOSES CALLED GENESIS

THE CREATION • ADAM AND EVE • THE FALL • CAIN AND ABEL • NOAH BUILDS THE ARK • THE FLOOD • THE BOW OF THE COVENANT • THE TOWER OF BABEL • THE CALL OF ABRAM • GOD'S COVENANT WITH ABRAM • THE THREE VISITORS • THE BIRTH OF ISAAC • GOD TRIES ABRAHAM'S FAITH • ISAAC AND REBEKAH • JACOB AND ESAU • JACOB GETS ESAU'S BLESSING • JACOB'S DREAM AT BETHEL • THE DEATH OF ISAAC • JOSEPH'S DREAMS • JOSEPH SOLD INTO EGYPT • JOSEPH AND POTIPHAR'S WIFE • JOSEPH INTERPRETS DREAMS • PHARAOH'S DREAMS • JOSEPH AND HIS BRETHREN • JOSEPH MAKES HIMSELF KNOWN

Genesis

The Creation

Chapter 1

IN THE BEGINNING GOD CREATED THE HEAVEN AND the earth. [2]And the earth was without form, and void; and darkness was upon the face of the deep. And the spirit of God moved upon the face of the waters.

[3]And God said, "Let there be light": and there was light. [4]And God saw the light, that it was good: and God divided the light from the darkness. [5]And God called the light

THE CREATION OF THE ANIMALS *by an unknown artist*

GOD MAKING THE FIRMAMENT, *School of Raphael*

Day, and the darkness he called Night. And the evening and the morning were the first day.

[6]And God said, "Let there be a firmament in the midst of the waters, and let it divide the waters from the waters." [7]And God made the firmament, and divided the waters which were under the firmament from the waters which were above the firmament: and it was so. [8]And God called the firmament Heaven. And the evening and the morning were the second day.

[9]And God said, "Let the waters under the heaven be gathered together unto one place, and let the dry land appear": and it was so. [10]And God called the dry land Earth; and the gathering together of the waters called he Seas: and God saw that it was good.

[11]And God said, "Let the earth bring forth grass, the herb yielding seed, and the fruit tree yielding fruit after his kind, whose seed is in itself, upon the earth": and it was so. [12]And the earth brought forth grass, and herb yielding seed after his kind, and the tree yielding fruit, whose seed was in

itself, after his kind: and God saw that it was good. [13]And the evening and the morning were the third day.

[14]And God said, "Let there be lights in the firmament of the heaven to divide the day from the night; and let them be for signs, and for seasons, and for days, and years: [15]and let them be for lights in the firmament of the heaven to give light upon the earth": and it was so. [16]And God made two great lights; the greater light to rule the day, and the lesser light to rule the night: he made the stars also. [17]And God set them in the firmament of the heaven to give light upon the earth, [18]and to rule over the day and over the night, and to divide the light from the darkness: and God saw that it was good. [19]And the evening and the morning were the fourth day.

[20]And God said, "Let the waters bring forth abundantly the moving creature that hath life, and fowl that may fly above the earth in the open firmament of heaven." [21]And God created great whales, and every living creature that moveth, which the waters brought forth abundantly, after their kind, and every winged fowl after his kind: and God saw that it was good. [22]And God blessed them, saying, "Be fruitful, and multiply, and fill the waters in the seas, and let fowl multiply in the earth." [23]And the evening and the morning were the fifth day.

[24]And God said, "Let the earth bring forth the living creature after his kind, cattle, and creeping thing, and beast of the earth after his kind": and it was so. [25]And God made the beast of the earth after his kind, and cattle after their kind, and every thing that creepeth upon the earth after his kind: and God saw that it was good.

[26]And God said, "Let us make man in our image, after our likeness: and let them have dominion over the fish of the sea, and over the fowl of the air, and over the cattle, and over all the earth, and over every creeping thing that creepeth upon the earth." [27]So God created man in his own image, in the image of God created he him; male and female created he them. [28]And God blessed them, and God said unto them, "Be fruitful, and multiply, and replenish the earth, and subdue it: and have dominion over the fish of the sea, and over the fowl of the air, and over every living thing that moveth upon the earth."

Chapter 1

[29]And God said, "Behold, I have given you every herb bearing seed, which is upon the face of all the earth, and every tree, in the which is the fruit of a tree yielding seed; to you it shall be for meat. [30]And to every beast of the earth, and to every fowl of the air, and to every thing that creepeth upon the earth, wherein there is life, I have given every green herb for meat": and it was so.

[31]And God saw every thing that he had made, and, behold, it was very good. And the evening and the morning were the sixth day.

Chapter 2

THUS THE HEAVENS AND THE EARTH WERE FINISHED, AND all the host of them. [2]And on the seventh day God ended his work which he had made; and he rested on the seventh day from all his work which he had made. [3]And God blessed the seventh day, and sanctified it: because that in it he had rested from all his work which God created and made.

ADAM AND EVE

Chapter 2

THESE ARE THE GENERATIONS OF THE HEAVENS and of the earth when they were created, in the day that the LORD God made the earth and the heavens, [5]and every plant of the field before it was in the earth, and every herb of the field before it grew: for the LORD God had not caused it to rain upon the earth, and there was not a man to till the ground. [6]But there went up a mist from the earth, and watered the whole face of the ground. [7]And the LORD God formed man of the dust of the ground, and breathed into his nostrils the breath of life; and man became a living soul.

[8]And the LORD God planted a garden eastward in Eden; and there he put the man whom he had formed. [9]And out of the ground made the LORD God to grow every tree that is

pleasant to the sight, and good for food; the tree of life also in the midst of the garden, and the tree of knowledge of good and evil.

Chapter 2

[10]And a river went out to Eden to water the garden; and from thence it was parted, and became into four heads. [11]The name of the first is Pison: that is it which compasseth the whole land of Havilah, where there is gold; [12]and the

Above: GARDEN OF PARADISE AND THE FALL *by Lucas Cranach; facing page* THE GARDEN OF PARADISE *by Hieronymous Bosch*

gold of that land is good: there is bdellium and the onyx stone. [13]And the name of the second river is Gihon: the same is it that compasseth the whole land of Ethiopia. [14]And the name of the third river is Hiddekel: that is it which goeth toward the east of Assyria. And the fourth river is Euphrates.

Chapter 2

[15]And the LORD God took the man, and put him into the garden of Eden to dress it and to keep it. [16]And the LORD God commanded the man, saying, "Of every tree of the garden thou mayest freely eat: [17]but of the tree of the knowledge of good and evil, thou shalt not eat of it: for in the day that thou eatest thereof thou shalt surely die."

[18]And the LORD God said, "It is not good that the man should be alone; I will make him an help meet for him."

Chapter 2

[19]And out of the ground the LORD God formed every beast of the field, and every fowl of the air; and brought them unto Adam to see what he would call them: and whatsoever Adam called every living creature, that was the name thereof. [20]And Adam gave names to all cattle, and to the fowl of the air, and to every beast of the field; but for Adam there was not found an help meet for him.

[21]And the LORD God caused a deep sleep to fall upon Adam, and he slept: and he took one of his ribs and closed up the flesh instead thereof; [22]and the rib, which the LORD God had taken from man, made he a woman, and brought her unto the man.

[23]And Adam said, "This is now bone of my bones, and flesh of my flesh: she shall be called Woman, because she was taken out of Man." [24]Therefore shall a man leave his father and his mother, and shall cleave unto his wife: and they shall be one flesh.

[25]And they were both naked, the man and his wife, and were not ashamed.

THE FALL

Chapter 3

NOW THE SERPENT WAS MORE SUBTIL THAN any beast of the field which the LORD God had made. And he said unto the woman, "Yea, hath God said, 'Ye shall not eat of every tree of the garden'?"

[2]And the woman said unto the serpent, "We may eat of the fruit of the trees of the garden: [3]but of the fruit of the tree which is in the midst of the garden, God hath said, 'Ye shall not eat of it, neither shall ye touch it, lest ye die.' "

[4]And the serpent said unto the woman, "Ye shall not surely die: [5]for God doth know that in the day ye eat thereof, then your eyes shall be opened, and ye shall be as gods, knowing good and evil."

[6]And when the woman saw that the tree was good for food, and that it was pleasant to the eyes, and a tree to be desired to make one wise, she took of the fruit thereof, and did eat, and gave also unto her husband with her; and he

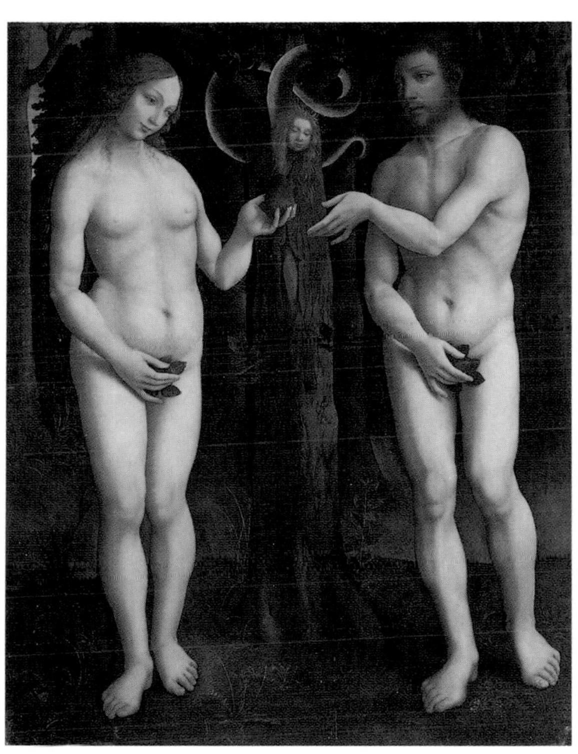

THE TEMPTATION OF ADAM *by the Master of Lucretia*

did eat. [7]And the eyes of them both were opened, and they knew that they were naked; and they sewed fig leaves together, and made themselves aprons.

[8]And they heard the voice of the LORD God walking in the garden in the cool of the day: and Adam and his wife hid themselves from the presence of the LORD God amongst the trees of the garden. [9]And the LORD God called unto Adam, and said unto him, "Where art thou?"

[10]And he said, "I heard thy voice in the garden, and I was afraid, because I was naked; and I hid myself."

[11]And he said, "Who told thee that thou wast naked? Hast thou eaten of the tree, whereof I commanded thee that thou shouldest not eat?"

[12]And the man said, "The woman whom thou gavest to be with me, she gave me of the tree, and I did eat."

[13]And the LORD God said unto the woman, "What is this that thou hast done?"

And the woman said, "The serpent beguiled me, and I did eat."

[14]And the LORD God said unto the serpent, "Because thou hast done this, thou art cursed above all cattle, and above every beast of the field; upon thy belly shalt thou go, and dust shalt thou eat all the days of thy life: [15]and I will put enmity between thee and the woman, and between thy seed and her seed; it shall bruise thy head, and thou shalt bruise his heel."

[16]Unto the woman he said, "I will greatly multiply thy sorrow and thy conception; in sorrow thou shalt bring forth children; and thy desire shall be to thy husband, and he shall rule over thee."

[17]And unto Adam he said, "Because thou hast hearkened unto the voice of thy wife, and hast eaten of the tree, of which I commanded thee, saying, 'Thou shalt not eat of it': cursed is the ground for thy sake; in sorrow shalt thou eat of it all the days of thy life; [18]thorns also and thistles shall it bring forth to thee; and thou shalt eat the herb of the field; [19]in the sweat of thy face shalt thou eat bread, till thou return unto the ground; for out of it wast thou taken: for dust thou art, and unto dust shalt thou return."

[20]And Adam called his wife's name Eve; because she was the mother of all living.

[21]Unto Adam also and to his wife did the LORD God make coats of skins, and clothed them. [22]And the LORD God said, "Behold, the man is become as one of us, to know good and evil: and now, lest he put forth his hand, and take also of the tree of life, and eat, and live for ever": [23]Therefore the LORD God sent him forth from the garden of Eden, to till the ground from whence he was taken. [24]So he drove out the man; and he placed at the east of the garden of Eden Cherubims, and a flaming sword which turned every way, to keep the way of the tree of life.

Cain and Abel

Chapter 4

AND ADAM KNEW EVE HIS WIFE; AND SHE CONceived, and bare Cain, and said, "I have gotten a man from the LORD." [2]And she again bare his brother Abel.

And Abel was a keeper of sheep, but Cain was a tiller of the ground. [3]And in process of time it came to pass, that Cain brought of the fruit of the ground an offering unto the LORD. [4]And Abel, he also brought of the firstlings of his flock and of the fat thereof. And the LORD had respect unto Abel and to his offering: [5]but unto

ADAM AND EVE MOURNING THE DEATH OF ABEL *by Paolo de Matteis*

Chapter 4

Cain and to his offering he had not respect. And Cain was very wroth, and his countenance fell.

[6]And the LORD said unto Cain, "Why art thou wroth? and why is thy countenance fallen? [7]If thou doest well, shalt thou not be accepted? and if thou doest not well, sin lieth at the door. And unto thee shall be his desire, and thou shalt rule over him."

[8]And Cain talked with Abel his brother: and it came to pass, when they were in the field, that Cain rose up against Abel his brother, and slew him.

[9]And the LORD said unto Cain, "Where is Abel thy brother?"

And he said, "I know not: am I my brother's keeper?"

[10]And he said, "What hast thou done? The voice of thy brother's blood crieth unto me from the ground. [11]And now art thou cursed from the earth, which hath opened her mouth to receive thy brother's blood from thy hand; [12]when thou tillest the ground, it shall not henceforth yield unto thee her strength; a fugitive and a vagabond shalt thou be in the earth."

[13]And Cain said unto the LORD, "My punishment is greater than I can bear. [14]Behold, thou hast driven me out this day from the face of the earth; and from thy face shall I be hid; and I shall be a fugitive and a vagabond in the earth; and it shall come to pass, that every one that findeth me shall slay me."

[15]And the LORD said unto him, "Therefore whosoever slayeth Cain, vengeance shall be taken on him sevenfold." And the LORD set a mark upon Cain, lest any finding him should kill him. [16]And Cain went out from the presence of the LORD, and dwelt in the land of Nod, on the east of Eden . . .

Chapter 4

[25]And Adam knew his wife again; and she bare a son, and called his name Seth: "For God", said she, "hath appointed me another seed instead of Abel, whom Cain slew."

[26]And to Seth, to him also there was born a son; and he called his name Enos: then began men to call upon the name of the LORD.

Noah Builds the Ark

Chapter 6

THESE ARE THE GENERATIONS OF NOAH: Noah was a just man and perfect in his generations, and Noah walked with God. [10]And Noah begat three sons, Shem, Ham, and Japheth.

[11]The earth also was corrupt before God, and the earth was filled with violence. [12]And God looked upon the earth, and, behold, it was corrupt; for all flesh had corrupted his way upon the earth. [13]And God said unto Noah, "The end of all flesh is come before me; for the earth is filled with violence through them; and, behold, I will destroy them with the earth. [14]Make thee an ark of gopher wood; rooms shalt thou make in the ark, and shalt pitch it within and without with pitch. [15]And this is the fashion which thou shalt make it of: The length of the ark shall be three hundred cubits, the breadth of it fifty cubits, and the height of it thirty cubits. [16]A window shalt thou make to the ark,

BUILDING THE ARK, *School of Raphael*

Chapter 6

and in a cubit shalt thou finish it above; and the door of the ark shalt thou set in the side thereof; with lower, second, and third stories shalt thou make it. [17]And, behold, I, even I, do bring a flood of waters upon the earth, to destroy all flesh, wherein is the breath of life, from under heaven; and every thing that is in the earth shall die. [18]But with thee will I establish my covenant; and thou shalt come into the ark, thou, and thy sons, and thy wife, and thy sons' wives with thee. [19]And of every living thing of all flesh, two of every sort shalt thou bring into the ark, to keep them alive with thee; they shall be male and female. [20]Of fowls after their kind, and of cattle after their kind, of every creeping thing of the earth after his kind, two of every sort shall come unto thee, to keep them alive. [21]And take thou unto thee of all food that is eaten, and thou shalt gather it to thee; and it shall be for food for thee, and for them."

[22]Thus did Noah; according to all that God commanded him, so did he.

The Flood

Chapter 7

In the six hundredth year of Noah's life, in the second month, the seventeenth day of the month, the same day were all the fountains of the great deep broken up, and the windows of heaven were opened. [12]And the rain was upon the earth forty days and forty nights.

[13]In the selfsame day entered Noah, and Shem, and Ham, and Japheth, the sons of Noah, and Noah's wife, and the three wives of his sons with them, into the ark; [14]they, and every beast after his kind, and all the cattle after their kind, and every creeping thing that creepeth upon the earth after his kind, and every fowl after his kind, every bird of every sort. [15]And they went in unto Noah into the ark, two and two of all flesh, wherein is the breath of life. [16]And they that went in, went in male and female of all flesh, as God had commanded him: and the Lord shut him in.

[17]And the flood was forty days upon the earth; and the waters increased, and bare up the ark, and it was lift up

ANIMALS ENTERING THE ARK *by Jacob Savery II*

Chapter 7

above the earth. [18]And the waters prevailed, and were increased greatly upon the earth; and the ark went upon the face of the waters. [19]And the waters prevailed exceedingly upon the earth; and all the high hills, that were under the whole heaven, were covered. [20]Fifteen cubits upward did the waters prevail; and the mountains were covered. [21]And all flesh died that moved upon the earth, both of fowl, and of cattle, and of beast, and of every creeping thing that creepeth upon the earth, and every man: [22]all in whose nostrils was the breath of life, of all that was in the dry land, died. [23]And every living substance was destroyed which was upon the face of the ground, both man, and cattle, and the creeping things, and the fowl of the heaven; and they were destroyed from the earth: and Noah only remained alive, and they that were with him in the ark. And the waters prevailed upon the earth an hundred and fifty days.

ANIMALS ENTERING THE ARK *by Hans Jordaens III*

Chapter 8

AND GOD REMEMBERED NOAH, AND EVERY LIVING THING, and all the cattle that was with him in the ark: and God made a wind to pass over the earth, and the waters assuaged; [2]the fountains also of the deep and the windows

of heaven were stopped, and the rain from heaven was restrained; [3]and the waters returned from off the earth continually: and after the end of the hundred and fifty days the waters were abated. [4]And the ark rested in the seventh month, on the seventeenth day of the month, upon the mountains of Ararat. [5]And the waters decreased continually until the tenth month: in the tenth month, on the first day of the month, were the tops of the mountains seen.

[6]And it came to pass at the end of forty days, that Noah opened the window of the ark which he had made: [7]and he sent forth a raven, which went forth to and fro, until the waters were dried up from off the earth. [8]Also he sent forth a dove from him, to see if the waters were abated from off the face of the ground; [9]but the dove found no rest for the sole of her foot, and she returned unto him into the ark, for the waters were on the face of the whole earth: then he put forth his hand, and took her, and pulled her unto him into the ark. [10]And he stayed yet other seven days; and again he sent forth the dove out of the ark; [11]and the dove came in to him in the evening; and, lo, in her mouth was an olive leaf plucked off: so Noah knew that the waters were abated from off the earth. [12]And he stayed yet other seven days; and sent forth the dove; which returned not again unto him any more.

[13]And it came to pass in the six hundredth and first year, in the first month, the first day of the month, the waters were dried up from off the earth: and Noah removed the covering of the ark, and looked, and, behold, the face of the ground was dry. [14]And in the second month, on the seven and twentieth day of the month, was the earth dried.

[15]And God spake unto Noah, saying, [16]"Go forth of the ark, thou, and thy wife, and thy sons, and thy sons' wives with thee. [17]Bring forth with thee every living thing that is with thee, of all flesh, both of fowl, and of cattle, and of every creeping thing that creepeth upon the earth; that they may breed abundantly in the earth, and be fruitful, and multiply upon the earth."

[18]And Noah went forth, and his sons, and his wife, and his sons' wives with him: [19]every beast, every creeping thing, and every fowl, and whatsoever creepeth upon the earth, after their kinds, went forth out of the ark.

Chapter 8

[20]And Noah builded an altar unto the LORD; and took of every clean beast, and of every clean fowl, and offered burnt offerings on the altar. [21]And the LORD smelled a sweet savour; and the LORD said in his heart, "I will not again curse the ground any more for man's sake; for the imagination of man's heart is evil from his youth; neither will I again smite any more every thing living, as I have done. [22]While the earth remaineth, seedtime and harvest, and cold and heat, and summer and winter, and day and night shall not cease."

THE BOW OF THE COVENANT

Chapter 9

AND GOD BLESSED NOAH AND HIS SONS, AND SAID unto them, "Be fruitful, and multiply, and replenish the earth. [2]And the fear of you and the dread of you shall be upon every beast of the earth, and upon every fowl of the air, upon all that moveth upon the earth, and upon all the fishes of the sea; into your hand are they delivered. [3]Every

NOAH AND HIS FAMILY AFTER THE FLOOD *by Francesco Bassano II*

moving thing that liveth shall be meat for you; even as the green herb have I given you all things.

[4]"But flesh with the life thereof, which is the blood thereof, shall ye not eat. [5]And surely your blood of your lives will I require; at the hand of every beast will I require it, and at the hand of man; at the hand of every man's brother will I require the life of man. [6]Whoso sheddeth man's blood, by man shall his blood be shed: for in the image of God made he man. [7]And you, be ye fruitful, and multiply; bring forth abundantly in the earth, and multiply therein."

[8]And God spake unto Noah, and to his sons with him, saying, [9]"And I, behold, I establish my covenant with you, and with your seed after you; [10]and with every living creature that is with you, of the fowl, of the cattle, and of every beast of the earth with you; from all that go out of the ark, to every beast of the earth. [11]And I will establish my covenant with you; neither shall all flesh be cut off any more by the waters of a flood; neither shall there any more be a flood to destroy the earth."

[12]And God said, "This is the token of the covenant which I make between me and you and every living creature that is with you, for perpetual generations: [13]I do set my bow in the cloud, and it shall be for a token of a covenant between me and the earth. [14]And it shall come to pass, when I bring a cloud over the earth, that the bow shall be seen in the cloud: [15]and I will remember my covenant, which is between me and you and every living creature of all flesh; and the waters shall no more become a flood to destroy all flesh. [16]And the bow shall be in the cloud; and I will look upon it, that I may remember the everlasting covenant between God and every living creature of all flesh that is upon the earth."

[17]And God said unto Noah, "This is the token of the covenant, which I have established between me and all flesh that is upon the earth."

The Tower of Babel

Chapter 11

AND THE WHOLE EARTH WAS OF ONE LANGUAGE, and of one speech. [2]And it came to pass, as they journeyed from the east, that they found a plain in the land of Shinar; and they dwelt there.

[3]And they said to one another, "Go to, let us make brick, and burn them throughly." And they had brick for stone, and slime had they for mortar. [4]And they said, "Go to, let us build us a city and a tower, whose top may reach unto heaven; and let us make us a name, lest we be scattered abroad upon the face of the whole earth."

[5]And the LORD came down to see the city and the tower, which the children of men builded. [6]And the LORD said, "Behold, the people is one, and they have all one language; and this they begin to do: and now nothing will be re-

THE TOWER OF BABEL *by Pieter Breughel*

THE TOWER OF BABEL *by Abel Grimmer*

strained from them, which they have imagined to do. [7]Go to, let us go down, and there confound their language, that they may not understand one another's speech."

[8]So the LORD scattered them abroad from thence upon the face of all the earth: and they left off to build the city. [9]Therefore is the name of it called Babel; because the LORD did there confound the language of all the earth: and from thence did the LORD scatter them abroad upon the face of all the earth.

Chapter 12

THE JOURNEY TO CANAAN, *School of Raphael*

THE CALL OF ABRAM

Chapter 12

NOW THE LORD HAD SAID UNTO ABRAM, "GET thee out of thy country, and from thy kindred, and from thy father's house, unto a land that I will shew thee: [2]and I will make of thee a great nation, and I will bless thee, and make thy name great; and thou shalt be a blessing: [3]and I will bless them that bless thee, and curse him that curseth thee: and in thee shall all families of the earth be blessed."

[4]So Abram departed, as the LORD had spoken unto him; and Lot went with him: and Abram was seventy and five years old when he departed out of Haran. [5]And Abram took Sarai his wife, and Lot his brother's son, and all their substance that they had gathered, and the souls that they had gotten in Haran; and they went forth to go into the land of Canaan; and into the land of Canaan they came.

[6]And Abram passed through the land unto the place of Sichem, unto the plain of Moreh. And the Canaanite was then in the land. [7]And the LORD appeared unto Abram and said, "Unto thy seed will I give this land": and there builded he an altar unto the LORD, who appeared unto him.

God's Covenant with Abram

Chapter 17

And when Abram was ninety years old and nine, the Lord appeared to Abram, and said unto him, "I am the Almighty God; walk before me, and be thou perfect. [2]And I will make my covenant between me and thee, and will multiply thee exceedingly."

[3]And Abram fell on his face: and God talked with him, saying, [4]"As for me, behold, my covenant is with thee, and thou shalt be a father of many nations. [5]Neither shall thy name any more be called Abram, but thy name shall be Abraham; for a father of many nations have I made thee. [6]And I will make thee exceeding fruitful, and I will make nations of thee, and kings shall come out of thee. [7]And I will establish my covenant between me and thee and thy seed after thee in their generations for an everlasting covenant, to be a God unto thee, and to thy seed after thee. [8]And I will give unto thee, and to thy seed after thee, the land wherein thou art a stranger, all the land of Canaan, for an everlasting possession; and I will be their God."

[9]And God said unto Abraham, "Thou shalt keep my covenant therefore, thou, and thy seed after thee in their generations. [10]This is my covenant, which ye shall keep, between me and you and thy seed after thee; Every man child among you shall be circumcised. [11]And ye shall circumcise the flesh of your foreskin; and it shall be a token of the covenant betwixt me and you. [12]And he that is eight days old shall be circumcised among you, every man child in your generations, he that is born in the house, or bought with money of any stranger, which is not of thy seed. [13]He that is born in thy house, and he that is bought with thy money, must needs be circumcised: and my covenant shall be in your flesh for an everlasting covenant. [14]And the uncircumcised man child whose flesh of his foreskin is not circumcised, that soul shall be cut off from his people; he hath broken my covenant."

[15]And God said unto Abraham, "As for Sarai thy wife, thou shalt not call her name Sarai, but Sarah shall her

Chapter 17

name be. [16]And I will bless her, and give thee a son also of her; yea, I will bless her, and she shall be a mother of nations; kings of people shall be of her."

The Three Visitors

Chapter 18

AND THE LORD APPEARED UNTO HIM IN THE plains of Mamre: and he sat in the tent door in the heat of the day; [2]and he lift up his eyes and looked, and, lo, three men stood by him: and when he saw them, he ran to meet them from the tent door, and bowed himself toward the ground, [3]and said, "My Lord, if now I have found favour in thy sight, pass not away, I pray thee, from thy servant: [4]let a

ABRAHAM AND THE THREE ANGELS *by Sebastien Bourdon*

Chapter 18

little water, I pray you, be fetched, and wash your feet, and rest yourselves under the tree: [5]and I will fetch a morsel of bread, and comfort ye your hearts; after that ye shall pass on: for therefore are ye come to your servant."

And they said, "So do, as thou hast said."

[6]And Abraham hastened into the tent unto Sarah, and said, "Make ready quickly three measures of fine meal, knead it, and make cakes upon the hearth."

[7]And Abraham ran unto the herd, and fetched a calf tender and good, and gave it unto a young man; and he hasted to dress it. [8]And he took butter, and milk, and the calf which he had dressed, and set it before them; and he stood by them under the tree, and they did eat.

[9]And they said unto him, "Where is Sarah thy wife?"

And he said, "Behold, in the tent."

[10]And he said, "I will certainly return unto thee according to the time of life; and, lo, Sarah thy wife shall have a son."

And Sarah heard it in the tent door, which was behind him. [11]Now Abraham and Sarah were old and well stricken in age; and it ceased to be with Sarah after the manner of women. [12]Therefore Sarah laughed within herself, saying, "After I am waxed old shall I have pleasure, my lord being old also?"

[13]And the LORD said unto Abraham, "Wherefore did Sarah laugh, saying, 'Shall I of a surety bear a child, which am old?' [14]Is any thing too hard for the LORD? At the time appointed I will return unto thee, according to the time of life, and Sarah shall have a son."

THE BIRTH OF ISAAC

Chapter 21

AND THE LORD VISITED SARAH AS HE HAD SAID, and the LORD did unto Sarah as he had spoken. [2]For Sarah conceived, and bare Abraham a son in his old age, at the set time of which God had spoken to him. [3]And Abraham called the name of his son that was born unto him, whom Sarah bare to him, Isaac. [4]And Abraham circumcised his

Chapter 21

son Isaac being eight days old, as God had commanded him. [5]And Abraham was an hundred years old, when his son Isaac was born unto him.

[6]And Sarah said, "God hath made me to laugh, so that all that hear will laugh with me." [7]And she said, "Who would have said unto Abraham, that Sarah should have given children suck? for I have born him a son in his old age."

God Tries Abraham's Faith

Chapter 22

And it came to pass after these things, that God did tempt Abraham, and said unto him, "Abraham": and he said, "Behold, here I am." [2]And he said, "Take now thy son, thine only son Isaac, whom thou lovest, and get thee into the land of Moriah; and offer him there for a burnt offering upon one of the mountains which I will tell thee of."

[3]And Abraham rose up early in the morning, and saddled his ass, and took two of his young men with him, and Isaac his son, and clave the wood for the burnt offering, and rose up, and went unto the place of which God had told him. [4]Then on the third day Abraham lifted up his eyes, and saw the place afar off. [5]And Abraham said unto his young men, "Abide ye here with the ass; and I and the lad will go yonder and worship, and come again to you."

[6]And Abraham took the wood of the burnt offering, and laid it upon Isaac his son; and he took the fire in his hand, and a knife; and they went both of them together. [7]And Isaac spake unto Abraham his father, and said, "My father": and he said, "Here am I, my son."

And he said, "Behold the fire and the wood: but where is the lamb for a burnt offering?"

[8]And Abraham said, "My son, God will provide himself a lamb for a burnt offering": so they went both of them together.

[9]And they came to the place which God had told him of; and Abraham built an altar there, and laid the wood in

THE SACRIFICE OF ISAAC *by Rembrandt*

order, and bound Isaac his son, and laid him on the altar upon the wood. [10]And Abraham stretched forth his hand, and took the knife to slay his son.

[11]And the angel of the LORD called unto him out of heaven, and said, "Abraham, Abraham": and he said, "Here am I."

Chapter 22

[12]And he said, "Lay not thine hand upon the lad, neither do thou any thing unto him: for now I know that thou fearest God, seeing thou hast not withheld thy son, thine only son from me."

[13]And Abraham lifted up his eyes, and looked, and behold behind him a ram caught in a thicket by his horns: and Abraham went and took the ram, and offered him up for a burnt offering in the stead of his son. [14]And Abraham called the name of that place Jehovah-jireh: as it is said to this day, "In the mount of the LORD it shall be seen."

[15]And the angel of the LORD called unto Abraham out of heaven the second time, [16]and said, "By myself have I sworn, saith the LORD, for because thou hast done this thing, and hast not withheld thy son, thine only son: [17]that in blessing I will bless thee, and in multiplying I will multiply thy seed as the stars of the heaven, and as the sand which is upon the sea shore; and thy seed shall possess the gate of his enemies; [18]and in thy seed shall all the nations of the earth be blessed; because thou hast obeyed my voice."

Isaac and Rebekah

Chapter 24

AND ABRAHAM WAS OLD, AND WELL STRICKEN IN age: and the LORD had blessed Abraham in all things. [2]And Abraham said unto his eldest servant of his house, that ruled over all that he had, "Put, I pray thee, thy hand under my thigh: [3]and I will make thee swear by the LORD, the God of heaven, and the God of the earth, that thou shalt not take a wife unto my son of the daughters of the Canaanites, among whom I dwell: [4]but thou shalt go unto my country, and to my kindred, and take a wife unto my son Isaac."

[5]And the servant said unto him, "Peradventure the woman will not be willing to follow me unto this land: must I needs bring thy son again unto the land from whence thou camest?"

[6]And Abraham said unto him, "Beware thou that thou bring not my son thither again. [7]The LORD God of heaven, which took me from my father's house, and from the land

of my kindred, and which spake unto me, and that sware unto me, saying, 'Unto thy seed will I give this land'; he shall send his angel before thee, and thou shalt take a wife unto my son from thence. [8]And if the woman will not be willing to follow thee, then thou shalt be clear from this my oath: only bring not my son thither again." [9]And the servant put his hand under the thigh of Abraham his master, and sware to him concerning that matter.

[10]And the servant took ten camels of the camels of his master, and departed; for all the goods of his master were in his hand: and he arose, and went to Mesopotamia, unto the city of Nahor. [11]And he made his camels to kneel down without the city by a well of water at the time of the evening, even the time that women go out to draw water.

[12]And he said, "O Lord God of my master Abraham, I pray thee, send me good speed this day, and shew kindness unto my master Abraham. [13]Behold, I stand here by the well of water; and the daughters of the men of the city come out to draw water: [14]and let it come to pass, that the damsel to whom I shall say, 'Let down thy pitcher, I pray thee, that I may drink'; and she shall say, 'Drink, and I will give thy camels drink also': let the same be she that thou hast appointed for thy servant Isaac; and thereby shall I know that thou hast shewed kindness unto my master."

[15]And it came to pass, before he had done speaking, that, behold, Rebekah came out, who was born to Bethuel, son of Milcah, the wife of Nahor, Abraham's brother, with her pitcher upon her shoulder. [16]And the damsel was very fair to look upon, a virgin, neither had any man known her: and she went down to the well, and filled her pitcher, and came up.

[17]And the servant ran to meet her, and said, "Let me, I pray thee, drink a little water of thy pitcher."

[18]And she said, "Drink, my lord": and she hasted, and let down her pitcher upon her hand, and gave him drink. [19]And when she had done giving him drink, she said, "I will draw water for thy camels also, until they have done drinking." [20]And she hasted, and emptied her pitcher into the trough, and ran again unto the well to draw water, and drew for all his camels. [21]And the man wondering at her held his peace, to wit whether the Lord had made his journey prosperous or not.

[22]And it came to pass, as the camels had done drinking, that the man took a golden earring of half a shekel weight, and two bracelets for her hands of ten shekels weight of gold; [23]and said, "Whose daughter art thou? Tell me, I pray thee: is there room in thy father's house for us to lodge in?"

[24]And she said unto him, "I am the daughter of Bethuel the son of Milcah, which she bare unto Nahor." [25]She said moreover unto him, "We have both straw and provender enough, and room to lodge in."

[26]And the man bowed down his head, and worshipped the LORD. [27]And he said, 'Blessed be the LORD God of my master Abraham, who hath not left destitute my master of his mercy and his truth: I being in the way, the LORD led me to the house of my master's brethren."

[28]And the damsel ran, and told them of her mother's house these things. [29]And Rebekah had a brother, and his name was Laban: and Laban ran out unto the man, unto the well. [30]And it came to pass, when he saw the earring and bracelets upon his sister's hands, and when he heard the words of Rebekah his sister, saying, "Thus spake the man unto me"; that he came unto the man; and, behold, he stood by the camels at the well. [31]And he said, "Come in, thou blessed of the LORD; wherefore standest thou without? for I have prepared the house, and room for the camels."

[32]And the man came into the house: and he ungirded his camels, and gave straw and provender for the camels, and water to wash his feet, and the men's feet that were with him. [33]And there was set meat before him to eat: but he said, "I will not eat, until I have told mine errand."

And he said, "Speak on."

[34]And he said, "I am Abraham's servant. [35]And the LORD hath blessed my master greatly; and he is become great: and he hath given him flocks, and herds, and silver, and gold, and menservants, and maidservants, and camels, and asses. [36]And Sarah my master's wife bare a son to my master when she was old: and unto him hath he given all that he hath. [37]And my master made me swear, saying, 'Thou shalt not take a wife to my son of the daughters of the Canaanites, in whose land I dwell: [38]but thou shalt go unto my father's house, and to my kindred, and take a wife unto my son.'

Eliezer and Rebecca at the Well, *after N. Poussin*

[39]"And I said unto my master, 'Peradventure the woman will not follow me.'

[40]"And he said unto me, 'The LORD, before whom I walk, will send his angel with thee, and prosper thy way; and thou shalt take a wife for my son of my kindred, and of my father's house: [41]then shalt thou be clear from this my oath, when thou comest to my kindred; and if they give not thee one, thou shalt be clear from my oath.'

[42]"And I came this day unto the well, and said, 'O LORD God of my master Abraham, if now thou do prosper my way which I go: [43]behold, I stand by the well of water; and it shall come to pass, that when the virgin cometh forth to draw water, and I say to her, "Give me, I pray thee, a little water of thy pitcher to drink"; [44]and she say to me, "Both drink thou, and I will also draw for thy camels": let the same be the woman whom the LORD hath appointed out for my master's son.'

[45]"And before I had done speaking in mine heart, behold, Rebekah came forth with her pitcher on her shoulder; and she went down unto the well, and drew water: and I said unto her, 'Let me drink, I pray thee.'

[46]"And she made haste, and let down her pitcher from her shoulder, and said, 'Drink, and I will give thy camels drink also': so I drank, and she made the camels drink also.

[47]"And I asked her, and said, 'Whose daughter art thou?'

"And she said, 'The daughter of Bethuel, Nahor's son, whom Milcah bare unto him': and I put the earring upon her face, and the bracelets upon her hands.

[48]"And I bowed down my head, and worshipped the LORD, and blessed the LORD God of my master Abraham, which had led me in the right way to take my master's brother's daughter unto his son. [49]And now if ye will deal kindly and truly with my master, tell me: and if not, tell me; that I may turn to the right hand, or to the left."

[50]Then Laban and Bethuel answered and said, "The thing proceedeth from the LORD: we cannot speak unto thee bad or good. [51]Behold, Rebekah is before thee, take her, and go, and let her be thy master's son's wife, as the LORD hath spoken."

[52]And it came to pass, that, when Abraham's servant heard their words, he worshipped the LORD, bowing himself to the earth. [53]And the servant brought forth jewels of silver, and jewels of gold, and raiment, and gave them to Rebekah: he gave also to her brother and to her mother precious things. [54]And they did eat and drink, he and the men that were with him, and tarried all night; and they rose up in the morning, and he said, "Send me away unto my master."

[55]And her brother and her mother said, "Let the damsel abide with us a few days, at the least ten; after that she shall go."

[56]And he said unto them, "Hinder me not, seeing the LORD hath prospered my way; send me away that I may go to my master."

[57]And they said, "We will call the damsel, and inquire at her mouth." [58]And they called Rebekah, and said unto her, "Wilt thou go with this man?"

And she said, "I will go."

Chapter 24

[59]And they sent away Rebekah their sister, and her nurse, and Abraham's servant, and his men. [60]And they blessed Rebekah, and said unto her, "Thou art our sister, be thou the mother of thousands of millions, and let thy seed possess the gate of those which hate them."

[61]And Rebekah arose, and her damsels, and they rode upon the camels, and followed the man: and the servant took Rebekah, and went his way.

[62]And Isaac came from the way of the well Lahai-roi; for he dwelt in the south country. [63]And Isaac went out to meditate in the field at the eventide: and he lifted up his eyes, and saw, and, behold, the camels were coming.

[64]And Rebekah lifted up her eyes, and when she saw Isaac, she lighted off the camel. [65]For she had said unto the servant, "What man is this that walketh in the field to meet us?" And the servant had said, "It is my master": therefore she took a veil, and covered herself.

[66]And the servant told Isaac all things that he had done. [67]And Isaac brought her into his mother Sarah's tent, and took Rebekah, and she became his wife; and he loved her: and Isaac was comforted after his mother's death.

Jacob and Esau

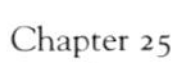

Chapter 25

And Isaac entreated the Lord for his wife, because she was barren: and the Lord was entreated of him, and Rebekah his wife conceived. [22]And the children struggled together within her; and she said, "If it be so, why am I thus?" And she went to inquire of the Lord.

[23]And the Lord said unto her, "Two nations are in thy womb, and two manner of people shall be separated from thy bowels; and the one people shall be stronger than the other people; and the elder shall serve the younger."

[24]And when her days to be delivered were fulfilled, behold, there were twins in her womb. [25]And the first came out red, all over like an hairy garment; and they called his name Esau. [26]And after that came his brother out, and his hand took hold on Esau's heel; and his name was called

ESAU SELLS HIS BIRTHRIGHT *by Michel Corneille the Elder*

Jacob: and Isaac was threescore years old when she bare them.

[27]And the boys grew: and Esau was a cunning hunter, a man of the field; and Jacob was a plain man, dwelling in tents. [28]And Isaac loved Esau, because he did eat of his venison: but Rebekah loved Jacob.

[29]And Jacob sod pottage: and Esau came from the field, and he was faint: [30]and Esau said to Jacob, "Feed me, I pray thee, with that same red pottage; for I am faint": therefore was his name called Edom.

[31]And Jacob said, "Sell me this day thy birthright."

[32]And Esau said, "Behold, I am at the point to die: and what profit shall this birthright do to me?"

[33]And Jacob said, "Swear to me this day"; and he sware unto him: and he sold his birthright unto Jacob.

[34]Then Jacob gave Esau bread and pottage of lentiles; and he did eat and drink, and rose up, and went his way: thus Esau despised his birthright.

Jacob Gets Esau's Blessing

Chapter 27

AND IT CAME TO PASS, THAT WHEN ISAAC WAS old, and his eyes were dim, so that he could not see, he called Esau his eldest son, and said unto him, "My son": and he said unto him, "Behold, here am I."

[2]And he said, "Behold now, I am old, I know not the day of my death: [3]now therefore take, I pray thee, thy weapons, thy quiver and thy bow, and go out to the field, and take me some venison; [4]and make me savoury meat, such as I love, and bring it to me, that I may eat; that my soul may bless thee before I die."

[5]And Rebekah heard when Isaac spake to Esau his son. And Esau went to the field to hunt for venison, and to bring it. [6]And Rebekah spake unto Jacob her son, saying,

ISAAC BLESSING JACOB *by Girolamo de Treviso*

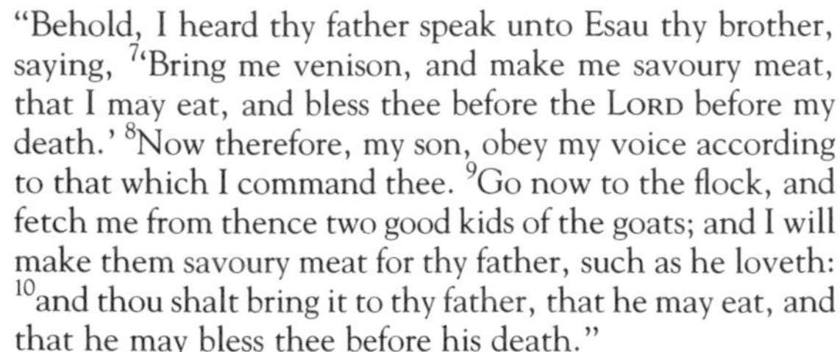

"Behold, I heard thy father speak unto Esau thy brother, saying, [7]'Bring me venison, and make me savoury meat, that I may eat, and bless thee before the LORD before my death.' [8]Now therefore, my son, obey my voice according to that which I command thee. [9]Go now to the flock, and fetch me from thence two good kids of the goats; and I will make them savoury meat for thy father, such as he loveth: [10]and thou shalt bring it to thy father, that he may eat, and that he may bless thee before his death."

[11]And Jacob said to Rebekah his mother, "Behold, Esau my brother is a hairy man, and I am a smooth man: [12]my father peradventure will feel me, and I shall seem to him as a deceiver; and I shall bring a curse upon me, and not a blessing."

[13]And his mother said unto him, "Upon me be thy curse, my son: only obey my voice, and go fetch me them."

[14]And he went, and fetched, and brought them to his mother: and his mother made savoury meat, such as his father loved. [15]And Rebekah took goodly raiment of her eldest son Esau, which were with her in the house, and put them upon Jacob her younger son: [16]and she put the skins of the kids of the goats upon his hands, and upon the smooth of his neck: [17]and she gave the savoury meat and the bread, which she had prepared, into the hand of her son Jacob.

[18]And he came unto his father, and said, "My father": and he said, "Here am I; who art thou, my son?"

[19]And Jacob said unto his father, "I am Esau thy firstborn; I have done according as thou badest me: arise, I pray thee, sit and eat of my venison, that thy soul may bless me."

[20]And Isaac said unto his son, "How is it that thou hast found it so quickly, my son?"

And he said, "Because the LORD thy God brought it to me."

[21]And Isaac said unto Jacob, "Come near, I pray thee, that I may feel thee, my son, whether thou be my very son Esau or not."

[22]And Jacob went near unto Isaac his father; and he felt him, and said, "The voice is Jacob's voice, but the hands are the hands of Esau." [23]And he discerned him not, because his hands were hairy, as his brother Esau's hands: so he blessed him. [24]And he said, "Art thou my very son Esau?"

And he said, "I am."

[25]And he said, "Bring it near to me, and I will eat of my son's venison, that my soul may bless thee."

And he brought it near to him, and he did eat: and he brought him wine, and he drank. [26]And his father Isaac said unto him, "Come near now, and kiss me, my son."

[27]And he came near, and kissed him: and he smelled the smell of his raiment, and blessed him, and said, "See, the smell of my son is as the smell of a field which the LORD hath blessed: [28]therefore God give thee of the dew of heaven, and the fatness of the earth, and plenty of corn and wine: [29]let people serve thee, and nations bow down to thee: be lord over thy brethren, and let thy mother's sons bow down to thee: cursed be every one that curseth thee, and blessed be he that blesseth thee."

[30]And it came to pass, as soon as Isaac had made an end of blessing Jacob, and Jacob was yet scarce gone out from the presence of Isaac his father, that Esau his brother came in from his hunting. [31]And he also had made savoury meat, and brought it unto his father, and said unto his father, "Let my father arise, and eat of his son's venison, that thy soul may bless me."

[32]And Isaac his father said unto him, "Who art thou?"

And he said, "I am thy son, thy firstborn Esau."

[33]And Isaac trembled very exceedingly, and said, "Who? Where is he that hath taken venison, and brought it me, and I have eaten of all before thou camest, and have blessed him? Yea, and he shall be blessed."

[34]And when Esau heard the words of his father, he cried with a great and exceeding bitter cry, and said unto his father, "Bless me, even me also, O my father."

[35]And he said, "Thy brother came with subtilty, and hath taken away thy blessing."

[36]And he said, "Is not he rightly named Jacob? for he hath supplanted me these two times: he took away my birthright; and, behold, now he hath taken away my blessing." And he said, "Hast thou not reserved a blessing for me?"

[37]And Isaac answered and said unto Esau, "Behold, I have made him thy lord, and all his brethren have I given to him for servants; and with corn and wine have I sustained him: and what shall I do now unto thee, my son?"

[38]And Esau said unto his father, "Hast thou but one blessing, my father? Bless me, even me also, O my father." And Esau lifted up his voice, and wept.

[39]And Isaac his father answered and said unto him, "Behold, thy dwelling shall be the fatness of the earth, and of the dew of heaven from above; [40]and by thy sword shalt thou live, and shalt serve thy brother; and it shall come to pass when thou shalt have the dominion, that thou shalt break his yoke from off thy neck."

JACOB'S DREAM *by Ludovico Cardi da Cigoli*

Jacob's Dream at Bethel

Chapter 28

AND JACOB WENT OUT FROM BEERSHEBA, AND went toward Haran. [11]And he lighted upon a certain place, and tarried there all night, because the sun was set; and he took of the stones of that place, and put them for his pillows, and lay down in that place to sleep. [12]And he dreamed, and behold a ladder set up on the earth, and the top of it reached to heaven: and behold the angels of God ascending and descending on it. [13]And, behold, the LORD stood above it, and said, "I am the LORD God of Abraham thy father, and the God of Isaac: the land whereon thou liest, to thee will I give it, and to thy seed: [14]and thy seed shall be as the dust of the earth, and thou shalt spread abroad to the west, and to the east, and to the north, and to the south: and in thee and in thy seed shall all the families of the earth be blessed. [15]And, behold, I am with thee, and will keep thee in all places whither thou goest, and will bring thee again into this land; for I will not leave thee, until I have done that which I have spoken to thee of."

[16]And Jacob awaked out of his sleep, and he said, "Surely the LORD is in this place; and I knew it not." [17]And he was afraid, and said, "How dreadful is this place! This is none other but the house of God, and this is the gate of heaven."

The Death of Isaac

Chapter 35

NOW THE SONS OF JACOB WERE TWELVE:
[23]The sons of Leah; Reuben, Jacob's firstborn, and Simeon, and Levi, and Judah, and Issachar, and Zebulun:
[24]The sons of Rachel; Joseph, and Benjamin:
[25]And the sons of Bilhah, Rachel's handmaid; Dan, and Naphtali:
[26]And the sons of Zilpah, Leah's handmaid; Gad, and Asher: these are the sons of Jacob, which were born to him in Padan-aram.

Chapter 35

[27]And Jacob came unto Isaac his father unto Mamre, unto the city of Arbah, which is Hebron, where Abraham and Isaac sojourned. [28]And the days of Isaac were an hundred and fourscore years. [29]And Isaac gave up the ghost, and died, and was gathered unto his people, being old and full of days: and his sons Esau and Jacob buried him.

Joseph's Dreams

Chapter 37

And Jacob dwelt in the land wherein his father was a stranger, in the land of Canaan.

[2]These are the generations of Jacob.

Joseph, being seventeen years old, was feeding the flock with his brethren; and the lad was with the sons of Bilhah, and with the sons of Zilpah, his father's wives: and Joseph brought unto his father their evil report.

[3]Now Israel loved Joseph more than all his children, because he was the son of his old age: [4]and he made him a coat of many colours.

[5]And Joseph dreamed a dream, and he told it his brethren: and they hated him yet the more. [6]And he said unto them, "Hear, I pray you, this dream which I have dreamed: [7]For, behold, we were binding sheaves in the field, and, lo, my sheaf arose, and also stood upright; and, behold, your sheaves stood round about, and made obeisance to my sheaf."

[8]And his brethren said to him, "Shalt thou indeed reign over us? or shalt thou indeed have dominion over us?" And they hated him yet the more for his dreams, and for his words.

[9]And he dreamed yet another dream, and told it his brethren, and said, "Behold, I have dreamed a dream more; and, behold, the sun and the moon and the eleven stars made obeisance to me."

[10]And he told it to his father, and to his brethren: and his father rebuked him, and said unto him, "What is this dream that thou hast dreamed? Shall I and thy mother and thy brethren indeed come to bow down ourselves to thee to

the earth?" [11]And his brethren envied him; but his father observed the saying.

[12]And his brethren went to feed their father's flock in Shechem.

JOSEPH SOLD INTO EGYPT

AND ISRAEL SAID UNTO JOSEPH, "DO NOT THY brethren feed the flock in Shechem? Come, and I will send thee unto them."

And he said to him, "Here am I."

[14]And he said to him, "Go, I pray thee, see whether it be well with thy brethren, and well with the flocks; and bring me word again." So he sent him out of the vale of Hebron, and he came to Shechem.

[15]And a certain man found him, and, behold, he was wandering in the field: and the man asked him, saying, "What seekest thou?"

[16]And he said, "I seek my brethren: tell me, I pray thee, where they feed their flocks."

[17]And the man said, "They are departed hence; for I heard them say, 'Let us go to Dothan.'"

And Joseph went after his brethren, and found them in Dothan. [18]And when they saw him afar off, even before he came near unto them, they conspired against him to slay him.

[19]And they said one to another, "Behold, this dreamer cometh. [20]Come now therefore, and let us slay him, and cast him into some pit, and we will say, 'Some evil beast hath devoured him': and we shall see what will become of his dreams."

[21]And Reuben heard it, and he delivered him out of their hands; and said, "Let us not kill him." [22]And Reuben said unto them, "Shed no blood, but cast him into this pit that is in the wilderness, and lay no hand upon him"; that he might rid him out of their hands, to deliver him to his father again. [23]And it came to pass, when Joseph was come unto his brethren, that they stript Joseph out of his coat, his coat of many colours that was on him; [24]and they took

JOSEPH'S COAT BEING PRESENTED TO HIS FATHER, *circle of D. Fiasella*

him, and cast him into a pit: and the pit was empty, there was no water in it.

[25]And they sat down to eat bread: and they lifted up their eyes and looked, and, behold, a company of Ishmeelites came from Gilead with their camels bearing spicery and balm and myrrh, going to carry it down to Egypt.

[26]And Judah said unto his brethren, "What profit is it if we slay our brother, and conceal his blood? [27]Come, and let us sell him to the Ishmeelites, and let not our hand be upon him; for he is our brother and our flesh." And his brethren were content.

[28]Then there passed by Midianites merchantmen; and they drew and lifted up Joseph out of the pit, and sold Joseph to the Ishmeelites for twenty pieces of silver: and they brought Joseph into Egypt.

[29]And Reuben returned unto the pit; and, behold, Joseph was not in the pit; and he rent his clothes. [30]And he returned unto his brethren, and said, "The child is not; and I, whither shall I go?"

[31]And they took Joseph's coat, and killed a kid of the goats, and dipped the coat in the blood; [32]and they sent the coat of many colours, and they brought it to their father;

Chapter 37

and said, "This have we found; know now whether it be thy son's coat or no."

[33]And he knew it, and said, "It is my son's coat; an evil beast hath devoured him; Joseph is without doubt rent in pieces."

[34]And Jacob rent his clothes, and put sackcloth upon his loins, and mourned for his son many days. [35]And all his sons and all his daughters rose up to comfort him; but he refused to be comforted; and he said, "For I will go down into the grave unto my son mourning." Thus his father wept for him.

Joseph and Potiphar's Wife

Chapter 39

AND JOSEPH WAS BROUGHT DOWN TO EGYPT; AND Potiphar, an officer of Pharaoh, captain of the guard, an Egyptian, bought him of the hands of the Ishmeelites, which had brought him down thither.

[2]And the LORD was with Joseph, and he was a prosperous man; and he was in the house of his master the Egyptian. [3]And his master saw that the LORD was with him, and that the LORD made all that he did to prosper in his hand. [4]And Joseph found grace in his sight, and he served him: and he made him overseer over his house, and all that he had he put into his hand. [5]And it came to pass from the time that he had made him overseer in his house, and over all that he had, that the LORD blessed the Egyptian's house for Joseph's sake; and the blessing of the LORD was upon all that he had in the house, and in the field. [6]And he left all that he had in Joseph's hand; and he knew not aught he had, save the bread which he did eat.

And Joseph was a goodly person, and well favoured. [7]And it came to pass after these things, that his master's wife cast her eyes upon Joseph; and she said, "Lie with me."

[8]But he refused, and said unto his master's wife, "Behold, my master wotteth not what is with me in the house, and he hath committed all that he hath to my hand; [9]there is none greater in this house than I; neither hath he

kept back any thing from me but thee, because thou art his wife: how then can I do this great wickedness, and sin against God?" [10]And it came to pass, as she spake to Joseph day by day, that he hearkened not unto her, to lie by her, or to be with her.

[11]And it came to pass about this time, that Joseph went into the house to do his business; and there was none of the men of the house there within. [12]And she caught him by his garment, saying, "Lie with me": and he left his garment in her hand, and fled, and got him out.

[13]And it came to pass, when she saw that he had left his garment in her hand, and was fled forth, [14]that she called unto the men of her house, and spake unto them, saying, "See, he hath brought in an Hebrew unto us to mock us; he came in unto me to lie with me, and I cried with a loud voice: [15]and it came to pass, when he heard that I lifted up my voice and cried, that he left his garment with me, and fled, and got him out."

[16]And she laid up his garment by her, until his lord came home. [17]And she spake unto him according to these words, saying, "The Hebrew servant, which thou hast brought unto us, came in unto me to mock me: [18]and it came to pass, as I lifted up my voice and cried, that he left his garment with me, and fled out."

[19]And it came to pass, when his master heard the words of his wife, which she spake unto him, saying, "After this manner did thy servant to me"; that his wrath was kindled. [20]And Joseph's master took him, and put him into the prison, a place where the king's prisoners were bound: and he was there in the prison.

[21]But the Lord was with Joseph, and shewed him mercy, and gave him favour in the sight of the keeper of the prison. [22]And the keeper of the prison committed to Joseph's hand all the prisoners that were in the prison; and whatsoever they did there, he was the doer of it. [23]The keeper of the prison looked not to any thing that was under his hand; because the Lord was with him, and that which he did, the Lord made it to prosper.

Joseph Interprets Dreams

Chapter 40

AND IT CAME TO PASS AFTER THESE THINGS, THAT the butler of the king of Egypt and his baker had offended their lord the king of Egypt. [2]And Pharaoh was wroth against two of his officers, against the chief of the butlers, and against the chief of the bakers. [3]And he put them in ward in the house of the captain of the guard, into the prison, the place where Joseph was bound. [4]And the captain of the guard charged Joseph with them, and he served them: and they continued a season in ward.

[5]And they dreamed a dream both of them, each man his dream in one night, each man according to the interpretation of his dream, the butler and the baker of the king of Egypt, which were bound in the prison.

[6]And Joseph came in unto them in the morning, and looked upon them, and, behold, they were sad. [7]And he asked Pharaoh's officers that were with him in the ward of his lord's house, saying, "Wherefore look ye so sadly today?"

[8]And they said unto him, "We have dreamed a dream, and there is no interpreter of it."

And Joseph said unto them, "Do not interpretations belong to God? Tell me them, I pray you."

[9]And the chief butler told his dream to Joseph, and said to him, "In my dream, behold, a vine was before me; [10]and in the vine were three branches: and it was as though it budded, and her blossoms shot forth; and the clusters thereof brought forth ripe grapes: [11]and Pharaoh's cup was in my hand: and I took the grapes, and pressed them into Pharaoh's cup, and I gave the cup into Pharaoh's hand."

[12]And Joseph said unto him, "This is the interpretation of it: The three branches are three days: [13]yet within three days shall Pharaoh lift up thine head, and restore thee unto thy place: and thou shalt deliver Pharaoh's cup into his hand, after the former manner when thou wast his butler. [14]But think on me when it shall be well with thee, and shew kindness, I pray thee, unto me, and make mention of me unto Pharaoh, and bring me out of this house: [15]for indeed I

Chapter 40

was stolen away out of the land of the Hebrews: and here also have I done nothing that they should put me into the dungeon."

[16]When the chief baker saw that the interpretation was good, he said unto Joseph, "I also was in my dream, and, behold, I had three white baskets on my head: [17]and in the uppermost basket there was of all manner of bakemeats for Pharaoh; and the birds did eat them out of the basket upon my head."

[18]And Joseph answered and said, "This is the interpretation thereof: The three baskets are three days: [19]yet within three days shall Pharaoh lift up thy head from off thee, and shall hang thee on a tree; and the birds shall eat thy flesh from off thee."

[20]And it came to pass the third day, which was Pharaoh's birthday, that he made a feast unto all his servants: and he lifted up the head of the chief butler and of the chief baker among his servants. [21]And he restored the chief butler unto his butlership again; and he gave the cup into Pharaoh's hand: [22]but he hanged the chief baker: as Joseph had interpreted to them.

[23]Yet did not the chief butler remember Joseph, but forgat him.

Pharaoh's Dreams

Chapter 41

And it came to pass at the end of two full years, that Pharaoh dreamed: and, behold, he stood by the river. [2]And, behold, there came up out of the river seven well favoured kine and fatfleshed; and they fed in a meadow. [3]And, behold, seven other kine came up after them out of the river, ill favoured and leanfleshed; and stood by the other kine upon the brink of the river. [4]And the ill favoured and leanfleshed kine did eat up the seven well favoured and fat kine. So Pharaoh awoke.

[5]And he slept and dreamed the second time: and, behold, seven ears of corn came up upon one stalk, rank and good. [6]And, behold, seven thin ears and blasted with

the east wind sprung up after them. [7]And the seven thin ears devoured the seven rank and full ears. And Pharaoh awoke, and, behold, it was a dream.

[8]And it came to pass in the morning that his spirit was troubled; and he sent and called for all the magicians of Egypt, and all the wise men thereof: and Pharaoh told them his dream; but there was none that could interpret them unto Pharaoh.

[9]Then spake the chief butler unto Pharaoh, saying, "I do remember my faults this day: [10]Pharaoh was wroth with his servants, and put me in ward in the captain of the guard's

Joseph Interpreting Pharaoh's Dreams, *circle of Sigismondo Coccapani*

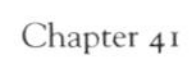

house, both me and the chief baker: [11]and we dreamed a dream in one night, I and he; we dreamed each man according to the interpretation of his dream. [12]And there was there with us a young man, an Hebrew, servant to the captain of the guard; and we told him, and he interpreted to us our dreams; to each man according to his dream he did interpret. [13]And it came to pass, as he interpreted to us, so it was; me he restored unto mine office, and him he hanged."

Chapter 41

[14]Then Pharaoh sent and called Joseph, and they brought him hastily out of the dungeon: and he shaved himself, and changed his raiment, and came in unto Pharaoh.

[15]And Pharaoh said unto Joseph, "I have dreamed a dream, and there is none that can interpret it: and I have heard say of thee, that thou canst understand a dream to interpret it."

[16]And Joseph answered Pharaoh, saying, "It is not in me: God shall give Pharaoh an answer of peace."

[17]And Pharaoh said unto Joseph, "In my dream, behold, I stood upon the bank of the river: [18]and, behold, there came up out of the river seven kine, fatfleshed and well favoured; and they fed in a meadow: [19]and, behold, seven other kine came up after them, poor and very ill favoured and leanfleshed, such as I never saw in all the land of Egypt for badness: [20]and the lean and the ill favoured kine did eat up the first seven fat kine: [21]and when they had eaten them up, it could not be known that they had eaten them; but they were still ill favoured, as at the beginning. So I awoke.

[22]"And I saw in my dream, and, behold, seven ears came up in one stalk, full and good: [23]and, behold, seven ears, withered, thin, and blasted with the east wind, sprung up after them: [24]and the thin ears devoured the seven good ears: and I told this unto the magicians; but there was none that could declare it to me."

[25]And Joseph said unto Pharaoh, "The dream of Pharaoh is one: God hath shewed Pharaoh what he is about to do. [26]The seven good kine are seven years; and the seven good ears are seven years: the dream is one. [27]And the seven thin and ill favoured kine that came up after them are seven years; and the seven empty ears blasted with the east wind shall be seven years of famine.

[28]"This is the thing which I have spoken unto Pharaoh: What God is about to do he sheweth unto Pharaoh. [29]Behold, there come seven years of great plenty throughout all the land of Egypt: [30]and there shall arise after them seven years of famine; and all the plenty shall be forgotten in the land of Egypt; and the famine shall consume the land; [31]and the plenty shall not be known in the land by reason of that famine following; for it shall be very grievous. [32]And for that the dream was doubled unto Pharaoh

Chapter 41

twice; it is because the thing is established by God, and God will shortly bring it to pass.

[33]"Now therefore let Pharaoh look out a man discreet and wise, and set him over the land of Egypt. [34]Let Pharaoh do this, and let him appoint officers over the land, and take up the fifth part of the land of Egypt in the seven plenteous years. [35]And let them gather all the food of those good years that come, and lay up corn under the hand of Pharaoh, and let them keep food in the cities. [36]And that food shall be for store to the land against the seven years of famine, which shall be in the land of Egypt; that the land perish not through the famine."

[37]And the thing was good in the eyes of Pharaoh, and in the eyes of all his servants. [38]And Pharaoh said unto his servants, "Can we find such a one as this is, a man in whom the spirit of God is?"

[39]And Pharaoh said unto Joseph, "Forasmuch as God hath shewed thee all this, there is none so discreet and wise as thou art: [40]thou shalt be over my house, and according unto thy word shall all my people be ruled: only in the throne will I be greater than thou."

[41]And Pharaoh said unto Joseph, "See, I have set thee over all the land of Egypt." [42] And Pharaoh took off his ring from his hand, and put it upon Joseph's hand, and arrayed him in vestures of fine linen, and put a gold chain about his neck; [43]and he made him to ride in the second chariot which he had; and they cried before him, "Bow the knee": and he made him ruler over all the land of Egypt.

Joseph and his Brethren

Chapter 41

AND UNTO JOSEPH WERE BORN TWO SONS BEFORE the years of famine came, which Asenath the daughter of Potipherah priest of On bare unto him. [51]And Joseph called the name of the firstborn Manasseh: "For God", said he, "hath made me forget all my toil, and all my father's house." [52]And the name of the second called he Ephraim:

Chapter 41

"For God hath caused me to be fruitful in the land of my affliction."

[53]And the seven years of plenteousness, that was in the land of Egypt, were ended. [54]And the seven years of dearth began to come, according as Joseph had said: and the dearth was in all lands; but in all the land of Egypt there was bread. [55]And when all the land of Egypt was famished, the people cried to Pharaoh for bread: and Pharaoh said unto all the Egyptians, "Go unto Joseph; what he saith to you, do."

[56]And the famine was over all the face of the earth: and Joseph opened all the storehouses, and sold unto the Egyptians; and the famine waxed sore in the land of Egypt. [57]And all countries came into Egypt to Joseph for to buy corn; because that the famine was so sore in all lands.

Chapter 42

NOW WHEN JACOB SAW THAT THERE WAS CORN IN EGYPT, Jacob said unto his sons, "Why do ye look one upon another?" [2]And he said, "Behold, I have heard that there is corn in Egypt: get you down thither, and buy for us from thence; that we may live, and not die."

[3]And Joseph's ten brethren went down to buy corn in Egypt. [4]But Benjamin, Joseph's brother, Jacob sent not with his brethren; for he said, "Lest peradventure mischief

JOSEPH'S BROTHERS IN EGYPT *by Giovanni de Bartolommeo*

Chapter 42

befall him." [5]And the sons of Israel came to buy corn among those that came: for the famine was in the land of Canaan.

[6]And Joseph was the governor over the land, and he it was that sold to all the people of the land: and Joseph's brethren came, and bowed down themselves before him with their faces to the earth.

Joseph Makes Himself Known

Chapter 45

THEN JOSEPH COULD NOT REFRAIN HIMSELF before all them that stood by him; and he cried, "Cause every man to go out from me." [2]And there stood no man with him, while Joseph made himself known unto his brethren. [2]And he wept aloud: and the Egyptians and the house of Pharaoh heard.

[3]And Joseph said unto his brethren, "I am Joseph; doth my father yet live?" And his brethren could not answer him; for they were troubled at his presence.

[4]And Joseph said unto his brethren, "Come near to me, I pray you." And they came near. And he said, "I am Joseph your brother, whom ye sold into Egypt. [5]Now therefore be not grieved, nor angry with yourselves, that ye sold me hither: for God did send me before you to preserve life. [6]For these two years hath the famine been in the land: and yet there are five years, in the which there shall neither be earing nor harvest. [7]And God sent me before you to preserve you a posterity in the earth, and to save your lives by a great deliverance.

[8]"So now it was not you that sent me hither, but God: and he hath made me a father to Pharaoh, and lord of all his house, and a ruler throughout all the land of Egypt. [9]Haste ye, and go up to my father, and say unto him, 'Thus saith thy son Joseph, God hath made me lord of all Egypt: come down unto me, tarry not: [10]and thou shalt dwell in the land of Goshen, and thou shalt be near unto me, thou, and thy children, and thy children's children, and thy flocks, and thy herds, and all that thou hast: [11]and there

Chapter 45

will I nourish thee; for yet there are five years of famine; lest thou, and thy household, and all that thou hast, come to poverty.'

[12]"And, behold, your eyes see, and the eyes of my brother Benjamin, that it is my mouth that speaketh unto you. [13]And ye shall tell my father of all my glory in Egypt, and of all that ye have seen; and ye shall haste and bring down my father hither."

[14]And he fell upon his brother Benjamin's neck, and wept; and Benjamin wept upon his neck. [15]Moreover he kissed all his brethren, and wept upon them: and after that his brethren talked with him.

[16]And the fame thereof was heard in Pharaoh's house, saying, "Joseph's brethren are come": and it pleased Pharaoh well, and his servants. [17]And Pharaoh said unto Joseph, "Say unto thy brethren, 'This do ye; lade your beasts, and go, get you unto the land of Canaan; [18]and take your father and your households, and come unto me: and I will give you the good of the land of Egypt, and ye shall eat the fat of the land.'"

Chapters & Verses
FROM
THE SECOND BOOK OF MOSES
CALLED
EXODUS

THE BIRTH OF MOSES • MOSES FLEES TO MIDIAN • MOSES AND THE BURNING BUSH • THE PASSOVER • THE EXODUS • CROSSING THE RED SEA • QUAIL AND MANNA • AT MOUNT SINAI • THE TEN COMMANDMENTS • THE TABERNACLE AND THE ARK • THE SABBATH • THE GOLDEN CALF • THE TABLES OF STONE RENEWED

The Birth of Moses

Chapter 1

NOW THESE ARE THE NAMES OF THE CHILDREN of Israel, which came into Egypt; every man and his household came with Jacob. [2]Reuben, Simeon, Levi, and Judah, [3]Issachar, Zebulun, and Benjamin, [4]Dan, and Naphtali, Gad, and Asher. [5]And all the souls that came out of the loins of Jacob were seventy souls: for Joseph was in Egypt already.

[6]And Joseph died, and all his brethren, and all that generation. [7]And the children of Israel were fruitful, and increased abundantly, and multiplied, and waxed exceeding mighty; and the land was filled with them.

[8]Now there arose up a new king over Egypt, which knew not Joseph. [9]And he said unto his people, "Behold, the people of the children of Israel are more and mightier than we: [10]come on, let us deal wisely with them; lest they multiply, and it come to pass, that, when there falleth out any war, they join also unto our enemies, and fight against us, and so get them up out of the land."

Moses Saved from the River *by Sebastien Bourdon*

MOSES FOUND IN THE BULLRUSHES *by Giovanni Romanelli*

[11]Therefore they did set over them taskmasters to afflict them with their burdens. And they built for Pharaoh treasure cities, Pithom and Raamses. [12]But the more they afflicted them, the more they multiplied and grew. And they were grieved because of the children of Israel. [13]And the Egyptians made the children of Israel to serve with rigour: [14]and they made their lives bitter with hard

Chapter 1

bondage, in mortar, and in brick, and in all manner of service in the field: all their service, wherein they made them serve, was with rigour.

[15]And the king of Egypt spake to the Hebrew midwives, of which the name of the one was Shiphrah, and the name of the other Puah: [16]and he said, "When ye do the office of a midwife to the Hebrew women, and see them upon the stools; if it be a son, then ye shall kill him: but if it be a daughter, then she shall live." [17]But the midwives feared God, and did not as the king of Egypt commanded them, but saved the men children alive. [18]And the king of Egypt called for the midwives, and said unto them, "Why have ye done this thing, and have saved the men children alive?"

[19]And the midwives said unto Pharaoh, "Because the Hebrew women are not as the Egyptian women; for they are lively, and are delivered ere the midwives come in unto them."

[20]Therefore God dealt well with the midwives: and the people multiplied, and waxed very mighty. [21]And it came to pass, because the midwives feared God, that he made them houses.

[22]And Pharaoh charged all his people, saying, "Every son that is born ye shall cast into the river, and every daughter ye shall save alive."

Chapter 2

AND THERE WENT A MAN OF THE HOUSE OF LEVI, AND TOOK to wife a daughter of Levi. [2]And the woman conceived, and bare a son: and when she saw him that he was a goodly child, she hid him three months. [3]And when she could not longer hide him, she took for him an ark of bulrushes, and daubed it with slime and with pitch, and put the child therein; and she laid it in the flags by the river's brink. [4]And his sister stood afar off, to wit what would be done to him.

[5]And the daughter of Pharaoh came down to wash herself at the river; and her maidens walked along by the river's side; and when she saw the ark among the flags, she sent her maid to fetch it. [6]And when she had opened it, she

saw the child: and, behold, the babe wept. And she had compassion on him, and said, "This is one of the Hebrews' children."

[7]Then said his sister to Pharaoh's daughter, "Shall I go and call to thee a nurse of the Hebrew women, that she may nurse the child for thee?"

[8]And Pharaoh's daughter said to her, "Go." And the maid went and called the child's mother. [9]And Pharaoh's daughter said unto her, "Take this child away, and nurse it for me, and I will give thee thy wages." And the woman took the child, and nursed it. [10]And the child grew, and she brought him unto Pharaoh's daughter, and he became her son. And she called his name Moses: and she said, "Because I drew him out of the water."

Moses Flees to Midian

AND IT CAME TO PASS IN THOSE DAYS, WHEN Moses was grown, that he went out unto his brethren, and looked on their burdens: and he spied an Egyptian smiting an Hebrew, one of his brethren. [12]And he looked this way and that way, and when he saw that there was no man, he slew the Egyptian, and hid him in the sand. [13]And when he went out the second day, behold, two men of the Hebrews strove together: and he said to him that did the wrong, "Wherefore smitest thou thy fellow?"

[14]And he said, "Who made thee a prince and a judge over us? Intendest thou to kill me, as thou killedst the Egyptian?" And Moses feared, and said, "Surely this thing is known."

[15]Now when Pharaoh heard this thing, he sought to slay Moses. But Moses fled from the face of Pharaoh, and dwelt in the land of Midian: and he sat down by a well. [16]Now the priest of Midian had seven daughters: and they came and drew water, and filled the troughs to water their father's flock. [17]And the shepherds came and drove them away: but Moses stood up and helped them, and watered their flock.

MOSES DEFENDS JETHRO'S DAUGHTERS *by Rosso Fiorentino*

[18]And when they came to Reuel their father, he said, "How is it that ye are come so soon today?"

[19]And they said, "An Egyptian delivered us out of the hand of the shepherds, and also drew water enough for us, and watered the flock."

[20]And he said unto his daughters, "And where is he? Why is it that ye have left the man? Call him, that he may eat bread."

Chapter 2

Moses and Jethro's Daughters *by Carol Saraceni*

Chapter 2

[21]And Moses was content to dwell with the man: and he gave Moses Zipporah his daughter. [22]And she bare him a son, and he called his name Gershom: for he said, "I have been a stranger in a strange land."

[23]And it came to pass in process of time, that the king of Egypt died: and the children of Israel sighed by reason of the bondage, and they cried, and their cry came up unto God by reason of the bondage. [24]And God heard their groaning, and God remembered his covenant with Abraham, with Isaac, and with Jacob. [25]And God looked upon the children of Israel, and God had respect unto them.

Moses and the Burning Bush

Chapter 3

Now Moses kept the flock of Jethro his father in law, the priest of Midian: and he led the flock to the backside of the desert, and came to the mountain of God, even to Horeb. [2]And the angel of the Lord appeared unto him in a flame of fire out of the midst of a bush: and he looked, and, behold, the bush was burned with fire, and the bush was not consumed. [3]And Moses said, "I will now turn aside, and see this great sight, why the bush is not burnt."

[4]And when the LORD saw that he turned aside to see, God called unto him out of the midst of the bush, and said, "Moses, Moses."

And he said, "Here am I.'

[5]And he said, "Draw not nigh hither: put off thy shoes from off thy feet, for the place whereon thou standest is holy ground." [6]Moreover he said, "I am the God of thy father, the God of Abraham, the God of Isaac, and the God of Jacob." And Moses hid his face; for he was afraid to look upon God.

[7]And the LORD said, "I have surely seen the affliction of my people which are in Egypt, and have heard their cry by reason of their taskmasters; for I know their sorrows; [8]and I am come down to deliver them out of the hand of the Egyptians, and to bring them up out of that land unto a good land and a large, unto a land flowing with milk and honey; unto the place of the Canaanites, and the Hittites, and the Amorites, and the Perizzites, and the Hivites, and the Jebusites. [9]Now therefore, behold, the cry of the children of Israel is come unto me: and I have also seen the oppression wherewith the Egyptians oppress them. [10]Come now therefore, and I will send thee unto Pharaoh, that thou mayest bring forth my people the children of Israel out of Egypt."

[11]And Moses said unto God, "Who am I, that I should go unto Pharaoh, and that I should bring forth the children of Israel out of Egypt?"

[12]And he said, "Certainly I will be with thee; and this shall be a token unto thee, that I have sent thee: When thou hast brought forth the people out of Egypt, ye shall serve God upon this mountain."

[13]And Moses said unto God, "Behold, when I come unto the children of Israel, and shall say unto them, 'The God of your fathers hath sent me unto you'; and they shall say to me, 'What is his name?' what shall I say unto them?"

[14]And God said unto Moses, "I AM THAT I AM": and he said, "Thus shalt thou say unto the children of Israel, 'I AM hath sent me unto you.'"

[15]And God said moreover unto Moses, "Thus shalt thou

Chapter 3

say unto the children of Israel, 'The LORD God of your fathers, the God of Abraham, the God of Isaac, and the God of Jacob, hath sent me unto you': this is my name for ever, and this is my memorial unto all generations.

[16]"Go, and gather the elders of Israel together, and say unto them, 'The LORD God of your fathers, the God of Abraham, of Isaac and of Jacob, appeared unto me, saying, I have surely visited you, and seen that which is done to you in Egypt: [17]and I have said, I will bring you up out of the affliction of Egypt unto the land of the Canaanites, and the Hittites, and the Amorites, and the Perizzites, and the Hivites, and the Jebusites, unto a land flowing with milk and honey.'"

THE PASSOVER

Chapter 12

AND THE LORD SPAKE UNTO MOSES AND AARON IN the land of Egypt, saying, [2]"This month shall be unto you the beginning of months: it shall be the first month of the year to you. [3]Speak ye unto all the congregation of Israel, saying, In the tenth day of this month they shall take to them every man a lamb, according to the house of their fathers, a lamb for an house: [4]and if the household be too little for the lamb, let him and his neighbour next unto his house take it according to the number of the souls; every man according to his eating shall make your count for the lamb. [5]Your lamb shall be without blemish, a male of the first year: ye shall take it out from the sheep, or from the goats: [6]and ye shall keep it up unto the fourteenth day of the same month: and the whole assembly of the congregation of Israel shall kill it in the evening. [7]And they shall take of the blood, and strike it on the two side posts and on the upper door post of the houses, wherein they shall eat it. [8]And they shall eat the flesh in that night, roast with fire, and unleavened bread; and with bitter herbs they shall eat it. [9]Eat not of it raw, nor sodden at all with water, but roast with fire; his head with his legs, and with the purtenance thereof. [10]And ye

THE PASSOVER *by Dirck Bouts*

shall let nothing of it remain until the morning; and that which remaineth of it until the morning ye shall burn with fire. [11]And thus shall ye eat it; with your loins girded, your shoes on your feet, and your staff in your hand; and ye shall eat it in haste: it is the LORD's passover.

[12]"For I will pass through the land of Egypt this night, and will smite all the firstborn in the land of Egypt, both man and beast; and against all the gods of Egypt I will

Chapter 12

execute judgment: I am the LORD. 13 And the blood shall be to you for a token upon the houses where ye are: and when I see the blood, I will pass over you, and the plague shall not be upon you to destroy you, when I smite the land of Egypt.

14 "And this day shall be unto you for a memorial; and ye shall keep it a feast to the LORD throughout your generations; ye shall keep it a feast by an ordinance for ever . . .

Chapter 12

26 "And it shall come to pass, when your children shall say unto you, 'What mean ye by this service?' 27 that ye shall say, 'It is the sacrifice of the LORD's passover, who passed over the houses of the children of Israel in Egypt, when he smote the Egyptians, and delivered our houses.'" And the people bowed the head and worshipped. 28 And the children of Israel went away, and did as the LORD had commanded Moses and Aaron, so did they.

THE EXODUS

Chapter 12

AND IT CAME TO PASS, THAT AT MIDNIGHT THE LORD smote all the firstborn in the land of Egypt, from the firstborn of Pharaoh that sat on his throne unto the firstborn of the captive that was in the dungeon; and all the firstborn of cattle. 30 And Pharaoh rose up in the night, he, and all his servants, and all the Egyptians; and there was a great cry in Egypt; for there was not a house where there was not one dead.

31 And he called for Moses and Aaron by night, and said, "Rise up, and get you forth from among my people, both ye and the children of Israel; and go, serve the LORD, as ye have said. 32 Also take your flocks and your herds, as ye have said, and be gone; and bless me also."

33 And the Egyptians were urgent upon the people, that they might send them out of the land in haste; for they said,

Chapter 12

"We be all dead men." [34]And the people took their dough before it was leavened, their kneadingtroughs being bound up in their clothes upon their shoulders. [35]And the children of Israel did according to the word of Moses; and they borrowed of the Egyptians jewels of silver, and jewels of gold, and raiment: [36]and the LORD gave the people favour in the sight of the Egyptians, so that they lent unto them such things as they required. And they spoiled the Egyptians.

[37]And the children of Israel journeyed from Rameses to Succoth, about six hundred thousand on foot that were men, beside children. [38]And a mixed multitude went up also with them; and flocks, and herds, even very much cattle. [39]And they baked unleavened cakes of the dough which they brought forth out of Egypt, for it was not leavened; because they were thrust out of Egypt, and could not tarry, neither had they prepared for themselves any victual.

[40]Now the sojourning of the children of Israel, who dwelt in Egypt, was four hundred and thirty years. [41]And it came to pass at the end of the four hundred and thirty years, even the selfsame day it came to pass, that all the hosts of the LORD went out from the land of Egypt. [42]It is a night to be much observed unto the LORD for bringing them out from the land of Egypt: this is that night of the LORD to be observed of all the children of Israel in their generations.

CROSSING THE RED SEA

Chapter 14

AND IT WAS TOLD THE KING OF EGYPT THAT THE people fled: and the heart of Pharaoh and of his servants was turned against the people, and they said, "Why have we done this, that we have let Israel go from serving us?" [6]And he made ready his chariot, and took his people with him: [7]and he took six hundred chosen chariots, and all the chariots of Egypt, and captains over every one of them. [8]And the LORD hardened the heart of Pharaoh king of Egypt, and he pursued after the children of Israel: and the children of Israel went out with an high hand. [9]But the Egyptians pursued after them, all the horses and chariots of Pharaoh, and his horsemen, and his army, and overtook them encamping by the sea, beside Pi-hahiroth, before Baal-zephon.

[10]And when Pharaoh drew nigh, the children of Israel lifted up their eyes, and, behold, the Egyptians marched after them; and they were sore afraid: and the children of Israel cried out unto the LORD. [11]And they said unto Moses, "Because there were no graves in Egypt, hast thou taken us away to die in the wilderness? Wherefore hast thou dealt thus with us, to carry us forth out of Egypt? [12]Is not this the word that we did tell thee in Egypt, saying, 'Let us alone, that we may serve the Egyptians'? For it had been better for us to serve the Egyptians, than that we should die in the wilderness."

[13]And Moses said unto the people, "Fear ye not, stand still, and see the salvation of the LORD, which he will shew to you to day: for the Egyptians whom ye have seen to day, ye shall see them again no more for ever. [14]The LORD shall fight for you, and ye shall hold your peace."

[15]And the LORD said unto Moses, "Wherefore criest thou unto me? Speak unto the children of Israel, that they go forward: [16]but lift thou up thy rod, and stretch out thine hand over the sea, and divide it: and the children of Israel shall go on dry ground through the midst of the sea. [17]And I, behold, I will harden the hearts of the Egyptians, and they shall follow them: and I will get me honour upon Pharaoh, and upon all his host, upon his chariots, and upon his horsemen. [18]And the Egyptians shall know that I am the LORD, when I have gotten me honour upon Pharaoh, upon his chariots, and upon his horsemen."

[19]And the angel of God, which went before the camp of Israel, removed and went behind them; and the pillar of the cloud went from before their face, and stood behind them: [20]and it came between the camp of the Egyptians and the camp of Israel; and it was a cloud and darkness to them, but it gave light by night to these: so that the one came not near the other all the night.

[21]And Moses stretched out his hand over the sea; and the LORD caused the sea to go back by a strong east wind all that night, and made the sea dry land, and the waters were

Chapter 14

Crossing the Red Sea, *Flemish School*

Chapter 14

divided. [22]And the children of Israel went into the midst of the sea upon the dry ground: and the waters were a wall unto them on their right hand, and on their left.

[23]And the Egyptians pursued, and went in after them to the midst of the sea, even all Pharaoh's horses, his chariots, and his horsemen. [24]And it came to pass, that in the morning watch the Lord looked unto the host of the Egyptians through the pillar of fire and of the cloud, and troubled the host of the Egyptians, [25]and took off their chariot wheels, that they drave them heavily: so that the Egyptians said, "Let us flee from the face of Israel; for the Lord fighteth for them against the Egyptians."

[26]And the Lord said unto Moses, "Stretch out thine hand over the sea, that the waters may come again upon the Egyptians, upon their chariots, and upon their horsemen." [27]And Moses stretched forth his hand over the sea, and the sea returned to his strength when the morning appeared; and the Egyptians fled against it; and the Lord overthrew the Egyptians in the midst of the sea. [28]And the waters returned, and covered the chariots, and the horsemen, and all the host of Pharaoh that came into the sea after them; there remained not so much as one of them.

Chapter 14

[29]But the children of Israel walked upon dry land in the midst of the sea; and the waters were a wall unto them on their right hand, and on their left. [30]Thus the LORD saved Israel that day out of the hand of the Egyptians; and Israel saw the Egyptians dead upon the sea shore. [31]And Israel saw that great work which the LORD did upon the Egyptians: and the people feared the LORD, and believed the LORD, and his servant Moses.

QUAIL AND MANNA

Chapter 15

AND THEY CAME TO ELIM, WHERE WERE TWELVE wells of water, and threescore and ten palm trees: and they encamped there by the waters.

Chapter 16

AND THEY TOOK THEIR JOURNEY FROM ELIM, AND ALL THE congregation of the children of Israel came unto the wilderness of Sin, which is between Elim and Sinai, on the fifteenth day of the second month after their departing out of the land of Egypt. [2]And the whole congregation of the children of Israel murmured against Moses and Aaron in the wilderness: [3]and the children of Israel said unto them, "Would to God we had died by the hand of the LORD in the land of Egypt, when we sat by the flesh pots, and when we did eat bread to the full; for ye have brought us forth into this wilderness, to kill this whole assembly with hunger."

[4]Then said the LORD unto Moses, "Behold, I will rain bread from heaven for you; and the people shall go out and gather a certain rate every day, that I may prove them, whether they will walk in my law, or no. [5]And it shall come to pass, that on the sixth day they shall prepare that which they bring in; and it shall be twice as much as they gather daily."

[6]And Moses and Aaron said unto all the children of Israel, "At even, then ye shall know that the LORD hath brought you out from the land of Egypt: [7]and in the morning, then ye shall see the glory of the LORD; for that he heareth your murmurings against the LORD: and what are we, that ye murmur against us?"

[8]And Moses said, "This shall be, when the LORD shall give you in the evening flesh to eat, and in the morning bread to the full; for that the LORD heareth your murmurings which ye murmur against him: and what are we? Your murmurings are not against us, but against the LORD."

[9]And Moses spake unto Aaron, "Say unto all the congregation of the children of Israel, 'Come near before the LORD: for he hath heard your murmurings.'"

[10]And it came to pass, as Aaron spake unto the whole congregation of the children of Israel, that they looked toward the wilderness, and, behold, the glory of the LORD appeared in the cloud.

[11]And the LORD spake unto Moses, saying, [12]"I have heard the murmurings of the children of Israel: speak unto them, saying, 'At even ye shall eat flesh, and in the morning ye shall be filled with bread; and ye shall know that I am the LORD your God.'"

[13]And it came to pass, that at even the quails came up, and covered the camp: and in the morning the dew lay round about the host. [14]And when the dew that lay was gone up, behold, upon the face of the wilderness there lay a small round thing, as small as the hoar frost on the ground. [15]And when the children of Israel saw it, they said to one another, "It is manna": for they wist not what it was.

And Moses said unto them, "This is the bread which the LORD hath given you to eat. [16]This is the thing which the LORD hath commanded, 'Gather of it every man according to his eating, an omer for every man, according to the number of your persons; take ye every man for them which are in his tents.'"

[17]And the children of Israel did so, and gathered, some more, some less. And when they did mete it with an omer, he that gathered much had nothing over, and he that gathered little had no lack; they gathered every man according to his eating.

At Mount Sinai

Chapter 19

In the third month, when the children of Israel were gone forth out of the land of Egypt, the same day came they into the wilderness of Sinai. [2]For they were departed from Rephidim, and were come to the desert of Sinai, and had pitched in the wilderness; and there Israel camped before the mount.

[3]And Moses went up unto God, and the Lord called unto him out of the mountain, saying, "Thus shalt thou say to the house of Jacob, and tell the children of Israel; [4]'Ye have seen what I did unto the Egyptians, and how I bare you on eagles' wings, and brought you unto myself. [5]Now therefore, if ye will obey my voice indeed, and keep my covenant, then ye shall be a peculiar treasure unto me above all people: for all the earth is mine: [6]and ye shall be unto me a kingdom of priests, and an holy nation.' These are the words which thou shalt speak unto the children of Israel."

The Ten Commandments

Chapter 19

And Moses brought forth the people out of the camp to meet with God; and they stood at the nether part of the mount. [18]And mount Sinai was altogether on a smoke, because the Lord descended upon it in fire: and the smoke thereof ascended as the smoke of a furnace, and the whole mount quaked greatly. [19]And when the voice of the trumpet sounded long, and waxed louder and louder, Moses spake, and God answered him by a voice.

[20]And the Lord came down upon mount Sinai, on the top of the mount: and the Lord called Moses up to the top of the mount; and Moses went up. [21]And the Lord said unto Moses, "Go down, charge the people, lest they break through unto the Lord to gaze, and many of them perish. [22]And let the priests also, which come

Chapter 19

THE COLUMN OF SMOKE, *School of Raphael*

Chapter 19

near to the LORD, sanctify themselves, lest the LORD break forth upon them."

23 And Moses said unto the LORD, "The people cannot come up to mount Sinai: for thou chargedst us, saying, 'Set bounds about the mount, and sanctify it.'"

24 And the LORD said unto him, "Away, get thee down, and thou shalt come up, thou, and Aaron with thee: but let not the priests and the people break through to come up unto the LORD, lest he break forth upon them."

25 So Moses went down unto the people, and spake unto them.

Chapter 20

AND GOD SPAKE ALL THESE WORDS, SAYING,

2 "I am the LORD thy God, which have brought thee out of the land of Egypt, out of the house of bondage.

3 "Thou shalt have no other gods before me.

4 "Thou shalt not make unto thee any graven image, or any likeness of any thing that is in heaven above, or that is

in the earth beneath, or that is in the water under the earth: [5]thou shalt not bow down thyself to them, nor serve them: for I the LORD thy God am a jealous God, visiting the iniquity of the fathers upon the children unto the third and fourth generation of them that hate me: [6]and shewing mercy unto thousands of them that love me, and keep my commandments.

[7]"Thou shalt not take the name of the LORD thy God in vain; for the LORD will not hold him guiltless that taketh his name in vain.

[8]"Remember the sabbath day, to keep it holy. [9]Six days shalt thou labour, and do all thy work: [10]but the seventh day is the sabbath of the LORD thy God: in it thou shalt not do any work, thou, nor thy son, nor thy daughter, thy manservant, nor thy maidservant, nor thy cattle, nor thy stranger that is within thy gates: [11]for in six days the LORD made heaven and earth, the sea, and all that in them is, and rested the seventh day: wherefore the LORD blessed the sabbath day, and hallowed it.

[12]"Honour thy father and thy mother: that thy days may be long upon the land which the LORD thy God giveth thee.

[13]"Thou shalt not kill.

[14]"Thou shalt not commit adultery.

[15]"Thou shalt not steal.

[16]"Thou shalt not bear false witness against thy neighbour.

[17]"Thou shalt not covet thy neighbour's house, thou shalt not covet thy neighbour's wife, nor his manservant, nor his maidservant, nor his ox, nor his ass, nor any thing that is thy neighbour's."

[18]And all the people saw the thunderings, and the lightnings, and the noise of the trumpet, and the mountain smoking: and when the people saw it, they removed, and stood afar off. [19]And they said unto Moses, "Speak thou with us, and we will hear: but let not God speak with us, lest we die."

[20]And Moses said unto the people, "Fear not: for God is come to prove you, and that his fear may be before your faces, that ye sin not."

[21]And the people stood afar off, and Moses drew near unto the thick darkness where God was.

The Tabernacle and the Ark

Chapter 24

AND MOSES WENT UP INTO THE MOUNT, AND A cloud covered the mount. [16]And the glory of the LORD abode upon mount Sinai, and the cloud covered it six days: and the seventh day he called unto Moses out of the midst of the cloud. [17]And the sight of the glory of the LORD was like devouring fire on the top of the mount in the eyes of the children of Israel. [18]And Moses went into the midst of the cloud, and gat him up into the mount: and Moses was in the mount forty days and forty nights.

Chapter 25

AND THE LORD SPAKE UNTO MOSES, SAYING, [2]"SPEAK UNTO the children of Israel, that they bring me an offering: of every man that giveth it willingly with his heart ye shall take my offering. [3]And this is the offering which ye shall take of them; gold, and silver, and brass, [4]and blue, and purple, and scarlet, and fine linen, and goats' hair, [5]and rams' skins dyed red, and badgers' skins, and shittim wood, [6]oil for the light, spices for anointing oil, and for sweet incense, [7]onyx stones, and stones to be set in the ephod, and in the breastplate.

[8]"And let them make me a sanctuary; that I may dwell among them. [9]According to all that I shew thee, after the pattern of the tabernacle, and the pattern of all the instruments thereof, even so shall ye make it.

[10]"And they shall make an ark of shittim wood: two cubits and a half shall be the length thereof, and a cubit and a half the breadth thereof, and a cubit and a half the height thereof. [11]And thou shalt overlay it with pure gold, within and without shalt thou overlay it, and shalt make upon it a crown of gold round about. [12]And thou shalt cast four rings of gold for it, and put them in the four corners thereof; and two rings shall be in the one side of it, and two rings in the other side of it. [13]And thou shalt make staves of shittim wood, and overlay them with gold. [14]And thou

Chapter 25

shalt put the staves into the rings by the sides of the ark, that the ark may be borne with them. [15]The staves shall be in the rings of the ark: they shall not be taken from it. [16]And thou shalt put into the ark the testimony which I shall give thee.

[17]"And thou shalt make a mercy seat of pure gold: two cubits and a half shall be the length thereof, and a cubit and a half the breadth thereof. [18]And thou shalt make two cherubims of gold, of beaten work shalt thou make them, in the two ends of the mercy seat. [19]And make one cherub on the one end, and the other cherub on the other end: even of the mercy seat shall ye make the cherubims on the two ends thereof. [20]And the cherubims shall stretch forth their wings on high, covering the mercy seat with their wings, and their faces shall look one to another; toward the mercy seat shall the faces of the cherubims be. [21]And thou shalt put the mercy seat above upon the ark; and in the ark thou shalt put the testimony that I shall give thee. [22]And there I will meet with thee, and I will commune with thee from above the mercy seat, from between the two cherubims which are upon the ark of the testimony, of all things which I will give thee in commandment unto the children of Israel."

The Sabbath

Chapter 31

And the Lord spake unto Moses, saying, [13]"Speak thou also unto the children of Israel, saying, 'Verily my sabbaths ye shall keep: for it is a sign between me and you throughout your generations; that ye may know that I am the Lord that doth sanctify you.

[14]"'Ye shall keep the sabbath therefore; for it is holy unto you: every one that defileth it shall surely be put to death: for whosoever doeth any work therein, that soul shall be cut off from among his people. [15]Six days may work be done; but in the seventh is the sabbath of rest, holy to the Lord. whosoever doeth any work in the sabbath day, he shall surely be put to death. [16]Wherefore the children of

Chapter 31

Israel shall keep the sabbath, to observe the sabbath throughout their generations, for a perpetual covenant. [17]It is a sign between me and the children of Israel for ever: for in six days the LORD made heaven and earth, and on the seventh day he rested, and was refreshed.'"

[18]And he gave unto Moses, when he had made an end of communing with him upon mount Sinai, two tables of testimony, tables of stone, written with the finger of God.

THE GOLDEN CALF

Chapter 32

AND WHEN THE PEOPLE SAW THAT MOSES DELAYED to come down out of the mount, the people gathered themselves together unto Aaron, and said unto him, "Up, make us gods, which shall go before us; for as for this Moses, the man that brought us up out of the land of Egypt, we wot not what is become of him."

[2]And Aaron said unto them, "Break off the golden earrings, which are in the ears of your wives, of your sons, and of your daughters, and bring them unto me." [3]And all the people brake off the golden earrings which were in their ears, and brought them unto Aaron. [4]And he received them at their hand, and fashioned it with a graving tool, after he had made it a molten calf: and they said, "These be thy gods, O Israel, which brought thee up out of the land of Egypt."

[5]And when Aaron saw it, he built an altar before it; and Aaron made proclamation, and said, "To morrow is a feast to the LORD." [6]And they rose up early on the morrow, and offered burnt offerings, and brought peace offerings; and the people sat down to eat and to drink, and rose up to play.

[7]And the LORD said unto Moses, "Go, get thee down; for thy people, which thou broughtest out of the land of Egypt, have corrupted themselves: [8]they have turned aside quickly out of the way which I commanded them: they have made them a molten calf, and have worshipped it, and have sacrificed thereunto, and said, 'These be thy

MOSES ON MOUNT SINAI AND THE ADORATION OF THE GOLDEN CALF by *Cosimo Rosselli*

gods, O Israel, which have brought thee up out of the land of Egypt.'"

[9]And the LORD said unto Moses, "I have seen this people, and, behold, it is a stiffnecked people: [10]now therefore let me alone, that my wrath may wax hot against them, and that I may consume them: and I will make of thee a great nation."

[11]And Moses besought the LORD his God, and said, "LORD, why doth thy wrath wax hot against thy people, which thou hast brought forth out of the land of Egypt with great power, and with a mighty hand? [12]Wherefore should the Egyptians speak, and say, 'For mischief did he bring them out, to slay them in the mountains, and to consume them from the face of the earth'? Turn from thy fierce wrath, and repent of this evil against thy people. [13]Remember Abraham, Isaac, and Israel, thy servants, to whom

thou swarest by thine own self, and saidst unto them, 'I will multiply your seed as the stars of heaven, and all this land that I have spoken of will I give unto your seed, and they shall inherit it for ever.'" [14]And the LORD repented of the evil which he thought to do unto his people.

[15]And Moses turned, and went down from the mount, and the two tables of the testimony were in his hand: the tables were written on both their sides; on the one side and on the other were they written. [16]And the tables were the work of God, and the writing was the writing of God, graven upon the tables.

[17]And when Joshua heard the noise of the people as they shouted, he said unto Moses, "There is a noise of war in the camp."

[18]And he said, "It is not the voice of them that shout for mastery, neither is it the voice of them that cry for being overcome: but the noise of them that sing do I hear."

[19]And it came to pass, as soon as he came nigh unto the camp, that he saw the calf, and the dancing: and Moses' anger waxed hot, and he cast the tables out of his hands, and brake them beneath the mount. [20]And he took the calf which they had made, and burnt it in the fire, and ground it to powder, and strawed it upon the water, and made the children of Israel drink of it.

[21]And Moses said unto Aaron, "What did this people unto thee, that thou hast brought so great a sin upon them?"

[22]And Aaron said, "Let not the anger of my lord wax hot: thou knowest the people, that they are set on mischief. [23]For they said unto me, 'Make us gods, which shall go before us: for as for this Moses, the man that brought us up out of the land of Egypt, we wot not what is become of him.' [24]And I said unto them, 'Whosoever hath any gold, let them break it off.' So they gave it me: then I cast it into the fire, and there came out this calf."

[25]And when Moses saw that the people were naked; (for Aaron had made them naked unto their shame among their enemies:) [26]then Moses stood in the gate of the camp, and said, "Who is on the LORD's side? Let him come unto me." And all the sons of Levi gathered themselves together unto him.

[27]And he said unto them, "Thus saith the LORD God of

Chapter 32

Israel, 'Put every man his sword by his side, and go in and out from gate to gate throughout the camp, and slay every man his brother, and every man his companion, and every man his neighbour.'" [28]And the children of Levi did according to the word of Moses: and there fell of the people that day about three thousand men. [29]For Moses had said, "Consecrate yourselves to day to the LORD, even every man upon his son, and upon his brother; that he may bestow upon you a blessing this day."

[30]And it came to pass on the morrow, that Moses said unto the people, "Ye have sinned a great sin: and now I will go up unto the LORD; peradventure I shall make an atonement for your sin."

[31]And Moses returned unto the LORD, and said, "Oh, this people have sinned a great sin, and have made them gods of gold. [32]Yet now, if thou wilt forgive their sin – ; and if not, blot me, I pray thee, out of thy book which thou hast written."

[33]And the LORD said unto Moses, "Whosoever hath sinned against me, him will I blot out of my book. [34]Therefore now go, lead the people unto the place of which I have spoken unto thee: behold, mine Angel shall go before thee: nevertheless in the day when I visit I will visit their sin upon them."

[35]And the LORD plagued the people, because they made the calf, which Aaron made.

THE TABLES OF STONE RENEWED

Chapter 34

AND THE LORD SAID UNTO MOSES, "HEW THEE TWO tables of stone like unto the first: and I will write upon these tables the words that were written in the first tables, which thou brakest. [2]And be ready in the morning, and come up in the morning unto mount Sinai, and present thyself there to me in the top of the mount. [3]And no man shall come up with thee, neither let any man be seen throughout all the mount; neither let the flocks nor herds feed before that mount."

Chapter 34

MOSES AND THE TABLETS OF LAW *by Raphael*

Chapter 34

[4]And he hewed two tables of stone like unto the first; and Moses rose up early in the morning, and went up unto mount Sinai, as the LORD had commanded him, and took in his hand the two tables of stone. [5]And the LORD descended in the cloud, and stood with him there, and proclaimed the name of the LORD. [6]And the LORD passed by before him, and proclaimed, "The LORD, The LORD God, merciful and gracious, longsuffering, and abundant in goodness and truth, [7]keeping mercy for thousands, forgiving iniquity and transgression and sin, and that will by no means clear the guilty; visiting the iniquity of the fathers upon the children, and upon the children's children, unto the third and to the fourth generation."

[8]And Moses made haste, and bowed his head toward the earth, and worshipped. And he said, [9]"If now I have found grace in thy sight, O Lord, let my Lord, I pray thee, go among us; for it is a stiffnecked people; and pardon our iniquity and our sin, and take us for thine inheritance."

[10]And he said, "Behold, I make a covenant: before all thy people I will do marvels, such as have not been done in all the earth, nor in any nation: and all the people among which thou art shall see the work of the LORD: for it is a terrible thing that I will do with thee."

Chapters & Verses
FROM
THE THIRD, FOURTH & FIFTH
BOOKS OF MOSES
CALLED

LEVITICUS NUMBERS & DEUTERONOMY

THE DAY OF ATONEMENT • LEAVING SINAI • WATER FROM THE ROCK • MOSES SPEAKS TO ISRAEL • MOSES COMMANDS OBEDIENCE TO GOD • MOSES COMMANDS THE FEAR OF THE LORD • THE OFFER OF LIFE OR DEATH • THE DEATH OF MOSES

LEVITICUS

The Day of Atonement

Chapter 16

AND THE LORD SAID UNTO MOSES, “SPEAK UNTO Aaron thy brother, that he come not at all times into the holy place within the veil before the mercy seat, which is upon the ark; that he die not; for I will appear in the cloud upon the mercy seat.

[3]“Thus shall Aaron come into the holy place: with a young bullock for a sin offering, and a ram for a burnt offering. [4]He shall put on the holy linen coat, and he shall have the linen breeches upon his flesh, and shall be girded with a linen girdle, and with the linen mitre shall he be attired: these are holy garments; therefore shall he wash his flesh in water, and so put them on. [5]And he shall take of the congregation of the children of Israel two kids of the goats for a sin offering, and one ram for a burnt offering.

[6]“And Aaron shall offer his bullock of the sin offering, which is for himself, and make an atonement for himself, and for his house. [7]And he shall take the two goats, and present them before the Lord at the door of the tabernacle of the congregation. [8]And Aaron shall cast lots upon the two goats; one lot for the Lord, and the other lot for the scapegoat. [9]And Aaron shall bring the goat upon which the Lord’s lot fell, and offer him for a sin offering. [10]But the goat, on which the lot fell to be the scapegoat, shall be presented alive before the Lord, to make an atonement with him, and to let him go for a scapegoat into the wilderness.

[11]“And Aaron shall bring the bullock of the sin offering, which is for himself, and shall make an atonement for himself, and for his house, and shall kill the bullock of the sin offering which is for himself: [12]and he shall take a censer full of burning coals of fire from off the altar before the

Chapter 16

Lord, and his hands full of sweet incense beaten small, and bring it within the veil: [13]and he shall put the incense upon the fire before the Lord, that the cloud of the incense may cover the mercy seat that is upon the testimony, that he die not: [14]and he shall take of the blood of the bullock, and sprinkle it with his finger upon the mercy seat eastward; and before the mercy seat shall he sprinkle of the blood with his finger seven times.

[15]"Then shall he kill the goat of the sin offering, that is for the people, and bring his blood within the veil, and do with that blood as he did with the blood of the bullock, and sprinkle it upon the mercy seat, and before the mercy seat: [16]and he shall make an atonement for the holy place, because of the uncleanness of the children of Israel, and because of their transgressions in all their sins: and so shall he do for the tabernacle of the congregation, that remaineth among them in the midst of their uncleanness. [17]And there shall be no man in the tabernacle of the congregation when he goeth in to make an atonement in the holy place, until he come out, and have made an atonement for himself, and for his household, and for all the congregation of Israel."

NUMBERS

Leaving Sinai

Chapter 9

And on the day that the tabernacle was reared up the cloud covered the tabernacle, namely, the tent of the testimony: and at even there was upon the tabernacle as it were the appearance of fire, until the morning. [16]So it was alway: the cloud covered it by day, and the appear-

Chapter 9

ance of fire by night. [17]And when the cloud was taken up from the tabernacle, then after that the children of Israel journeyed: and in the place where the cloud abode, there the children of Israel pitched their tents. [18]At the commandment of the LORD the children of Israel journeyed, and at the commandment of the LORD they pitched: as long as the cloud abode upon the tabernacle they rested in their tents. [19]And when the cloud tarried long upon the tabernacle many days, then the children of Israel kept the charge of the LORD, and journeyed not. [20]And so it was, when the cloud was a few days upon the tabernacle; according to the commandment of the LORD they abode in their tents, and according to the commandment of the LORD they journeyed. [21]And so it was, when the cloud abode from even unto the morning, and that the cloud was taken up in the morning, then they journeyed: whether it was by day or by night that the cloud was taken up, they journeyed. [22]Or whether it were two days, or a month, or a year, that the cloud tarried upon the tabernacle, remaining thereon, the children of Israel abode in their tents, and journeyed not: but when it was taken up, they journeyed. [23]At the commandment of the LORD they rested in the tents, and at the commandment of the LORD they journeyed: they kept the charge of the LORD, at the commandment of the LORD by the hand of Moses.

WATER FROM THE ROCK

Chapter 20

THEN CAME THE CHILDREN OF ISRAEL, EVEN THE whole congregation, into the desert of Zin in the first month: and the people abode in Kadesh; and Miriam died there, and was buried there.

[2]And there was no water for the congregation: and they gathered themselves together against Moses and against Aaron. [3]And the people chode with Moses, and spake, saying, "Would God that we had died when our brethren died before the LORD! [4]And why have ye brought up the congregation of the LORD into this wilderness, that we and our

MOSES STRIKES WATER FROM THE ROCK *by Raphael*

cattle should die there? [5]And wherefore have ye made us to come up out of Egypt, to bring us in unto this evil place? It is no place of seed, or of figs, or of vines, or of pomegranates; neither is there any water to drink."

[6]And Moses and Aaron went from the presence of the assembly unto the door of the tabernacle of the congregation, and they fell upon their faces: and the glory of the LORD appeared unto them. [7]And the LORD spake unto Moses, saying, [8]"Take the rod, and gather thou the assembly together, thou, and Aaron thy brother, and speak ye unto the rock before their eyes; and it shall give forth his water, and thou shalt bring forth to them water out of the rock: so thou shalt give the congregation and their beasts drink."

[9]And Moses took the rod from before the LORD, as he commanded him. [10]And Moses and Aaron gathered the congregation together before the rock, and he said unto them, "Hear now, ye rebels; must we fetch you water out of this rock?" [11]And Moses lifted up his hand, and with his rod he smote the rock twice: and the water came out abundantly, and the congregation drank, and their beasts also.

Chapter 20

[12]And the LORD spake unto Moses and Aaron, "Because ye believed me not, to sanctify me in the eyes of the children of Israel, therefore ye shall not bring this congregation into the land which I have given them."

DEUTERONOMY

MOSES SPEAKS TO ISRAEL

Chapter 1

THESE BE THE WORDS WHICH MOSES SPAKE UNTO all Israel on this side Jordan in the wilderness, in the plain over against the Red sea, between Paran, and Tophel, and Laban, and Hazeroth, and Dizahab. [2](There are eleven days' journey from Horeb by the way of mount Seir unto Kadesh-barnea.)

[3]And it came to pass in the fortieth year, in the eleventh month, on the first day of the month, that Moses spake unto the children of Israel, according unto all that the LORD had given him in commandment unto them; [4]after he had slain Sihon the king of the Amorites, which dwelt in Heshbon, and Og the king of Bashan, which dwelt at Astaroth in Edrei: [5]on this side Jordan, in the land of Moab, began Moses to declare this law, saying, [6]"The LORD our God spake unto us in Horeb, saying, 'Ye have dwelt long enough in this mount: [7]turn you, and take your journey, and go to the mount of the Amorites, and unto all the places nigh thereunto, in the plain, in the hills, and in the vale, and in the south, and by the sea side, to the land of the Canaanites, and unto Lebanon, unto the great river, the river Euphrates. [8]Behold, I have set the land before you: go in and possess the land which the LORD sware unto your fathers, Abraham, Isaac, and Jacob, to give unto them and to their seed after them.'"

Moses Commands Obedience to God

"NOW THEREFORE HEARKEN, O ISRAEL, unto the statutes and unto the judgments, which I teach you, for to do them, that ye may live, and go in and possess the land which the LORD God of your fathers giveth you. [2]Ye shall not add unto the word which I command you, neither shall ye diminish aught from it, that ye may keep the commandments of the LORD your God which I command you . . .

Chapter 4

[32]"For ask now of the days that are past, which were before thee, since the day that God created man upon the earth, and ask from the one side of heaven unto the other, whether there hath been any such thing as this great thing is, or hath been heard like it? [33]Did ever people hear the voice of God speaking out of the midst of the fire, as thou hast heard, and live? [34]Or hath God assayed to go and take him a nation from the midst of another nation, by temptations, by signs, and by wonders, and by war, and by a mighty hand, and by a stretched out arm, and by great terrors, according to all that the LORD your God did for you in Egypt before your eyes?

Chapter 4

[35]"Unto thee it was shewed, that thou mightest know that the LORD he is God; there is none else beside him. [36]Out of heaven he made thee to hear his voice, that he might instruct thee: and upon earth he shewed thee his great fire; and thou heardest his words out of the midst of the fire. [37]And because he loved thy fathers, therefore he chose their seed after them, and brought thee out in his sight with his mighty power out of Egypt; [38]to drive out nations from before thee greater and mightier than thou art, to bring thee in, to give thee their land for an inheritance, as it is this day.

[39]"Know therefore this day, and consider it in thine heart, that the LORD he is God in heaven above, and upon

Chapter 4

the earth beneath: there is none else. [40]Thou shalt keep therefore his statutes, and his commandments, which I command thee this day, that it may go well with thee, and with thy children after thee, and that thou mayest prolong thy days upon the earth, which the LORD thy God giveth thee, for ever."

MOSES COMMANDS THE FEAR OF THE LORD

Chapter 10

"AND NOW, ISRAEL, WHAT DOTH THE LORD thy God require of thee, but to fear the LORD thy God, to walk in all his ways, and to love him, and to serve the LORD thy God with all thy heart and with all thy soul, [13]to keep the commandments of the LORD, and his statutes, which I command thee this day for thy good?

TESTAMENT AND DEATH OF MOSES *by Luca Signorelli*

Chapter 10

[14]"Behold, the heaven and the heaven of heavens is the LORD's thy God, the earth also, with all that therein is. [15]Only the LORD had a delight in thy fathers to love them, and he chose their seed after them, even you above all people, as it is this day. [16]Circumcise therefore the foreskin of your heart, and be no more stiffnecked. [17]For the LORD your God is God of gods, and Lord of lords, a great God, a mighty, and a terrible, which regardeth not persons, nor taketh reward: [18]he doth execute the judgment of the fatherless and widow, and loveth the stranger, in giving him food and raiment. [19]Love ye therefore the stranger: for ye were strangers in the land of Egypt. [20]Thou shalt fear the LORD thy God; him shalt thou serve, and to him shalt thou cleave, and swear by his name. [21]He is thy praise, and he is thy God, that hath done for thee these great and terrible things, which thine eyes have seen. [22]Thy fathers went down into Egypt with threescore and ten persons; and now the LORD thy God hath made thee as the stars of heaven for multitude.

Chapter 11

"THEREFORE THOU SHALT LOVE THE LORD THY GOD, AND keep his charge, and his statutes, and his judgments, and his commandments, alway."

THE OFFER OF LIFE OR DEATH

Chapter 30

"FOR THIS COMMANDMENT WHICH I COMMAND thee this day, it is not hidden from thee, neither is it far off. [12]It is not in heaven, that thou shouldest say, 'Who shall go up for us to heaven, and bring it unto us, that we may hear it, and do it?' [13]Neither is it beyond the sea, that thou shouldest say, 'Who shall go over the sea for us, and bring it unto us, that we may hear it, and do it?' [14]But the word is very nigh unto thee, in thy mouth, and in thy heart, that thou mayest do it.

Chapter 30

[15]"See, I have set before thee this day life and good, and death and evil; [16]in that I command thee this day to love the LORD thy God, to walk in his ways, and to keep his commandments and his statutes and his judgments, that thou mayest live and multiply: and the LORD thy God shall bless thee in the land whither thou goest to possess it.

[17]"But if thine heart turn away, so that thou wilt not hear, but shalt be drawn away, and worship other gods, and serve them; [18]I denounce unto you this day, that ye shall surely perish, and that ye shall not prolong your days upon the land, whither thou passest over Jordan to go to possess it.

[19]"I call heaven and earth to record this day against you, that I have set before you life and death, blessing and cursing: therefore choose life, that both thou and thy seed may live: [20]that thou mayest love the LORD thy God, and that thou mayest obey his voice, and that thou mayest cleave unto him: for he is thy life, and the length of thy days: that thou mayest dwell in the land which the LORD sware unto thy fathers, to Abraham, to Isaac, and to Jacob, to give them."

The Death of Moses

Chapter 34

AND MOSES WENT UP FROM THE PLAINS OF MOAB unto the mountain of Nebo, to the top of Pisgah, that is over against Jericho. And the LORD shewed him all the land of Gilead, unto Dan, [2]and all Naphtali, and the land of Ephraim, and Manasseh, and all the land of Judah, unto the utmost sea, [3]and the south, and the plain of the valley of Jericho, the city of palm trees, unto Zoar. [4]And the LORD said unto him, "This is the land which I sware unto Abraham, unto Isaac, and unto Jacob, saying, I will give it unto thy seed: I have caused thee to see it with thine eyes, but thou shalt not go over thither."

[5]So Moses the servant of the LORD died there in the land of Moab, according to the word of the LORD. [6]And he buried him in a valley in the land of Moab, over against

Beth-peor: but no man knoweth of his sepulchre unto this day. [7]And Moses was an hundred and twenty years old when he died: his eye was not dim, nor his natural force abated. [8]And the children of Israel wept for Moses in the plains of Moab thirty days: so the days of weeping and mourning for Moses were ended.

[9]And Joshua the son of Nun was full of the spirit of wisdom; for Moses had laid his hands upon him: and the children of Israel hearkened unto him, and did as the LORD commanded Moses.

[10]And there arose not a prophet since in Israel like unto Moses, whom the LORD knew face to face, [11]in all the signs and the wonders, which the LORD sent him to do in the land of Egypt to Pharaoh, and to all his servants, and to all his land, [12]and in all that mighty hand, and in all the great terror which Moses shewed in the sight of all Israel.

God surrounded by Fire, *Illuminated manuscript*

Chapters & Verses
FROM
THE BOOKS OF

JOSHUA JUDGES & RUTH

THE PROMISED LAND • RAHAB AND THE SPIES • CROSSING THE JORDAN • THE FALL OF JERICHO • ISRAEL'S WICKEDNESS • DEBORAH • GIDEON • GIDEON DEFEATS THE MIDIANITES • THE BIRTH OF SAMSON • SAMSON AND DELILAH • NAOMI AND RUTH • RUTH AND BOAZ • RUTH'S MARRIAGE

JOSHUA

The Promised Land

Chapter 1

NOW AFTER THE DEATH OF MOSES THE SERVANT of the LORD it came to pass, that the LORD spake unto Joshua the son of Nun, Moses' minister, saying, [2]"Moses my servant is dead; now therefore arise, go over this Jordan, thou, and all this people, unto the land which I do give to them, even to the children of Israel. [3]Every place that the sole of your foot shall tread upon, that have I given unto you, as I said unto Moses. [4]From the wilderness and this Lebanon even unto the great river, the river Euphrates, all the land of the Hittites, and unto the great sea toward the going down of the sun, shall be your coast. [5]There shall not any man be able to stand before thee all the days of thy life: as I was with Moses, so I will be with thee: I will not fail thee, nor forsake thee.

[6]"Be strong and of a good courage: for unto this people shalt thou divide for an inheritance the land, which I sware unto their fathers to give them. [7]Only be thou strong and very courageous, that thou mayest observe to do according to all the law, which Moses my servant commanded thee: turn not from it to the right hand or to the left, that thou mayest prosper whithersoever thou goest. [8]This book of the law shall not depart out of thy mouth; but thou shalt meditate therein day and night, that thou mayest observe to do according to all that is written therein: for then thou shalt make thy way prosperous, and then thou shalt have good success. [9]Have not I commanded thee? Be strong and of a good courage; be not afraid, neither be thou dismayed: for the LORD thy God is with thee whithersoever thou goest."

Rahab and the Spies

Chapter 2

AND JOSHUA THE SON OF NUN SENT OUT OF SHITtim two men to spy secretly, saying, "Go view the land, even Jericho." And they went, and came into an harlot's house, named Rahab, and lodged there.

[2]And it was told the king of Jericho, saying, "Behold, there came men in hither to night of the children of Israel to search out the country." [3]And the king of Jericho sent unto Rahab, saying, "Bring forth the men that are come to thee, which are entered into thine house: for they be come to search out all the country."

[4]And the woman took the two men, and hid them, and said thus, "There came men unto me, but I wist not whence they were: [5]and it came to pass about the time of shutting of the gate, when it was dark, that the men went out: whither the men went I wot not: pursue after them quickly; for ye shall overtake them." [6]But she had brought them up to the roof of the house, and hid them with the stalks of flax, which she had laid in order upon the roof. [7]And the men pursued after them the way to Jordan unto the fords: and as soon as they which pursued after them were gone out, they shut the gate.

[8]And before they were laid down, she came up unto them upon the roof; [9]and she said unto the men, "I know that the LORD hath given you the land, and that your terror is fallen upon us, and that all the inhabitants of the land faint because of you. [10]For we have heard how the LORD dried up the water of the Red sea for you, when ye came out of Egypt; and what ye did unto the two kings of the Amorites, that were on the other side Jordan, Sihon and Og, whom ye utterly destroyed. [11]And as soon as we had heard these things, our hearts did melt, neither did there remain any more courage in any man, because of you: for the LORD your God, he is God in heaven above, and in earth beneath. [12]Now therefore, I pray you, swear unto me by the LORD, since I have shewed you kindness, that ye will also shew kindness unto my father's house, and give me a true token: [13]and that ye will save alive my father, and my

RAHAB AND THE SPIES, *School of Lombardy*

mother, and my brethren, and my sisters, and all that they have, and deliver our lives from death."

[14]And the men answered her, "Our life for yours, if ye utter not this our business. And it shall be, when the LORD hath given us the land, that we will deal kindly and truly with thee."

[15]Then she let them down by a cord through the window: for her house was upon the town wall, and she dwelt upon the wall. [16]And she said unto them, "Get you to the mountain, lest the pursuers meet you; and hide yourselves there three days, until the pursuers be returned: and afterward may ye go your way."

[17]And the men said unto her, "We will be blameless of this thine oath which thou hast made us swear. [18]Behold, when we come into the land, thou shalt bind this line of scarlet thread in the window which thou didst let us down by: and thou shalt bring thy father, and thy mother, and thy brethren, and all thy father's household, home unto thee. [19]And it shall be, that whosoever shall go out of the

Chapter 2

doors of thy house into the street, his blood shall be upon his head, and we will be guiltless: and whosoever shall be with thee in the house, his blood shall be on our head, if any hand be upon him. [20]And if thou utter this our business, then we will be quit of thine oath which thou hast made us to swear."

[21]And she said, "According unto your words, so be it." And she sent them away, and they departed: and she bound the scarlet line in the window.

[22]And they went, and came unto the mountain, and abode there three days, until the pursuers were returned: and the pursuers sought them throughout all the way, but found them not. [23]So the two men returned, and descended from the mountain, and passed over, and came to Joshua the son of Nun, and told him all things that befell them: [24]and they said unto Joshua, "Truly the LORD hath delivered into our hands all the land; for even all the inhabitants of the country do faint because of us."

CROSSING THE JORDAN

Chapter 3

AND JOSHUA ROSE EARLY IN THE MORNING; AND they removed from Shittim, and came to Jordan, he and all the children of Israel, and lodged there before they passed over. [2]And it came to pass after three days, that the officers went through the host; [3]and they commanded the people, saying, "When ye see the ark of the covenant of the LORD your God, and the priests the Levites bearing it, then ye shall remove from your place, and go after it. [4]Yet there shall be a space between you and it, about two thousand cubits by measure: come not near unto it, that ye may know the way by which ye must go: for ye have not passed this way heretofore."

[5]And Joshua said unto the people, "Sanctify yourselves: for to morrow the LORD will do wonders among you."

[6]And Joshua spake unto the priests, saying, "Take up the ark of the covenant, and pass over before the people." And

they took up the ark of the covenant, and went before the people.

[7]And the LORD said unto Joshua, "This day will I begin to magnify thee in the sight of all Israel, that they may know that, as I was with Moses, so I will be with thee. [8]And thou shalt command the priests that bear the ark of the covenant, saying, 'When ye are come to the brink of the water of Jordan, ye shall stand still in Jordan.'"

[9]And Joshua said unto the children of Israel, "Come hither, and hear the words of the LORD your God." [10]And Joshua said, "Hereby ye shall know that the living God is among you, and that he will without fail drive out from before you the Canaanites, and the Hittites, and the Hivites, and the Perizzites, and the Girgashites, and the Amorites, and the Jebusites. [11]Behold, the ark of the covenant of the LORD of all the earth passeth over before you into Jordan. [12]Now therefore take you twelve men out of the tribes of Israel, out of every tribe a man. [13]And it shall come to pass, as soon as the soles of the feet of the priests that bear the ark of the LORD, the Lord of all the earth, shall rest in the waters of Jordan, that the waters of Jordan shall be cut off from the waters that come down from above; and they shall stand upon an heap."

[14]And it came to pass, when the people removed from their tents, to pass over Jordan, and the priests bearing the ark of the covenant before the people; [15]and as they that bare the ark were come unto Jordan, and the feet of the priests that bare the ark were dipped in the brim of the water, (for Jordan overfloweth all his banks all the time of harvest,) [16]that the waters which came down from above stood and rose up upon an heap very far from the city Adam, that is beside Zaretan: and those that came down toward the sea of the plain, even the salt sea, failed, and were cut off: and the people passed over right against Jericho. [17]And the priests that bare the ark of the covenant of the LORD stood firm on dry ground in the midst of Jordan, and all the Israelites passed over on dry ground, until all the people were passed clean over Jordan.

The Fall of Jericho

Chapter 5

And it came to pass, when Joshua was by Jericho, that he lifted up his eyes and looked, and, behold, there stood a man over against him with his sword drawn in his hand: and Joshua went unto him, and said unto him, "Art thou for us, or for our adversaries?"

[14]And he said, "Nay; but as captain of the host of the Lord am I now come." And Joshua fell on his face to the earth, and did worship, and said unto him, "What saith my lord unto his servant?"

[15]And the captain of the Lord's host said unto Joshua, "Loose thy shoe from off thy foot; for the place whereon thou standest is holy." And Joshua did so.

Chapter 6

Now Jericho was straitly shut up because of the children of Israel: none went out, and none came in.

[2]And the Lord said unto Joshua, "See, I have given into thine hand Jericho, and the king thereof, and the mighty men of valour. [3]And ye shall compass the city, all ye men of war, and go round about the city once. Thus shalt thou do six days. [4]And seven priests shall bear before the ark seven trumpets of rams' horns: and the seventh day ye shall compass the city seven times, and the priests shall blow with the trumpets. [5]And it shall come to pass, that when they make a long blast with the ram's horn, and when ye hear the sound of the trumpet, all the people shall shout with a great shout; and the wall of the city shall fall down flat, and the people shall ascend up every man straight before him."

[6]And Joshua the son of Nun called the priests, and said unto them, "Take up the ark of the covenant, and let seven priests bear seven trumpets of rams' horns before the ark of the Lord." [7]And he said unto the people, "Pass on, and compass the city, and let him that is armed pass on before the ark of the Lord."

[8]And it came to pass, when Joshua had spoken unto the people, that the seven priests bearing the seven trumpets of rams' horns passed on before the LORD, and blew with the trumpets: and the ark of the covenant of the LORD followed them. [9]And the armed men went before the priests that blew with the trumpets, and the rearward came after the ark, the priests going on, and blowing with the trumpets. [10]And Joshua had commanded the people, saying, "Ye shall not shout, nor make any noise with your voice, neither shall any word proceed out of your mouth, until the day I bid you shout; then shall ye shout." [11]So the ark of the LORD compassed the city, going about it once: and they came into the camp, and lodged in the camp.

[12]And Joshua rose early in the morning, and the priests took up the ark of the LORD. [13]And seven priests bearing seven trumpets of rams' horns before the ark of the LORD went on continually, and blew with the trumpets: and the armed men went before them; but the rearward came after the ark of the LORD, the priests going on, and blowing with the trumpets. [14]And the second day they compassed the city once, and returned into the camp: so they did six days.

[15]And it came to pass on the seventh day, that they rose early about the dawning of the day, and compassed the city after the same manner seven times: only on that day they compassed the city seven times. [16]And it came to pass at the seventh time, when the priests blew with the trumpets, Joshua said unto the people, "Shout; for the LORD hath given you the city. [17]And the city shall be accursed, even it, and all that are therein, to the LORD: only Rahab the harlot shall live, she and all that are with her in the house, because she hid the messengers that we sent. [18]And ye, in any wise keep yourselves from the accursed thing, lest ye make yourselves accursed, when ye take of the accursed thing, and make the camp of Israel a curse, and trouble it. [19]But all the silver, and gold, and vessels of brass and iron, are consecrated unto the LORD: they shall come into the treasury of the LORD."

[20]So the people shouted when the priests blew with the trumpets: and it came to pass, when the people heard the sound of the trumpet, and the people shouted with a great shout, that the wall fell down flat, so that the people went up into the city, every man straight before him, and they

THE FALL OF JERICHO *by Jean Fouquet*

took the city. [21]And they utterly destroyed all that was in the city, both man and woman, young and old, and ox, and sheep, and ass, with the edge of the sword.

[22]But Joshua had said unto the two men that had spied out the country, "Go into the harlot's house, and bring out thence the woman, and all that she hath, as ye sware unto her." [23]And the young men that were spies went in, and brought out Rahab, and her father, and her mother, and her brethren, and all that she had; and they brought out all her kindred, and left them without the camp of Israel.

[24]And they burnt the city with fire, and all that was therein: only the silver, and the gold, and the vessels of brass and of iron, they put into the treasury of the house of

Chapter 6

the Lord. 25 And Joshua saved Rahab the harlot alive, and her father's household, and all that she had; and she dwelleth in Israel even unto this day; because she hid the messengers, which Joshua sent to spy out Jericho.

26 And Joshua adjured them at that time, saying, "Cursed be the man before the Lord, that riseth up and buildeth this city Jericho: he shall lay the foundation thereof in his firstborn, and in his youngest son shall he set up the gates of it."

27 So the Lord was with Joshua; and his fame was noised throughout all the country.

JUDGES

Israel's Wickedness

Chapter 2

And when Joshua had let the people go, the children of Israel went every man unto his inheritance to possess the land. 7 And the people served the Lord all the days of Joshua, and all the days of the elders that outlived Joshua, who had seen all the great works of the Lord, that he did for Israel.

8 And Joshua the son of Nun, the servant of the Lord, died, being an hundred and ten years old. 9 And they buried him in the border of his inheritance in Timnath-heres, in the mount of Ephraim, on the north side of the hill Gaash.

10 And also all that generation were gathered unto their fathers: and there arose another generation after them, which knew not the Lord, not yet the works which he had done for Israel. 11 And the children of Israel did evil in the sight of the Lord, and served Baalim: 12 and they forsook the Lord God of their fathers, which brought them out of

Chapter 2

the land of Egypt, and followed other gods, of the gods of the people that were round about them, and bowed themselves unto them, and provoked the LORD to anger. [13]And they forsook the LORD, and served Baal and Ashtaroth. [14]And the anger of the LORD was hot against Israel, and he delivered them into the hands of spoilers that spoiled them, and he sold them into the hands of their enemies round about, so that they could not any longer stand before their enemies. [15]Whithersoever they went out, the hand of the LORD was against them for evil, as the LORD had said, and as the LORD had sworn unto them: and they were greatly distressed.

[16]Nevertheless the LORD raised up judges, which delivered them out of the hand of those that spoiled them. [17]And yet they would not hearken unto their judges, but they went a whoring after other gods, and bowed themselves unto them: they turned quickly out of the way which their fathers walked in, obeying the commandments of the LORD; but they did not so. [18]And when the LORD raised them up judges, then the LORD was with the judge, and delivered them out of the hand of their enemies all the days of the judge: for it repented the LORD because of their groanings by reason of them that oppressed them and vexed them. [19]And it came to pass, when the judge was dead, that they returned, and corrupted themselves more than their fathers, in following other gods to serve them, and to bow down unto them; they ceased not from their own doings, nor from their stubborn way.

DEBORAH

Chapter 4

AND THE CHILDREN OF ISRAEL AGAIN DID EVIL IN the sight of the LORD, when Ehud was dead. [2]And the LORD sold them into the hand of Jabin king of Canaan, that reigned in Hazor; the captain of whose host was Sisera, which dwelt in Harosheth of the Gentiles. [3]And the children of Israel cried unto the LORD: for he had nine hundred chariots of iron; and twenty years he mightily oppressed the children of Israel.

[4]And Deborah, a prophetess, the wife of Lapidoth, she judged Israel at that time. [5]And she dwelt under the palm tree of Deborah between Ramah and Bethel in mount Ephraim: and the children of Israel came up to her for judgment. [6]And she sent and called Barak the son of Abinoam out of Kedesh-naphtali, and said unto him, "Hath not the LORD God of Israel commanded, saying, 'Go and draw toward mount Tabor, and take with thee ten thousand men of the children of Naphtali and of the children of Zebulun? [7]And I will draw unto thee to the river Kishon Sisera, the captain of Jabin's army, with his chariots and his multitude; and I will deliver him into thine hand.'"

[8]And Barak said unto her, "If thou wilt go with me, then I will go: but if thou wilt not go with me, then I will not go."

[9]And she said, "I will surely go with thee: notwithstanding the journey that thou takest shall not be for thine honour; for the LORD shall sell Sisera into the hand of a woman." And Deborah arose, and went with Barak to Kedesh. [10]And Barak called Zebulun and Naphtali to Kedesh; and he went up with ten thousand men at his feet: and Deborah went up with him.

[11]Now Heber the Kenite, which was of the children of Hobab the father in law of Moses, had severed himself from the Kenites, and pitched his tent unto the plain of Zaanaim, which is by Kedesh.

[12]And they shewed Sisera that Barak the son of Abinoam was gone up to mount Tabor. [13]And Sisera gathered together all his chariots, even nine hundred chariots of iron, and all the people that were with him, from Harosheth of the Gentiles unto the river of Kishon.

[14]And Deborah said unto Barak, "Up; for this is the day in which the LORD hath delivered Sisera into thine hand: is not the LORD gone out before thee?" So Barak went down from mount Tabor, and ten thousand men after him. [15]And the LORD discomfited Sisera, and all his chariots, and all his host, with the edge of the sword before Barak; so that Sisera lighted down off his chariot, and fled away on his feet. [16]But Barak pursued after the chariots, and after the host, unto Harosheth of the Gentiles: and all the host

The Creation of Adam *by Michelangelo*

of Sisera fell upon the edge of the sword; and there was not a man left.

[17]Howbeit Sisera fled away on his feet to the tent of Jael the wife of Heber the Kenite: for there was peace between Jabin the king of Hazor and the house of Heber the Kenite.

[18]And Jael went out to meet Sisera, and said unto him, "Turn in, my lord, turn in to me; fear not." And when he had turned in unto her into the tent, she covered him with a mantle.

[19]And he said unto her, "Give me, I pray thee, a little water to drink; for I am thirsty." And she opened a bottle of milk, and gave him drink, and covered him.

[20]Again he said unto her, "Stand in the door of the tent, and it shall be, when any man doth come and inquire of thee, and say, 'Is there any man here?' that thou shalt say, 'No.'"

Chapter 4

[21]Then Jael Heber's wife took a nail of the tent, and took an hammer in her hand, and went softly unto him, and smote the nail into his temples, and fastened it into the ground: for he was fast asleep and weary. So he died.

[22]And, behold, as Barak pursued Sisera, Jael came out to meet him, and said unto him, "Come, and I will shew thee the man whom thou seekest." And when he came into her tent, behold, Sisera lay dead, and the nail was in his temples.

[23]So God subdued on that day Jabin the king of Canaan before the children of Israel.

Gideon

Chapter 6

AND THE CHILDREN OF ISRAEL DID EVIL IN THE sight of the LORD: and the LORD delivered them into the hand of Midian seven years. [2]And the hand of Midian prevailed against Israel: and because of the Midianites the children of Israel made them the dens which are in the mountains, and caves, and strong holds. [3]And so it was, when Israel had sown, that the Midianites came up, and the Amalekites, and the children of the east, even they came up against them; [4]and they encamped against them, and destroyed the increase of the earth, till thou come unto Gaza, and left no sustenance for Israel, neither sheep, nor ox, nor ass. [5]For they came up with their cattle and their tents, and they came as grasshoppers for multitude; for both they and their camels were without number: and they entered into the land to destroy it. [6]And Israel was greatly impoverished because of the Midianites; and the children of Israel cried unto the LORD.

[7]And it came to pass, when the children of Israel cried unto the LORD because of the Midianites, [8]that the LORD sent a prophet unto the children of Israel, which said unto them, "Thus saith the LORD God of Israel, I brought you up from Egypt, and brought you forth out of the house of bondage; [9]and I delivered you out of the hand of the Egyptians, and out of the hand of all that oppressed you,

Chapter 6

and drave them out from before you, and gave you their land; [10]and I said unto you, 'I am the LORD your God; fear not the gods of the Amorites, in whose land ye dwell': but ye have not obeyed my voice."

[11]And there came an angel of the LORD, and sat under an oak which was in Ophrah, that pertained unto Joash the Abiezrite: and his son Gideon threshed wheat by the winepress, to hide it from the Midianites. [12]And the angel of the LORD appeared unto him, and said unto him, "The LORD is with thee, thou mighty man of valour."

[13]And Gideon said unto him, "Oh my Lord, if the LORD be with us, why then is all this befallen us? and where be all his miracles which our fathers told us of, saying, 'Did not the LORD bring us up from Egypt?' But now the LORD hath forsaken us, and delivered us into the hands of the Midianites."

[14]And the LORD looked upon him, and said, "Go in this thy might, and thou shalt save Israel from the hand of the Midianites: have not I sent thee?"

[15]And he said unto him, "Oh my Lord, wherewith shall I save Israel? Behold, my family is poor in Manasseh, and I am the least in my father's house."

[16]And the LORD said unto him, "Surely I will be with thee, and thou shalt smite the Midianites as one man."

GIDEON DEFEATS THE MIDIANITES

Chapter 7

THEN JERUBBAAL, WHO IS GIDEON, AND ALL the people that were with him, rose up early, and pitched beside the well of Harod: so that the host of the Midianites were on the north side of them, by the hill of Moreh, in the valley. [2]And the LORD said unto Gideon, "The people that are with thee are too many for me to give the Midianites into their hands, lest Israel vaunt themselves against me, saying, 'Mine own hand hath saved me.' [3]Now therefore go to, proclaim in the ears of the people, saying, 'Whosoever is fearful and afraid, let him return and depart early from mount Gilead.'" And there

Detail of God, *by Michelangelo*

returned of the people twenty and two thousand; and there remained ten thousand.

[4]And the Lord said unto Gideon, "The people are yet too many; bring them down unto the water, and I will try them for thee there: and it shall be, that of whom I say unto thee, 'This shall go with thee', the same shall go with thee; and of whomsoever I say unto thee, 'This shall not go with thee', the same shall not go."

[5]So he brought down the people unto the water: and the Lord said unto Gideon, "Every one that lappeth of the water with his tongue, as a dog lappeth, him shalt thou set by himself; likewise every one that boweth down upon his knees to drink." [6]And the number of them that lapped, putting their hand to their mouth, were three hundred men: but all the rest of the people bowed down upon their knees to drink water.

[7]And the Lord said unto Gideon, "By the three hundred men that lapped will I save you, and deliver the Midianites into thine hand: and let all the other people go every man unto his place." [8]So the people took victuals in their hand,

and their trumpets: and he sent all the rest of Israel every man unto his tent, and retained those three hundred men: and the host of Midian was beneath him in the valley.

[9]And it came to pass the same night, that the LORD said unto him, "Arise, get thee down unto the host; for I have delivered it into thine hand. [10]But if thou fear to go down, go thou with Phurah thy servant down to the host: [11]and thou shalt hear what they say; and afterward shall thine hands to be strengthened to go down unto the host." Then went he down with Phurah his servant unto the outside of the armed men that were in the host. [12]And the Midianites and the Amalekites and all the children of the east lay along in the valley like grasshoppers for multitude; and their camels were without number, as the sand by the sea side for multitude.

[13]And when Gideon was come, behold, there was a man that told a dream unto his fellow, and said, "Behold, I dreamed a dream, and, lo, a cake of barley bread tumbled into the host of Midian, and came unto a tent, and smote it that it fell, and overturned it, that the tent lay along."

[14]And his fellow answered and said, "This is nothing else save the sword of Gideon the son of Joash, a man of Israel: for into his hand hath God delivered Midian, and all the host."

[15]And it was so, when Gideon heard the telling of the dream, and the interpretation thereof, that he worshipped, and returned into the host of Israel, and said, "Arise; for the LORD hath delivered into your hand the host of Midian." [16]And he divided the three hundred men into three companies, and he put a trumpet in every man's hand, with empty pitchers, and lamps within the pitchers. [17]And he said unto them, "Look on me, and do likewise: and, behold, when I come to the outside of the camp, it shall be that, as I do, so shall ye do. [18]When I blow with a trumpet, I and all that are with me, then blow ye the trumpets also on every side of all the camp, and say, 'The sword of the LORD, and of Gideon.'"

[19]So Gideon, and the hundred men that were with him, came unto the outside of the camp in the beginning of the middle watch; and they had but newly set the watch: and they blew the trumpets, and brake the pitchers that were in their hands. [20]And the three companies blew the trumpets,

Chapter 7

and brake the pitchers, and held the lamps in their left hands, and the trumpets in their right hands to blow withal: and they cried, "The sword of the Lord, and of Gideon." [21]And they stood every man in his place round about the camp: and all the host ran, and cried, and fled.

[22]And the three hundred blew the trumpets, and the Lord set every man's sword against his fellow, even throughout all the host: and the host fled to Beth-shittah in Zererath, and to the border of Abel-meholah, unto Tabbath. [23]And the men of Israel gathered themselves together out of Naphtali, and out of Asher, and out of all Manasseh, and pursued after the Midianites. [24]And Gideon sent messengers throughout all mount Ephraim, saying, "Come down against the Midianites, and take before them the waters unto Beth-barah and Jordan."

Then all the men of Ephraim gathered themselves together, and took the waters unto Beth-barah and Jordan. [25]And they took two princes of the Midianites, Oreb and Zeeb; and they slew Oreb upon the rock Oreb, and Zeeb they slew at the winepress of Zeeb, and pursued Midian, and brought the heads of Oreb and Zeeb to Gideon on the other side Jordan.

The Birth of Samson

Chapter 13

AND THE CHILDREN OF ISRAEL DID EVIL AGAIN IN the sight of the Lord; and the Lord delivered them into the hand of the Philistines forty years.

[2]And there was a certain man of Zorah, of the family of the Danites, whose name was Manoah; and his wife was barren, and bare not. [3]And the angel of the Lord appeared unto the woman, and said unto her, "Behold now, thou art barren, and bearest not: but thou shalt conceive, and bear a son. [4]Now therefore beware, I pray thee, and drink not wine nor strong drink, and eat not any unclean thing: [5]for, lo, thou shalt conceive, and bear a son: and no razor shall come on his head: for the

child shall be a Nazarite unto God from the womb: and he shall begin to deliver Israel out of the hand of the Philistines."

[6]Then the woman came and told her husband, saying, "A man of God came unto me, and his countenance was like the countenance of an angel of God, very terrible: but I asked him not whence he was, neither told he me his name: [7]but he said unto me, 'Behold, thou shalt conceive, and bear a son; and now drink no wine nor strong drink, neither eat any unclean thing: for the child shall be a Nazarite to God from the womb to the day of his death.'"

[8]Then Manoah entreated the Lord, and said, "O my Lord, let the man of God which thou didst send come again unto us, and teach us what we shall do unto the child that shall be born."

[9]And God hearkened to the voice of Manoah; and the angel of God came again unto the woman as she sat in the field: but Manoah her husband was not with her. [10]And the woman made haste, and ran, and shewed her husband, and said unto him, "Behold, the man hath appeared unto me, that came unto me the other day."

[11]And Manoah arose, and went after his wife, and came to the man, and said unto him, "Art thou the man that spakest unto the woman?"

And he said, "I am."

[12]And Manoah said, "Now let thy words come to pass. How shall we order the child, and how shall we do unto him?"

[13]And the angel of the Lord said unto Manoah, "Of all that I said unto the woman let her beware. [14]She may not eat of any thing that cometh of the vine, neither let her drink wine or strong drink, nor eat any unclean thing: all that I commanded her let her observe."

[15]And Manoah said unto the angel of the Lord, "I pray thee, let us detain thee, until we shall have made ready a kid for thee."

[16]And the angel of the Lord said unto Manoah, "Though thou detain me, I will not eat of thy bread: and if thou wilt offer a burnt offering, thou must offer it unto the Lord." For Manoah knew not that he was an angel of the Lord.

Chapter 13

[17]And Manoah said unto the angel of the Lord, "What is thy name, that when thy sayings come to pass we may do thee honour?"

[18]And the angel of the Lord said unto him, "Why askest thou thus after my name, seeing it is secret?" [19]So Manoah took a kid with a meat offering, and offered it upon a rock unto the Lord: and the angel did wondrously; and Manoah and his wife looked on. [20]For it came to pass, when the flame went up toward heaven from off the altar, that the angel of the Lord ascended in the flame of the altar. And Manoah and his wife looked on it, and fell on their faces to the ground. [21]But the angel of the Lord did no more appear to Manoah and to his wife. Then Manoah knew that he was an angel of the Lord.

[22]And Manoah said unto his wife, "We shall surely die, because we have seen God."

[23]But his wife said unto him, "If the Lord were pleased to kill us, he would not have received a burnt offering and a meat offering at our hands, neither would he have shewed us all these things, nor would as at this time have told us such things as these."

[24]And the woman bare a son, and called his name Samson: and the child grew, and the Lord blessed him. [25]And the spirit of the Lord began to move him at times in the camp of Dan between Zorah and Eshtaol.

Samson and Delilah

Chapter 16

THEN WENT SAMSON TO GAZA, AND SAW THERE an harlot, and went in unto her. [2]And it was told the Gazites, saying, "Samson is come hither." And they compassed him in, and laid wait for him all night in the gate of the city, and were quiet all the night, saying, "In the morning, when it is day, we shall kill him."

[3]And Samson lay till midnight, and arose at midnight, and took the doors of the gate of the city, and the two posts, and went away with them, bar and all, and put them

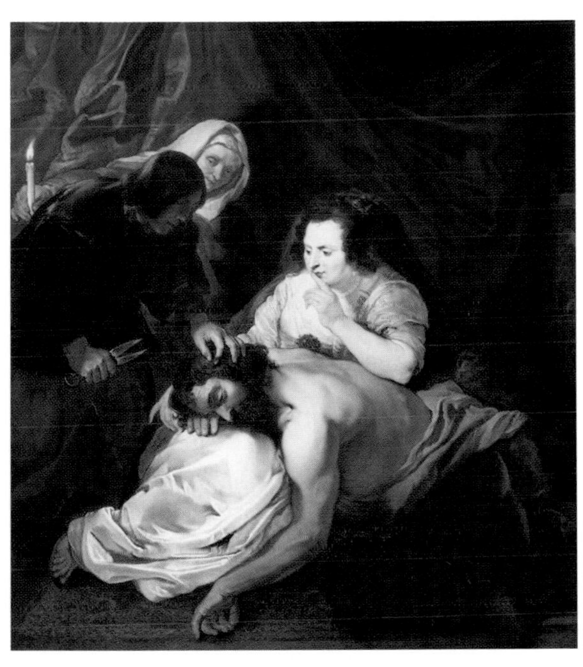

Samson and Delilah *by Pieter Claesz Soutman*

upon his shoulders, and carried them up to the top of an hill that is before Hebron.

[4]And it came to pass afterward, that he loved a woman in the valley of Sorek, whose name was Delilah. [5]And the lords of the Philistines came up unto her, and said unto her, "Entice him, and see wherein his great strength lieth, and by what means we may prevail against him, that we may bind him to afflict him: and we will give thee every one of us eleven hundred pieces of silver."

[6]And Delilah said to Samson, "Tell me, I pray thee, wherein thy great strength lieth, and wherewith thou mightest be bound to afflict thee."

[7]And Samson said unto her, "If they bind me with seven green withs that were never dried, then shall I be weak, and be as another man."

[8]Then the lords of the Philistines brought up to her seven green withs which had not been dried, and she bound him with them. [9]Now there were men lying in wait, abiding with her in the chamber. And she said unto him, "The Philistines be upon thee, Samson." And he brake the withs, as a thread of tow is broken when it toucheth the fire. So his strength was not known.

[10]And Delilah said unto Samson, "Behold, thou hast mocked me, and told me lies: now tell me, I pray thee, wherewith thou mightest be bound."

[11]And he said unto her, "If they bind me fast with new ropes that never were occupied, then shall I be weak, and be as another man."

[12]Delilah therefore took new ropes, and bound him therewith, and said unto him, "The Philistines be upon thee, Samson." And there were liers in wait abiding in the chamber. And he brake them from off his arms like a thread.

[13]And Delilah said unto Samson, "Hitherto thou hast mocked me, and told me lies: tell me wherewith thou mightest be bound."

And he said unto her, "If thou weavest the seven locks of my head with the web." [14]And she fastened it with the pin, and said unto him, "The Philistines be upon thee, Samson." And he awaked out of his sleep, and went away with the pin of the beam, and with the web.

[15]And she said unto him, "How canst thou say, 'I love thee,' when thine heart is not with me? Thou hast mocked me these three times, and hast not told me wherein thy great strength lieth."

[16]And it came to pass, when she pressed him daily with her words, and urged him, so that his soul was vexed unto death: [17]that he told her all his heart, and said unto her, "There hath not come a razor upon mine head; for I have been a Nazarite unto God from my mother's womb: if I be shaven, then my strength will go from me, and I shall become weak, and be like any other man."

[18]And when Delilah saw that he had told her all his heart, she sent and called for the lords of the Philistines,

saying, "Come up this once, for he hath shewed me all his heart." Then the lords of the Philistines came up unto her, and brought money in their hand. [19]And she made him sleep upon her knees; and she called for a man, and she caused him to shave off the seven locks of his head; and she began to afflict him, and his strength went from him.

[20]And she said, "The Philistines be upon thee, Samson."

And he awoke out of his sleep, and said, "I will go out as at other times before, and shake myself." And he wist not that the LORD was departed from him.

[21]But the Philistines took him, and put out his eyes, and brought him down to Gaza, and bound him with fetters of brass; and he did grind in the prison house. [22]Howbeit the hair of his head began to grow again after he was shaven.

[23]Then the lords of the Philistines gathered them together for to offer a great sacrifice unto Dagon their god, and to rejoice: for they said, "Our god hath delivered Samson our enemy into our hand."

[24]And when the people saw him, they praised their god: for they said, "Our god hath delivered into our hands our enemy, and the destroyer of our country, which slew many of us."

[25]And it came to pass, when their hearts were merry, that they said, "Call for Samson, that he may make us sport." And they called for Samson out of the prison house; and he made them sport: and they set him between the pillars.

[26]And Samson said unto the lad that held him by the hand, "Suffer me that I may feel the pillars whereupon the house standeth, that I may lean upon them." [27]Now the house was full of men and women; and all the lords of the Philistines were there; and there were upon the roof about three thousand men and women, that beheld while Samson made sport. [28]And Samson called unto the LORD, and said, "O Lord GOD, remember me, I pray thee, and strengthen me, I pray thee, only this once, O God, that I may be at once avenged of the Philistines for my two eyes." [29]And Samson took hold of the two middle pillars upon which the house stood, and on which it was borne up, of the one with his right hand, and of the other with his left. [30]And Samson said, "Let me die with the Philistines." And

Chapter 16 he bowed himself with all his might; and the house fell upon the lords, and upon all the people that were therein. So the dead which he slew at his death were more than they which he slew in his life.

[31]Then his brethren and all the house of his father came down, and took him, and brought him up, and buried him between Zorah and Eshtaol in the buryingplace of Manoah his father. And he judged Israel twenty years.

RUTH

Naomi and Ruth

Chapter 1

NOW IT CAME TO PASS IN THE DAYS WHEN THE judges ruled, that there was a famine in the land. And a certain man of Bethlehem-judah went to sojourn in the country of Moab, he, and his wife, and his two sons. [2]And the name of the man was Elimelech, and the name of his wife Naomi, and the name of his two sons Mahlon and Chilion, Ephrathites of Bethlehem-judah. And they came into the country of Moab, and continued there.

[3]And Elimelech Naomi's husband died; and she was left, and her two sons. [4]And they took them wives of the women of Moab; the name of the one was Orpah, and the name of the other Ruth: and they dwelled there about ten years. [5]And Mahlon and Chilion died also both of them; and the woman was left of her two sons and her husband.

[6]Then she arose with her daughters in law, that she might return from the country of Moab: for she had heard in the country of Moab how that the LORD had visited his people in giving them bread. [7]Wherefore she went forth out of the place where she was, and her two daughters in

NAOMI AND RUTH, *attrib. Martin van Heemskerk*

law with her; and they went on the way to return unto the land of Judah.

[8]And Naomi said unto her two daughters in law, "Go, return each to her mother's house: the LORD deal kindly with you, as ye have dealt with the dead, and with me. [9]The LORD grant you that ye may find rest, each of you in the house of her husband."

Then she kissed them; and they lifted up their voice, and wept. [10]And they said unto her, "Surely we will return with thee unto thy people."

Chapter 1

[11]And Naomi said, "Turn again, my daughters: why will ye go with me? Are there yet any more sons in my womb, that they may be your husbands? [12]Turn again, my daughters, go your way; for I am too old to have an husband. If I should say, I have hope, if I should have an husband also to night, and should also bear sons: [13]would ye tarry for them till they were grown? Would ye stay for them from having husbands? Nay, my daughters; for it grieveth me much for your sakes that the hand of the LORD is gone out against me."

[14]And they lifted up their voice, and wept again: and Orpah kissed her mother in law; but Ruth clave unto her.

[15]And she said, "Behold, thy sister in law is gone back unto her people, and unto her gods: return thou after thy sister in law."

[16]And Ruth said, "Entreat me not to leave thee, or to return from following after thee: for whither thou goest, I will go; and where thou lodgest, I will lodge: thy people shall be my people, and thy God my God: [17]where thou diest, will I die, and there will I be buried: the LORD do so to me, and more also, if aught but death part thee and me." [18]When she saw that she was steadfastly minded to go with her, then she left speaking unto her.

[19]So they two went until they came to Bethlehem. And it came to pass, when they were come to Bethlehem, that all the city was moved about them, and they said, "Is this Naomi?"

[20]And she said unto them, "Call me not Naomi, call me Mara: for the Almighty hath dealt very bitterly with me. [21]I went out full, and the LORD hath brought me home again empty: why then call ye me Naomi, seeing the LORD hath testified against me, and the Almighty hath afflicted me?"

[22]So Naomi returned, and Ruth the Moabitess, her daughter in law, with her, which returned out of the country of Moab: and they came to Bethlehem in the beginning of barley harvest.

Ruth and Boaz

Chapter 2

AND NAOMI HAD A KINSMAN OF HER HUSBAND'S, A mighty man of wealth, of the family of Elimelech; and his name was Boaz.

[2]And Ruth the Moabitess said unto Naomi, "Let me now go to the field, and glean ears of corn after him in whose sight I shall find grace."

And she said unto her, "Go, my daughter." [3]And she went, and came, and gleaned in the field after the reapers: and her hap was to light on a part of the field belonging unto Boaz, who was of the kindred of Elimelech.

[4]And, behold, Boaz came from Bethlehem, and said unto the reapers, "The LORD be with you."

And they answered him, "The LORD bless thee."

[5]Then said Boaz unto his servant that was set over the reapers, "Whose damsel is this?"

[6]And the servant that was set over the reapers answered and said, "It is the Moabitish damsel that came back with Naomi out of the country of Moab: [7]and she said, 'I pray you, let me glean and gather after the reapers among the sheaves': so she came, and hath continued even from the morning until now, that she tarried a little in the house."

[8]Then said Boaz unto Ruth, "Hearest thou not, my daughter? Go not to glean in another field, neither go from hence, but abide here fast by my maidens: [9]let thine eyes be on the field that they do reap, and go thou after them: have I not charged the young men that they shall not touch thee? And when thou art athirst, go unto the vessels, and drink of that which the young men have drawn."

[10]Then she fell on her face, and bowed herself to the ground, and said unto him, "Why have I found grace in thine eyes, that thou shouldest take knowledge of me, seeing I am a stranger?"

[11]And Boaz answered and said unto her, "It hath fully been shewed me, all that thou hast done unto thy mother in law since the death of thine husband: and how thou hast left thy father and thy mother, and the land of thy nativity, and art come unto a people which thou knewest

Chapter 2

not heretofore. [12]The LORD recompense thy work, and a full reward be given thee of the LORD God of Israel, under whose wings thou art come to trust."

RUTH'S MARRIAGE

Chapter 4

AND BOAZ SAID UNTO THE ELDERS, AND UNTO ALL the people, "Ye are witnesses this day, that I have bought all that was Elimelech's, and all that was Chilion's and Mahlon's, of the hand of Naomi. [10]Moreover Ruth the Moabitess, the wife of Mahlon, have I purchased to be my wife, to raise up the name of the dead upon his inheritance, that the name of the dead be not cut off from among his brethren, and from the gate of his place: ye are witnesses this day."

[11]And all the people that were in the gate, and the elders, said, "We are witnesses. The LORD make the woman that is come into thine house like Rachel and like Leah, which two did build the house of Israel: and do thou worthily in Ephratah, and be famous in Bethlehem: [12]and let thy house be like the house of Pharez, whom Tamar bare unto Judah, of the seed which the LORD shall give thee of this young woman."

[13]So Boaz took Ruth, and she was his wife: and when he went in unto her, the LORD gave her conception, and she bare a son. [14]And the women said unto Naomi, "Blessed be the LORD, which hath not left thee this day without a kinsman, that his name may be famous in Israel. [15]And he shall be unto thee a restorer of thy life, and a nourisher of thine old age: for thy daughter in law, which loveth thee, which is better to thee than seven sons, hath born him."

[16]And Naomi took the child, and laid it in her bosom, and became nurse unto it. [17]And the women her neighbours gave it a name, saying, "There is a son born to Naomi"; and they called his name Obed: he is the father of Jesse, the father of David.

Chapters & Verses
FROM
THE FIRST & SECOND BOOKS OF SAMUEL

THE BIRTH OF SAMUEL • THE CALL OF SAMUEL • SAMUEL JUDGES ISRAEL • ISRAEL DESIRES A KING • SAMUEL ANOINTS SAUL • SAUL MADE KING • THE LORD REJECTS SAUL AS KING • SAMUEL ANOINTS DAVID • DAVID AND GOLIATH • SAUL'S JEALOUSY OF DAVID • DAVID FLEES TO SAMUEL • SAUL AND THE WITCH OF ENDOR • SAUL AND JONATHAN SLAIN • DAVID'S LAMENT FOR SAUL AND JONATHAN • DAVID BECOMES KING OF ISRAEL • DAVID DEFEATS THE PHILISTINES • DAVID BRINGS THE ARK TO JERUSALEM • GOD'S PROMISE TO DAVID • DAVID AND BATHSHEBA • NATHAN REBUKES DAVID

The Birth of Samuel

Chapter 1

NOW THERE WAS A CERTAIN MAN OF Ramathaim-zophim, of mount Ephraim, and his name was Elkanah, the son of Jeroham, the son of Elihu, the son of Tohu, the son of Zuph, an Ephrathite: [2]and he had two wives; the name of the one was Hannah, and the name of the other Penninah: and Penninah had children, but Hannah had no children.

[3]And this man went up out of his city yearly to worship and to sacrifice unto the LORD of hosts in Shiloh. And the two sons of Eli, Hophni and Phinehas, the priests of the LORD, were there. [4]And when the time was that Elkanah offered, he gave to Peninnah his wife, and to all her sons and her daughters, portions: [5]but unto Hannah he gave a worthy portion; for he loved Hannah: but the LORD had shut up her womb. [6]And her adversary also provoked her sore, for to make her fret, because the LORD had shut up her womb. [7]And as he did so year by year, when she went up to the house of the LORD, so she provoked her; therefore she wept, and did not eat. [8]Then said Elkanah her husband to her, "Hannah, why weepest thou? and why eatest thou not? and why is thy heart grieved? Am not I better to thee than ten sons?"

[9]So Hannah rose up after they had eaten in Shiloh, and after they had drunk. Now Eli the priest sat upon a seat by a post of the temple of the LORD. [10]And she was in bitterness of soul, and prayed unto the LORD, and wept sore. [11]And she vowed a vow, and said, "O LORD of hosts, if thou wilt indeed look on the affliction of thine handmaid, and remember me, and not forget thine handmaid, but wilt give unto thine handmaid a man child, then I will give him unto the LORD all the days of his life, and there shall be no razor come upon his head."

[12]And it came to pass, as she continued praying before the LORD, that Eli marked her mouth. [13]Now Hannah, she spake in her heart; only her lips moved, but her voice was not heard: therefore Eli thought she had been drunken.

14And Eli said unto her, "How long wilt thou be drunken? Put away thy wine from thee."

15And Hannah answered and said, "No, my lord, I am a woman of a sorrowful spirit: I have drunk neither wine nor strong drink, but have poured out my soul before the LORD. 16Count not thine handmaid for a daughter of Belial: for out of the abundance of my complaint and grief have I spoken hitherto."

17Then Eli answered and said, "Go in peace: and the God of Israel grant thee thy petition that thou hast asked of him."

18And she said, "Let thine handmaid find grace in thy sight." So the woman went her way, and did eat, and her countenance was no more sad.

19And they rose up in the morning early, and worshipped before the LORD, and returned, and came to their house to Ramah: and Elkanah knew Hannah his wife; and the LORD remembered her. 20Wherefore it came to pass, when the time was come about after Hannah had conceived, that she bare a son, and called his name Samuel, saying, "Because I have asked him of the LORD."

21And the man Elkanah, and all his house, went up to offer unto the LORD the yearly sacrifice, and his vow. 22But Hannah went not up; for she said unto her husband, "I will not go up until the child be weaned, and then I will bring him, that he may appear before the LORD, and there abide for ever."

23And Elkanah her husband said unto her, "Do what seemeth thee good; tarry until thou have weaned him; only the LORD establish his word." So the woman abode, and gave her son suck until she weaned him.

24And when she had weaned him, she took him up with her, with three bullocks, and one ephah of flour, and a bottle of wine, and brought him unto the house of the LORD in Shiloh: and the child was young. 25And they slew a bullock, and brought the child to Eli. 26And she said, "Oh my lord, as thy soul liveth, my lord, I am the woman that stood by thee here, praying unto the LORD. 27For this child I prayed; and the LORD hath given me my petition which I asked of him: 28therefore also I have lent him to the LORD; as long as he liveth he shall be lent to the LORD." And he worshipped the LORD there.

The Call of Samuel

Chapter 3

AND THE CHILD SAMUEL MINISTERED UNTO THE LORD before Eli. And the word of the LORD was precious in those days; there was no open vision.

[2]And it came to pass at that time, when Eli was laid down in his place, and his eyes began to wax dim, that he could not see; [3]and ere the lamp of God went out in the temple of the LORD, where the ark of God was, and Samuel was laid down to sleep; [4]that the LORD called Samuel: and he answered, "Here am I."

[5]And he ran unto Eli, and said, "Here am I; for thou calledst me."

And he said, "I called not; lie down again." And he went and lay down.

[6]And the LORD called yet again, "Samuel." And Samuel arose and went to Eli, and said, "Here am I; for thou didst call me."

And he answered, "I called not, my son; lie down again."

[7]Now Samuel did not yet know the LORD, neither was the word of the LORD yet revealed to him.

[8]And the LORD called Samuel again the third time. And he arose and went to Eli, and said, "Here am I; for thou didst call me."

And Eli perceived that the LORD had called the child. [9]Therefore Eli said unto Samuel, "Go, lie down: and it shall be, if he call thee, that thou shalt say, 'Speak, LORD; for thy servant heareth.'" So Samuel went and lay down in his place.

[10]And the LORD came, and stood, and called as at other times, "Samuel, Samuel."

Then Samuel answered, "Speak; for thy servant heareth."

[11]And the LORD said to Samuel, "Behold, I will do a thing in Israel, at which both the ears of every one that heareth it shall tingle. [12]In that day I will perform against Eli all things which I have spoken concerning his house: when I begin, I will also make an end. [13]For I have told him

ELI INSTRUCTING SAMUEL *by Jan Lievens*

that I will judge his house for ever for the iniquity which he knoweth; because his sons made themselves vile, and he restrained them not. [14]And therefore I have sworn unto the house of Eli, that the iniquity of Eli's house shall not be purged with sacrifice nor offering for ever."

[15]And Samuel lay until the morning, and opened the doors of the house of the LORD. And Samuel feared to show Eli the vision. [16]Then Eli called Samuel, and said, "Samuel, my son."

And he answered, "Here am I."

[17]And he said, "What is the thing that the LORD hath said unto thee? I pray thee hide it not from me: God do so to thee, and more also, if thou hide any thing from me of all the things that he said unto thee." [18]And Samuel told him

Chapter 3

Chapter 3

every whit, and hid nothing from him. And he said, "It is the LORD: let him do what seemeth him good."

[19]And Samuel grew, and the LORD was with him, and did let none of his words fall to the ground. And all Israel from Dan even to Beersheba knew that Samuel was established to be a prophet of the LORD.

SAMUEL JUDGES ISRAEL

Chapter 7

AND SAMUEL SPAKE UNTO ALL THE HOUSE OF Israel, saying, "If ye do return unto the LORD with all your hearts, then put away the strange gods and Ashtaroth from among you, and prepare your hearts unto the LORD, and serve him only: and he will deliver you out of the hand of the Philistines." [4]Then the children of Israel did put away Baalim and Ashtaroth, and served the LORD only.

[5]And Samuel said, "Gather all Israel to Mizpeh, and I will pray for you unto the LORD." [6]And they gathered together to Mizpeh, and drew water, and poured it out before the LORD, and fasted on that day, and said there, "We have sinned against the LORD." And Samuel judged the children of Israel in Mizpeh. [7]And when the Philistines heard that the children of Israel were gathered together to Mizpeh, the lords of the Philistines went up against Israel. And when the children of Israel heard it, they were afraid of the Philistines. [8]And the children of Israel said to Samuel, "Cease not to cry unto the LORD our God for us, that he will save us out of the hand of the Philistines." [9]And Samuel took a sucking lamb, and offered it for a burnt offering wholly unto the LORD: and Samuel cried unto the LORD for Israel; and the LORD heard him.

[10]And as Samuel was offering up the burnt offering, the Philistines drew near to battle against Israel: but the LORD thundered with a great thunder on that day upon the Philistines, and discomfited them; and they were smitten before Israel. [11]And the men of Israel went out of Mizpeh, and pursued the Philistines, and smote them, until they came under Beth-car.

Chapter 7

[12]Then Samuel took a stone, and set it between Mizpeh and Shen, and called the name of it Ebenezer, saying, "Hitherto hath the LORD helped us."

[13]So the Philistines were subdued, and they came no more into the coast of Israel: and the hand of the LORD was against the Philistines all the days of Samuel. [14]And the cities which the Philistines had taken from Israel were restored to Israel, from Ekron even unto Gath; and the coasts thereof did Israel deliver out of the hands of the Philistines. And there was peace between Israel and the Amorites.

[15]And Samuel judged Israel all the days of his life.

ISRAEL DESIRES A KING

Chapter 8

AND IT CAME TO PASS, WHEN SAMUEL WAS OLD, that he made his sons judges over Israel. [2]Now the name of his firstborn was Joel; and the name of his second, Abiah: they were judges in Beersheba. [3]And his sons walked not in his ways, but turned aside after lucre, and took bribes, and perverted judgment.

[4]Then all the elders of Israel gathered themselves together, and came to Samuel unto Ramah, [5]and said unto him, "Behold, thou art old, and thy sons walk not in thy ways: now make us a king to judge us like all the nations."

[6]But the thing displeased Samuel, when they said, "Give us a king to judge us." And Samuel prayed unto the LORD. [7]And the LORD said unto Samuel, "Hearken unto the voice of the people in all that they say unto thee: for they have not rejected thee, but they have rejected me, that I should not reign over them. [8]According to all the works which they have done since the day that I brought them up out of Egypt even unto this day, wherewith they have forsaken me, and served other gods, so do they also unto thee. [9]Now therefore hearken unto their voice: howbeit yet protest solemnly unto them, and shew them the manner of the king that shall reign over them."

[10]And Samuel told all the words of the LORD unto the people that asked of him a king. [11]And he said, "This will

THE PROPHET SAMUEL *by Claude Vignon*

be the manner of the king that shall reign over you: he will take your sons, and appoint them for himself, for his chariots, and to be his horsemen; and some shall run before his chariots. [12]And he will appoint him captains over thousands, and captains over fifties; and will set them to ear his ground, and to reap his harvest, and to make his instruments of war, and instruments of his chariots. [13]And he will take your daughters to be confectionaries, and to be

Chapter 8

cooks, and to be bakers. [14]And he will take your fields, and your vineyards, and your oliveyards, even the best of them, and give them to his servants. [15]And he will take the tenth of your seed, and of your vineyards, and give to his officers, and to his servants. [16]And he will take your menservants, and your maidservants, and your goodliest young men, and your asses, and put them to his work. [17]He will take the tenth of your sheep: and ye shall be his servants. [18]And ye shall cry out in that day because of your king which ye shall have chosen you; and the LORD will not hear you in that day."

[19]Nevertheless the people refused to obey the voice of Samuel; and they said, "Nay; but we will have a king over us; [20]that we also may be like all the nations; and that our king may judge us, and go out before us, and fight our battles."

[21]And Samuel heard all the words of the people, and he rehearsed them in the ears of the LORD. [22]And the LORD said to Samuel, "Hearken unto their voice, and make them a king."

And Samuel said unto the men of Israel, "Go ye every man unto his city."

SAMUEL ANOINTS SAUL

Chapter 9

NOW THERE WAS A MAN OF BENJAMIN, WHOSE name was Kish, the son of Abiel, the son of Zeror, the son of Bechorath, the son of Aphiah, a Benjamite, a mighty man of power. [2]And he had a son, whose name was Saul, a choice young man, and a goodly: and there was not among the children of Israel a goodlier person than he: from his shoulders and upward he was higher than any of the people.

[3]And the asses of Kish Saul's father were lost. And Kish said to Saul his son, "Take now one of the servants with thee, and arise, go seek the asses." [4]And he passed through mount Ephraim, and passed through the land of Shalisha, but they found them not: then they passed through the

land of Shalim, and there they were not: and he passed through the land of the Benjamites, but they found them not.

[5]And when they were come to the land of Zuph, Saul said to his servant that was with him, "Come, and let us return; lest my father leave caring for the asses, and take thought for us."

[6]And he said unto him, "Behold now, there is in this city a man of God, and he is an honourable man; all that he saith cometh surely to pass: now let us go thither; peradventure he can shew us our way that we should go."

[7]Then said Saul to his servant, "But, behold, if we go, what shall we bring the man? for the bread is spent in our vessels, and there is not a present to bring to the man of God: what have we?"

[8]And the servant answered Saul again, and said, "Behold, I have here at hand the fourth part of a shekel of silver: that will I give to the man of God, to tell us our way." [9](Beforetime in Israel, when a man went to inquire of God, thus he spake, "Come, and let us go to the seer": for he that is now called a Prophet was beforetime called a Seer.)

[10]Then said Saul to his servant, "Well said; come, let us go." So they went unto the city where the man of God was.

[11]And as they went up the hill to the city, they found young maidens going out to draw water, and said unto them, "Is the seer here?"

[12]And they answered them, and said, "He is; behold, he is before you: make haste now, for he came to day to the city; for there is a sacrifice of the people to day in the high place: [13]as soon as ye be come into the city, ye shall straightway find him, before he go up to the high place to eat: for the people will not eat until he come, because he doth bless the sacrifice; and afterwards they eat that be bidden. Now therefore get you up; for about this time ye shall find him."

[14]And they went up into the city: and when they were come into the city, behold, Samuel came out against them, for to go up to the high place.

[15]Now the LORD had told Samuel in his ear a day before Saul came, saying, [16]"To morrow about this time I will send thee a man out of the land of Benjamin, and thou shalt

anoint him to be captain over my people Israel, that he may save my people out of the hand of the Philistines: for I have looked upon my people, because their cry is come unto me."

[17]And when Samuel saw Saul, the LORD said unto him, "Behold the man whom I spake to thee of! This same shall reign over my people."

[18]Then Saul drew near to Samuel in the gate, and said, "Tell me, I pray thee, where the seer's house is."

[19]And Samuel answered Saul, and said, "I am the seer: go up before me unto the high place; for ye shall eat with me to day, and to morrow I will let thee go, and will tell thee all that is in thine heart. [20]And as for thine asses that were lost three days ago, set not thy mind on them; for they are found. And on whom is all the desire of Israel? Is it not on thee, and on all thy father's house?"

[21]And Saul answered and said, "Am not I a Benjamite, of the smallest of the tribes of Israel? and my family the least of all the families of the tribe of Benjamin? Wherefore then speakest thou so to me?"

[22]And Samuel took Saul and his servant, and brought them into the parlour, and made them sit in the chiefest place among them that were bidden, which were about thirty persons. [23]And Samuel said unto the cook, "Bring the portion which I gave thee, of which I said unto thee, 'Set it by thee.'"

[24]And the cook took up the shoulder, and that which was upon it, and set it before Saul. And Samuel said, "Behold that which is left! Set it before thee, and eat: for unto this time hath it been kept for thee since I said, 'I have invited the people.'" So Saul did eat with Samuel that day.

[25]And when they were come down from the high place into the city, Samuel communed with Saul upon the top of the house. [26]And they arose early: and it came to pass about the spring of the day, that Samuel called Saul to the top of the house, saying, "Up, that I may send thee away." And Saul arose, and they went out both of them, he and Samuel, abroad. [27]And as they were going down to the end of the city, Samuel said to Saul, "Bid the servant pass on before us," (and he passed on,) "but stand thou still a while, that I may shew thee the word of God."

Chapter 10

SAUL ANOINTED KING *by Claude Lorrain*

Chapter 10

THEN SAMUEL TOOK A VIAL OF OIL, AND POURED IT UPON his head, and kissed him, and said, "Is it not because the LORD hath anointed thee to be captain over his inheritance?"

SAUL MADE KING

Chapter 10

AND SAMUEL CALLED THE PEOPLE TOGETHER UNTO the LORD to Mizpeh; [18]and said unto the children of Israel, "Thus saith the LORD God of Israel, 'I brought up Israel out of Egypt, and delivered you out of the hand of the Egyptians, and out of the hand of all kingdoms, and of them that oppressed you': [19]and ye have this day rejected your God, who himself saved you out of all your adversities and your tribulations; and ye have said unto him, 'Nay, but

Chapter 10

set a king over us.' Now therefore present yourselves before the LORD by your tribes, and by your thousands."

[20]And when Samuel had caused all the tribes of Israel to come near, the tribe of Benjamin was taken. [21]When he had caused the tribe of Benjamin to come near by their families, the family of Matri was taken, and Saul the son of Kish was taken: and when they sought him, he could not be found. [22]Therefore they inquired of the LORD further, if the man should yet come thither.

And the LORD answered, "Behold, he hath hid himself among the stuff."

[23]And they ran and fetched him thence: and when he stood among the people, he was higher than any of the people from his shoulders and upward. [24]And Samuel said to all the people, "See ye him whom the LORD hath chosen, that there is none like him among all the people?"

And all the people shouted, and said, "God save the king."

[25]Then Samuel told the people the manner of the kingdom, and wrote it in a book, and laid it up before the LORD. And Samuel sent all the people away, every man to his house.

[26]And Saul also went home to Gibeah; and there went with him a band of men, whose hearts God had touched.

THE LORD REJECTS SAUL AS KING

Chapter 14

NOW THE SONS OF SAUL WERE JONATHAN, AND Ishui, and Melchi-shua: and the names of his two daughters were these; the name of the firstborn Merab, and the name of the younger Michal: [50]and the name of Saul's wife was Ahinoam, the daughter of Ahimaaz: and the name of the captain of his host was Abner, the son of Ner, Saul's uncle. [51]And Kish was the father of Saul; and Ner the father of Abner was the son of Abiel.

[52]And there was sore war against the Philistines all the days of Saul: and when Saul saw any strong man, or any valiant man, he took him unto him.

Chapter 15

SAMUEL ALSO SAID UNTO SAUL, "THE LORD SENT ME TO anoint thee to be king over his people, over Israel: now therefore hearken thou unto the voice of the words of the LORD. [2]Thus saith the LORD of hosts, 'I remember that which Amalek did to Israel, how he laid wait for him in the way, when he came up from Egypt. [3]Now go and smite Amalek, and utterly destroy all that they have, and spare them not; but slay both man and woman, infant and suckling, ox and sheep, camel and ass.'"

[4]And Saul gathered the people together, and numbered them in Telaim, two hundred thousand footmen, and ten thousand men of Judah. [5]And Saul came to a city of Amalek, and laid wait in the valley. [6]And Saul said unto the Kenites, "Go, depart, get you down from among the Amalekites, lest I destroy you with them: for ye shewed kindness to all the children of Israel, when they came up out of Egypt." So the Kenites departed from among the Amalekites.

[7]And Saul smote the Amalekites from Havilah until thou comest to Shur, that is over against Egypt. [8]And he took Agag the king of the Amalekites alive, and utterly destroyed all the people with the edge of the sword. [9]But Saul and the people spared Agag, and the best of the sheep, and of the oxen, and of the fatlings, and the lambs, and all that was good, and would not utterly destroy them: but every thing that was vile and refuse, that they destroyed utterly.

[10]Then came the word of the LORD unto Samuel, saying, [11]"It repenteth me that I have set up Saul to be king: for he is turned back from following me, and hath not performed my commandments." And it grieved Samuel; and he cried unto the LORD all night.

[12]And when Samuel rose early to meet Saul in the morning, it was told Samuel, saying, "Saul came to Carmel, and, behold, he set him up a place, and is gone about, and passed on, and gone down to Gilgal."

[13]And Samuel came to Saul: and Saul said unto him, "Blessed be thou of the LORD: I have performed the commandment of the LORD."

[14]And Samuel said, "What meaneth then this bleating of the sheep in mine ears, and the lowing of the oxen which I hear?"

[15]And Saul said, "They have brought them from the Amalekites: for the people spared the best of the sheep and of the oxen, to sacrifice unto the LORD thy God; and the rest we have utterly destroyed."

[16]Then Samuel said unto Saul, "Stay, and I will tell thee what the LORD hath said to me this night."

And he said unto him, "Say on."

[17]And Samuel said, "When thou wast little in thine own sight, wast thou not made the head of the tribes of Israel, and the LORD anointed thee king over Israel? [18]And the LORD sent thee on a journey, and said, 'Go and utterly destroy the sinners the Amalekites, and fight against them until they be consumed.' [19]Wherefore then didst thou not obey the voice of the LORD, but didst fly upon the spoil, and didst evil in the sight of the LORD?"

[20]And Saul said unto Samuel, "Yea, I have obeyed the voice of the LORD, and have gone the way which the LORD sent me, and have brought Agag the king of Amalek, and have utterly destroyed the Amalekites. [21]But the people took of the spoil, sheep and oxen, the chief of the things which should have been utterly destroyed, to sacrifice unto the LORD thy God in Gilgal."

[22]And Samuel said, "Hath the LORD as great delight in burnt offerings and sacrifices, as in obeying the voice of the LORD? Behold, to obey is better than sacrifice, and to hearken than the fat of rams. [23]For rebellion is as the sin of witchcraft, and stubbornness is as iniquity and idolatry. Because thou hast rejected the word of the LORD, he hath also rejected thee from being king."

[24]And Saul said unto Samuel, "I have sinned: for I have transgressed the commandment of the LORD, and thy words: because I feared the people, and obeyed their voice. [25]Now therefore, I pray thee, pardon my sin, and turn again with me, that I may worship the LORD."

[26]And Samuel said unto Saul, "I will not return with thee, for thou hast rejected the word of the LORD, and the LORD hath rejected thee from being king over Israel."

[27]And as Samuel turned about to go away, he laid hold upon the skirt of his mantle, and it rent. [28]And Samuel said unto him, "The LORD hath rent the kingdom of Israel from thee this day, and hath given it to a neighbour of thine, that is better than thou. [29]And also the Strength of Israel

SAMUEL KILLS AGAG *by R. van Troyen*

will not lie nor repent: for he is not a man, that he should repent."

[30]Then he said, "I have sinned: yet honour me now, I pray thee, before the elders of my people, and before Israel, and turn again with me, that I may worship the LORD thy God." [31]So Samuel turned again after Saul; and Saul worshipped the LORD.

[32]Then said Samuel, "Bring ye hither to me Agag the king of the Amalekites."

And Agag came unto him delicately. And Agag said, "Surely the bitterness of death is past."

[33]And Samuel said, "As thy sword hath made women childless, so shall thy mother be childless among women." And Samuel hewed Agag in pieces before the LORD in Gilgal.

[34]Then Samuel went to Ramah; and Saul went up to his house to Gibeah of Saul. [35]And Samuel came no more to see Saul until the day of his death: nevertheless Samuel mourned for Saul: and the LORD repented that he had made Saul king over Israel.

Samuel Anoints David

Chapter 16

AND THE LORD SAID UNTO SAMUEL, "HOW LONG wilt thou mourn for Saul, seeing I have rejected him from reigning over Israel? Fill thine horn with oil, and go, I will send thee to Jesse the Bethlehemite: for I have provided me a king among his sons."

[2]And Samuel said, "How can I go? If Saul hear it, he will kill me."

And the LORD said, "Take an heifer with thee, and say, 'I am come to sacrifice to the LORD.' [3]And call Jesse to the sacrifice, and I will shew thee what thou shalt do: and thou shalt anoint unto me him whom I name unto thee."

[4]And Samuel did that which the LORD spake, and came to Bethlehem. And the elders of the town trembled at his coming, and said, "Comest thou peaceably?"

SAMUEL ANOINTING DAVID *by Mattia Preti*

Chapter 16

[5]And he said, "Peaceably: I am come to sacrifice unto the LORD: sanctify yourselves, and come with me to the sacrifice." And he sanctified Jesse and his sons, and called them to the sacrifice.

[6]And it came to pass, when they were come, that he looked on Eliab, and said, "Surely the LORD's anointed is before him."

[7]But the LORD said unto Samuel, "Look not on his countenance, or on the height of his stature; because I have refused him: for the LORD seeth not as man seeth; for man looketh on the outward appearance, but the LORD looketh on the heart."

[8]Then Jesse called Abinadab, and made him pass before Samuel. And he said, "Neither hath the LORD chosen this." [9]Then Jesse made Shammah to pass by. And he said, "Neither hath the LORD chosen this." [10]Again, Jesse made seven of his sons to pass before Samuel. And Samuel said unto Jesse, "The LORD hath not chosen these." [11]And Samuel said unto Jesse, "Are here all thy children?"

And he said, "There remaineth yet the youngest, and, behold, he keepeth the sheep."

And Samuel said unto Jesse, "Send and fetch him: for we will not sit down till he come hither."

[12]And he sent, and brought him in. Now he was ruddy, and withal of a beautiful countenance, and goodly to look to.

And the LORD said, "Arise, anoint him: for this is he."

[13]Then Samuel took the horn of oil, and anointed him in the midst of his brethren: and the spirit of the LORD came upon David from that day forward. So Samuel rose up, and went to Ramah.

DAVID AND GOLIATH

Chapter 17

NOW THE PHILISTINES GATHERED TOGETHER their armies to battle, and were gathered together at Shochoh, which belongeth to Judah, and pitched between Shochoh and Azekah, in Ephes-dammim. [2]And Saul and the men of Israel were gathered together, and pitched by

the valley of Elah, and set the battle in array against the Philistines. [3]And the Philistines stood on a mountain on the one side, and Israel stood on a mountain on the other side: and there was a valley between them.

[4]And there went out a champion of the camp of the Philistines, named Goliath, of Gath, whose height was six cubits and a span. [5]And he had an helmet of brass upon his head, and he was armed with a coat of mail; and the weight of the coat was five thousand shekels of brass. [6]And he had greaves of brass upon his legs, and a target of brass between his shoulders. [7]And the staff of his spear was like a weaver's beam; and his spear's head weighed six hundred shekels of iron: and one bearing a shield went before him.

[8]And he stood and cried unto the armies of Israel, and said unto them, "Why are ye come out to set your battle in array? Am I not a Philistine, and ye servants to Saul? Choose you a man for you, and let him come down to me. [9]If he be able to fight with me, and to kill me, then will we be your servants: but if I prevail against him, and kill him, then shall ye be our servants, and serve us." [10]And the Philistine said, "I defy the armies of Israel this day; give me a man, that we may fight together." [11]When Saul and all Israel heard those words of the Philistine, they were dismayed, and greatly afraid.

[12]Now David was the son of that Ephrathite of Bethlehem-judah, whose name was Jesse; and he had eight sons: and the man went among men for an old man in the days of Saul. [13]And the three eldest sons of Jesse went and followed Saul to the battle: and the names of his three sons that went to the battle were Eliab the firstborn, and next unto him Abinadab, and the third Shammah. [14]And David was the youngest: and the three eldest followed Saul. [15]But David went and returned from Saul to feed his father's sheep at Bethlehem.

[16]And the Philistine drew near morning and evening, and presented himself forty days.

[17]And Jesse said unto David his son, "Take now for thy brethren an ephah of this parched corn, and these ten loaves, and run to the camp to thy brethren; [18]and carry these ten cheeses unto the captain of their thousand, and look how thy brethren fare, and take their pledge." [19]Now

THE YOUNG DAVID *by Andrea Castagno*

Saul, and they, and all the men of Israel, were in the valley of Elah, fighting with the Philistines.

[20]And David rose up early in the morning, and left the sheep with a keeper, and took, and went, as Jesse had commanded him; and he came to the trench, as the host was going forth to the fight, and shouted for the battle. [21]Fc

Israel and the Philistines had put the battle in array, army against army. [22]And David left his carriage in the hand of the keeper of the carriage, and ran into the army, and came and saluted his brethren. [23]And as he talked with them, behold, there came up the champion, the Philistine of Gath, Goliath by name, out of the armies of the Philistines, and spake according to the same words: and David heard them. [24]And all the men of Israel, when they saw the man, fled from him, and were sore afraid.

[25]And the men of Israel said, "Have ye seen this man that is come up? Surely to defy Israel is he come up: and it shall be, that the man who killeth him, the king will enrich him with great riches, and will give him his daughter, and make his father's house free in Israel."

[26]And David spake to the men that stood by him, saying, "What shall be done to the man that killeth this Philistine, and taketh away the reproach from Israel? for who is this uncircumcised Philistine, that he should defy the armies of the living God?"

[27]And the people answered him after this manner, saying, "So shall it be done to the man that killeth him."

[28]And Eliab his eldest brother heard when he spake unto the men; and Eliab's anger was kindled against David, and he said, "Why camest thou down hither? and with whom hast thou left those few sheep in the wilderness? I know thy pride, and the naughtiness of thine heart; for thou art come down that thou mightest see the battle."

[29]And David said, "What have I now done? Is there not a cause?" [30]And he turned from him toward another, and spake after the same manner: and the people answered him again after the former manner. [31]And when the words were heard which David spake, they rehearsed them before Saul: and he sent for him.

[32]And David said to Saul, "Let no man's heart fail because of him; thy servant will go and fight with this Philistine."

[33]And Saul said to David, "Thou art not able to go against this Philistine to fight with him: for thou art but a youth, and he a man of war from his youth."

[34]And David said unto Saul, "Thy servant kept his father's sheep, and there came a lion, and a bear, and took a lamb out of the flock: [35]and I went out after him, and

smote him, and delivered it out of his mouth: and when he arose against me, I caught him by his beard, and smote him, and slew him. [36]Thy servant slew both the lion and the bear: and this uncircumcised Philistine shall be as one of them, seeing he hath defied the armies of the living God." [37]David said moreover, "The LORD that delivered me out of the paw of the lion, and out of the paw of the bear, he will deliver me out of the hand of this Philistine."

And Saul said unto David, "Go, and the LORD be with thee."

[38]And Saul armed David with his armour, and he put an helmet of brass upon his head; also he armed him with a coat of mail. [39]And David girded his sword upon his armour, and he assayed to go; for he had not proved it.

And David said unto Saul, "I cannot go with these; for I have not proved them." And David put them off him. [40]And he took his staff in his hand, and chose him five smooth stones out of the brook, and put them in a shepherd's bag which he had, even in a scrip; and his sling was in his hand: and he drew near to the Philistine.

[41]And the Philistine came on and drew near unto David; and the man that bare the shield went before him. [42]And when the Philistine looked about, and saw David, he disdained him: for he was but a youth, and ruddy, and of a fair countenance. [43]And the Philistine said unto David, "Am I a dog, that thou comest to me with staves?" And the Philistine cursed David by his gods. [44]And the Philistine said to David, "Come to me, and I will give thy flesh unto the fowls of the air, and to the beasts of the field."

THE TRIUMPH OF DAVID, *circle of Marten de Vos*

[45]Then said David to the Philistine, "Thou comest to me with a sword, and with a spear, and with a shield: but I come to thee in the name of the LORD of hosts, the God of the armies of Israel, whom thou hast defied. [46]This day will the LORD deliver thee into mine hand; and I will smite thee, and take thine head from thee; and I will give the carcases of the host of the Philistines this day unto the fowls of the air, and to the wild beasts of the earth; that all the earth may know that there is a God in Israel. [47]And all this assembly shall know that the LORD saveth not with sword and spear: for the battle is the LORD's, and he will give you into our hands."

[48]And it came to pass, when the Philistine arose, and came and drew nigh to meet David, that David hasted, and ran toward the army to meet the Philistine. [49]And David put his hand in his bag, and took thence a stone, and slang it, and smote the Philistine in his forehead, that the stone sunk into his forehead; and he fell upon his face to the earth.

[50]So David prevailed over the Philistine with a sling and with a stone, and smote the Philistine, and slew him; but there was no sword in the hand of David.

[51]Therefore David ran, and stood upon the Philistine, and took his sword, and drew it out of the sheath thereof, and slew him, and cut off his head therewith.

And when the Philistines saw their champion was dead, they fled. [52]And the men of Israel and of Judah arose, and shouted, and pursued the Philistines, until thou come to the valley, and to the gates of Ekron. And the wounded of the Philistines fell down by the way to Shaaraim, even unto Gath, and unto Ekron. [53]And the children of Israel returned from chasing after the Philistines, and they spoiled their tents. [54]And David took the head of the Philistine, and brought it to Jerusalem; but he put his armour in his tent.

[55]And when Saul saw David go forth against the Philistine, he said unto Abner, the captain of the host, "Abner, whose son is this youth?"

And Abner said, "As thy soul liveth, O king, I cannot tell."

[56]And the king said, "Inquire thou whose son the stripling is."

Chapter 17

David with the Head of Goliath *by Carlo Dolci*

Chapter 17

[57]And as David returned from the slaughter of the Philistine, Abner took him, and brought him before Saul with the head of the Philistine in his hand.

[58]And Saul said to him, "Whose son art thou, thou young man?" And David answered, "I am the son of th servant Jesse the Bethlehemite."

Saul's Jealousy of David

Chapter 18

AND IT CAME TO PASS, WHEN HE HAD MADE AN end of speaking unto Saul, that the soul of Jonathan was knit with the soul of David, and Jonathan loved him as his own soul. [2]And Saul took him that day, and would let him go no more home to his father's house. [3]Then Jonathan and David made a covenant, because he loved him as his own soul. [4]And Jonathan stripped himself of the robe that was upon him, and gave it to David, and his garments, even to his sword, and to his bow, and to his girdle.

[5]And David went out whithersoever Saul sent him, and behaved himself wisely: and Saul set him over the men of war, and he was accepted in the sight of all the people, and also in the sight of Saul's servants.

[6]And it came to pass as they came, when David was returned from the slaughter of the Philistine, that the women came out of all cities of Israel, singing and dancing, to meet

THE TRIUMPH OVER THE ASSYRIANS, *School of Raphael*

Chapter 18

king Saul, with tabrets, with joy, and with instruments of musick. [7]And the women answered one another as they played, and said, "Saul hath slain his thousands, and David his ten thousands."

[8]And Saul was very wroth, and the saying displeased him; and he said, "They have ascribed unto David ten thousands, and to me they have ascribed but thousands: and what can he have more but the kingdom?" [9]And Saul eyed David from that day and forward.

David Flees to Samuel

Chapter 19

AND SAUL SPAKE TO JONATHAN HIS SON, AND TO all his servants, that they should kill David. [2]But Jonathan Saul's son delighted much in David: and Jonathan told David, saying, "Saul my father seeketh to kill thee: now therefore, I pray thee, take heed to thyself until the morning, and abide in a secret place, and hide thyself: [3]and I will go out and stand beside my father in the field where thou art, and I will commune with my father of thee: and what I see, that I will tell thee."

[4]And Jonathan spake good of David unto Saul his father, and said unto him, "Let not the king sin against his servant, against David; because he hath not sinned against thee, and because his works have been to thee-ward very good: [5]for he did put his life in his hand, and slew the Philistine, and the LORD wrought a great salvation for all Israel: thou sawest it, and didst rejoice: wherefore then wilt thou sin against innocent blood, to slay David without a cause?"

[6]And Saul hearkened unto the voice of Jonathan: and Saul sware, "As the LORD liveth, he shall not be slain."

[7]And Jonathan called David, and Jonathan shewed him all those things. And Jonathan brought David to Saul, and he was in his presence, as in times past.

[8]And there was war again: and David went out, and fought with the Philistines, and slew them with a great slaughter; and they fled from him.

Chapter 19

[9]And the evil spirit from the LORD was upon Saul, as he sat in his house with his javelin in his hand: and David played with his hand. [10]And Saul sought to smite David even to the wall with the javelin; but he slipped away out of Saul's presence, and he smote the javelin into the wall: and David fled, and escaped that night.

[11]Saul also sent the messengers unto David's house, to watch him, and to slay him in the morning: and Michal David's wife told him, saying, "If thou save not thy life to night, to morrow thou shalt be slain." [12]So Michal let David down through a window: and he went, and fled, and escaped. [13]And Michal took an image, and laid it in the bed, and put a pillow of goats' hair for his bolster, and covered it with a cloth.

[14]And when Saul sent messengers to take David, she said, "He is sick."

[15]And Saul sent the messengers again to see David, saying, "Bring him up to me in the bed, that I may slay him." [16]And when the messengers were come in, behold, there was an image in the bed, with a pillow of goats' hair for his bolster.

[17]And Saul said unto Michal, "Why hast thou deceived me so, and sent away mine enemy, that he is escaped?"

And Michal answered Saul, "He said unto me, 'Let me go; why should I kill thee?'"

[18]So David fled, and escaped, and came to Samuel to Ramah, and told him all that Saul had done to him. And he and Samuel went and dwelt in Naioth.

SAUL AND THE WITCH OF ENDOR

Chapter 20

NOW SAMUEL WAS DEAD, AND ALL ISRAEL HAD lamented him, and buried him in Ramah, even in his own city. And Saul had put away those that had familiar spirits, and the wizards, out of the land.

[4]And the Philistines gathered themselves together, and came and pitched in Shunem: and Saul gathered all Israel together, and they pitched in Gilboa. [5]And when Saul saw

the host of the Philistines, he was afraid, and his heart greatly trembled. [6]And when Saul inquired of the LORD, the LORD answered him not, neither by dreams, nor by Urim, nor by prophets. [7]Then said Saul unto his servants, "Seek me a woman that hath a familiar spirit, that I may go to her, and inquire of her."

And his servants said to him, "Behold, there is a woman that hath a familiar spirit at Endor."

[8]And Saul disguised himself, and put on other raiment, and he went, and two men with him, and they came to the woman by night: and he said, "I pray thee, divine unto me by the familiar spirit, and bring me him up, whom I shall name unto thee."

[9]And the woman said unto him, "Behold, thou knowest what Saul hath done, how he hath cut off those that have familiar spirits, and the wizards, out of the land: wherefore then layest thou a snare for my life, to cause me to die?"

[10]And Saul sware to her by the LORD, saying, "As the LORD liveth, there shall no punishment happen to thee for this thing."

[11]Then said the woman, "Whom shall I bring up unto thee?"

And he said, "Bring me up Samuel."

[12]And when the woman saw Samuel, she cried with a loud voice: and the woman spake to Saul, saying, "Why hast thou deceived me? for thou art Saul."

[13]And the king said unto her, "Be not afraid: for what sawest thou?"

And the woman said unto Saul, "I saw gods ascending out of the earth."

[14]And he said unto her, "What form is he of?"

And she said, "An old man cometh up; and he is covered with a mantle."

And Saul perceived that it was Samuel, and he stooped with his face to the ground, and bowed himself.

[15]And Samuel said to Saul, "Why hast thou disquieted me, to bring me up?"

And Saul answered, "I am sore distressed; for the Philistines make war against me, and God is departed from me, and answereth me no more, neither by prophets, nor by dreams: therefore I have called thee, that thou mayest make known unto me what I shall do."

SAUL AND THE WITCH OF ENDOR *by Salvator Rosa*

[16]Then said Samuel, "Wherefore then dost thou ask of me, seeing the LORD is departed from thee, and is become thine enemy? [17]And the LORD hath done to him, as he spake by me: for the LORD hath rent the kingdom out of thine hand, and given it to thy neighbour, even to David: [18]because thou obeyedst not the voice of the LORD, nor executedst his fierce wrath upon Amalek, therefore hath the LORD done this thing unto thee this day. [19]Moreover the LORD will also deliver Israel with thee into the hand of

Chapter 28

SAUL AND THE WITCH OF ENDOR *by Cornelius van Oostenen*

Chapter 28

the Philistines: and to morrow shalt thou and thy sons be with me: the LORD also shall deliver the host of Israel into the hand of the Philistines."

SAUL AND JONATHAN SLAIN

Chapter 31

NOW THE PHILISTINES FOUGHT AGAINST Israel: and the men of Israel fled from before the Philistines, and fell down slain in mount Gilboa. [2]And the Philistines followed hard upon Saul and upon his sons; and the Philistines slew Jonathan, and Abinadab, and Malchi-shua, Saul's sons. [3]And the battle went sore against Saul, and the archers hit him; and he was sore wounded of the archers.

[4]Then said Saul unto his armourbearer, "Draw thy sword, and thrust me through therewith; lest these uncircumcised come and thrust me through, and abuse me."

But his armourbearer would not; for he was sore afraid. Therefore Saul took a sword, and fell upon it. [5]And when his armourbearer saw that Saul was dead, he fell likewise upon his sword, and died with him. [6]So Saul died, and his three sons, and his amourbearer, and all his men, that same day together.

[7]And when the men of Israel that were on the other side of the valley, and they that were on the other side Jordan, saw that the men of Israel fled, and that Saul and his sons were dead, they forsook the cities, and fled; and the Philistines came and dwelt in them.

[8]And it came to pass on the morrow, when the Philistines came to strip the slain, that they found Saul and his three sons fallen in mount Gilboa. [9]And they cut off his head, and stripped off his armour, and sent into the land of the Philistines round about, to publish it in the house of their idols, and among the people. [10]And they put his armour in the house of Ashtaroth: and they fastened his body to the wall of Beth-shan.

[11]And when the inhabitants of Jabesh-gilead heard of that which the Philistines had done to Saul; [12]all the valiant men arose, and went all night, and took the body of Saul and the bodies of his sons from the wall of Beth shan, and came to Jabesh, and burnt them there. [13]And they took their bones, and buried them under a tree at Jabesh, and fasted seven days.

THE SUICIDE OF SAUL *by Peter Breughel*

THE SECOND BOOK OF
SAMUEL

David's Lament for Saul and Jonathan

Chapter 1

THE BEAUTY OF ISRAEL IS SLAIN UPON THY HIGH places:
How are the mighty fallen!

[20]Tell it not in Gath,
Publish it not in the streets of Askelon;
Lest the daughters of the Philistines rejoice,
Lest the daughters of the uncircumcised triumph.

[21]Ye mountains of Gilboa,
Let there be no dew, neither let there be rain, upon you,
Nor fields of offerings:
For there the shield of the mighty is vilely cast away,
The shield of Saul, as though he had not been anointed with oil.
[22]From the blood of the slain, from the fat of the mighty,
The bow of Jonathan turned not back,
And the sword of Saul returned not empty.

[23]Saul and Jonathan were lovely and pleasant in their lives,
And in their death they were not divided:
They were swifter than eagles,
They were stronger than lions.

[24]Ye daughters of Israel, weep over Saul,
Who clothed you in scarlet, with other delights,
Who put on ornaments of gold upon your apparel.

Chapter 1

[25]How are the mighty fallen in the midst of the battle!
O Jonathan, thou wast slain in thine high places.
[26]I am distressed for thee, my brother Jonathan:
Very pleasant has thou been unto me:
Thy love to me was wonderful,
Passing the love of women.

[27]How are the mighty fallen,
And the weapons of war perished!

David Becomes King of Israel

Chapter 5

THEN CAME ALL THE TRIBES OF ISRAEL TO DAVID unto Hebron, and spake, saying, "Behold, we are thy bone and thy flesh. [2]Also in time past, when Saul was king over us, thou wast he that leddest out and broughtest in Israel: and the LORD said to thee, Thou shalt feed my people Israel, and thou shalt be a captain over Israel."

[3]So all the elders of Israel came to the king to Hebron; and king David made a league with them in Hebron before the LORD: and they anointed David king over Israel.

[4]David was thirty years old when he began to reign, and he reigned forty years. [5]In Hebron he reigned over Judah seven years and six months: and in Jerusalem he reigned thirty and three years over all Israel and Judah.

[6]And the king and his men went to Jerusalem unto the Jebusites, the inhabitants of the land: which spake unto David, saying, "Except thou take away the blind and the lame, thou shalt not come in hither": thinking, "David cannot come in hither." [7]Nevertheless David took the strong hold of Zion: the same is the city of David.

[8]And David said on that day, "Whosoever getteth up to the gutter, and smiteth the Jebusites, and the lame and the blind, that are hated of David's soul, he shall be chief and captain." Wherefore they said, "The blind and the lame shall not come into the house."

[9]So David dwelt in the fort, and called it the city of David. And David built round about from Millo and

Chapter 5

inward. [10]And David went on, and grew great, and the Lord God of hosts was with him.

[11]And Hiram king of Tyre sent messengers to David, and cedar trees, and carpenters, and masons: and they built David an house. [12]And David perceived that the Lord had established him king over Israel, and that he had exalted his kingdom for his people Israel's sake.

David Defeats the Philistines

Chapter 5

But when the Philistines heard that they had anointed David king over Israel, all the Philistines came up to seek David; and David heard of it, and went down to the hold. [18]The Philistines also came and spread themselves in the valley of Rephaim. [19]And David inquired of the Lord, saying, "Shall I go up to the Philistines? Wilt thou deliver them into mine hand?"

And the Lord said unto David, "Go up: for I will doubtless deliver the Philistines into thine hand."

[20]And David came to Baal-perazim, and David smote them there, and said, "The Lord hath broken forth upon mine enemies before me, as the breach of waters." Therefore he called the name of that place Baal-perazim. [21]And there they left their images, and David and his men burned them.

[22]And the Philistines came up yet again, and spread themselves in the valley of Rephaim. [23]And when David inquired of the Lord, he said, "Thou shalt not go up; but fetch a compass behind them, and come upon them over against the mulberry trees. [24]And let it be, when thou hearest the sound of a going in the tops of the mulberry trees, that then thou shalt bestir thyself: for then shall the Lord go out before thee, to smite the host of the Philistines." [25]And David did so, as the Lord had commanded him; and smote the Philistines from Geba until thou come to Gazer.

Facing page: David as King, *School of Amiens*

David Brings the Ark to Jerusalem

Chapter 6

AGAIN, DAVID HAD GATHERED TOGETHER ALL the chosen men of Israel, thirty thousand. [2]And David arose, and went with all the people that were with him from Baale of Judah, to bring up from thence the ark of God, whose name is called by the name of the LORD of hosts that dwelleth between the cherubims. [3]And they set the ark of God upon a new cart, and brought it out of the house of Abinadab that was in Gibeah: and Uzzah and Ahio, the sons of Abinadab, drave the new cart. [4]And they brought it out of the house of Abinadab which was at Gibeah, accompanying the ark of God: and Ahio went before the ark. [5]And David and all the house of Israel played before the LORD on all manner of instruments made of fir wood, even on harps, and on psalteries, and on timbrels, and on cornets, and on cymbals.

[6]And when they came to Nachon's threshingfloor, Uzzah put forth his hand to the ark of God, and took hold of it; for the oxen shook it. [7]And the anger of the LORD was kindled against Uzzah; and God smote him there for his error; and there he died by the ark of God.

[8]And David was displeased, because the LORD had made a breach upon Uzzah: and he called the name of the place Perez-uzzah to this day.

[9]And David was afraid of the LORD that day, and said, "How shall the ark of the LORD come to me?" [10]So David would not remove the ark of the LORD unto him into the city of David: but David carried it aside into the house of Obed-edom the Gittite. [11]And the ark of the LORD continued in the house of Obed-edom the Gittite three months: and the LORD blessed Obed-edom, and all his household.

[12]And it was told king David, saying, "The LORD hath blessed the house of Obed-edom, and all that pertaineth unto him, because of the ark of God." So David went and brought up the ark of God from the house of Obed-edom into the city of David with gladness. [13]And it was so, that when they that bare the ark of the LORD had gone six paces,

David Brings the Ark to Jerusalem

Chapter 6

THE CONSECRATION OF DAVID, *School of Raphael*

Chapter 6

he sacrificed oxen and fatlings. [14]And David danced before the LORD with all his might; and David was girded with a linen ephod. [15]So David and all the house of Israel brought up the ark of the LORD with shouting, and with the sound of the trumpet.

[16]And as the ark of the LORD came into the city of David, Michal Saul's daughter looked through a window, and saw king David leaping and dancing before the LORD; and she despised him in her heart.

[17]And they brought in the ark of the LORD, and set it in his place, in the midst of the tabernacle that David had pitched for it: and David offered burnt offerings and peace offerings before the LORD. [18]And as soon as David had made an end of offering burnt offerings and peace offerings, he blessed the people in the name of the LORD of hosts. [19]And he dealt among all the people, even among the whole multitude of Israel, as well to the women as men, to every one a cake of bread, and a good piece of flesh, and a flagon of wine. So all the people departed every one to his house.

Chapter 6

[20]Then David returned to bless his household. And Michal the daughter of Saul came out to meet David, and said, "How glorious was the king of Israel to day, who uncovered himself to day in the eyes of the handmaids of his servants, as one of the vain fellows shamelessly uncovereth himself!"

[21]And David said unto Michal, "It was before the LORD, which chose me before thy father, and before all his house, to appoint me ruler over the people of the LORD, over Israel: therefore will I play before the LORD. [22]And I will yet be more vile than thus, and will be base in mine own sight: and of the maidservants which thou hast spoken of, of them shall I be had in honour."

[23]Therefore Michal the daughter of Saul had no child unto the day of her death.

GOD'S PROMISE TO DAVID

Chapter 7

AND IT CAME TO PASS, WHEN THE KING SAT IN HIS house, and the LORD had given him rest round about from all his enemies; [2]that the king said unto Nathan the prophet, "See now, I dwell in an house of cedar, but the ark of God dwelleth within curtains."

[3]And Nathan said to the king, "Go, do all that is in thine heart: for the LORD is with thee."

[4]And it came to pass that night, that the word of the LORD came unto Nathan, saying,

[5]"Go and tell my servant David, 'Thus saith the LORD, Shalt thou build me an house for me to dwell in? [6]Whereas I have not dwelt in any house since the time that I brought up the children of Israel out of Egypt, even to this day, but have walked in a tent and in a tabernacle. [7]In all the places wherein I have walked with all the children of Israel spake I a word with any of the tribes of Israel, whom I commanded to feed my people Israel, saying, "Why build ye not me an house of cedar?"'

Chapter 7

[8]"Now therefore so shalt thou say unto my servant David, 'Thus saith the LORD of hosts, I took thee from the sheepcote, from following the sheep, to be ruler over my people, over Israel: [9]and I was with thee whithersoever thou wentest, and have cut off all thine enemies out of thy sight, and have made thee a great name, like unto the name of the great men that are in the earth. [10]Moreover I will appoint a place for my people Israel, and will plant them, that they may dwell in a place of their own, and move no more; neither shall the children of wickedness afflict them any more, as beforetime, [11]and as since the time that I commanded judges to be over my people Israel, and have caused thee to rest from all thine enemies.

"'Also the LORD telleth thee that he will make thee an house. [12]And when thy days be fulfilled, and thou shalt sleep with thy fathers, I will set up thy seed after thee, which shall proceed out of thy bowels, and I will establish his kingdom. [13]He shall build an house for my name, and I will stablish the throne of his kingdom for ever. [14]I will be his father, and he shall be my son. If he commit iniquity, I will chasten him with the rod of men, and with the stripes of the children of men: [15]but my mercy shall not depart away from him, as I took it from Saul, whom I put away before thee. [16]And thine house and thy kingdom shall be established for ever before thee: thy throne shall be established for ever.'"

[17]According to all these words, and according to all this vision, so did Nathan speak unto David.

David and Bathsheba

Chapter 11

AND IT CAME TO PASS, AFTER THE YEAR WAS EXpired, at the time when kings go forth to battle, that David sent Joab, and his servants with him, and all Israel; and they destroyed the children of Ammon, and besieged Rabbah. But David tarried still at Jerusalem.

[2]And it came to pass in an eveningtide, that David arose from off his bed, and walked upon the roof of the king's house: and from the roof he saw a woman washing herself; and the woman was very beautiful to look upon. [3]And David sent and inquired after the woman. And one said, "Is not this Bathsheba, the daughter of Eliam, the wife of Uriah the Hittite?" [4]And David sent messengers, and took her; and she came in unto him, and he lay with her; for she was purified from her uncleanness: and she returned unto her house. [5]And the woman conceived, and sent and told David, and said, "I am with child."

[6]And David sent to Joab, saying, "Send me Uriah the Hittite." And Joab sent Uriah to David. [7]And when Uriah was come unto him, David demanded of him how Joab did, and how the people did, and how the war prospered. [8]And David said to Uriah, "Go down to thy house, and wash thy feet." And Uriah departed out of the king's house, and there followed him a mess of meat from the king. [9]But Uriah slept at the door of the king's house with all the servants of his lord, and went not down to his house.

[10]And when they had told David, saying, "Uriah went not down unto his house," David said unto Uriah, "Camest thou not from thy journey? Why then didst thou not go down unto thine house?"

[11]And Uriah said unto David, "The ark, and Israel, and Judah, abide in tents; and my lord Joab, and the servants of my lord, are encamped in the open fields; shall I then go into mine house, to eat and to drink, and to lie with my wife? As thou livest, and as thy soul liveth, I will not do this thing."

[12]And David said to Uriah, "Tarry here to day also, and to morrow I will let thee depart." So Uriah abode in Jerusalem that day, and the morrow. [13]And when David had called him, he did eat and drink before him; and he made him drunk: and at even he went out to lie on his bed with the servants of his lord, but went not down to his house.

[14]And it came to pass in the morning, that David wrote a letter to Joab, and sent it by the hand of Uriah. [15]And he wrote in the letter, saying, "Set ye Uriah in the forefront of the hottest battle, and retire ye from him, that he may be smitten, and die."

[16]And it came to pass, when Joab observed the city, that he assigned Uriah unto a place where he knew that valiant men were. [17]And the men of the city went out, and fought with Joab: and there fell some of the people of the servants of David; and Uriah the Hittite died also.

[18]Then Joab sent and told David all the things concerning the war; [19]and charged the messenger, saying, "When thou hast made an end of telling the matters of the war unto the king, [20]and if so be that the king's wrath arise, and he say unto thee, 'Wherefore approached ye so nigh unto the city when ye did fight? Knew ye not that they would shoot from the wall? [21]Who smote Abimelech the son of Jerubbesheth? Did not a woman cast a piece of a millstone upon him from the wall, that he died in Thebez? Why went ye nigh the wall?' then say thou, 'Thy servant Uriah the Hittite is dead also.'"

[22]So the messenger went, and came and shewed David all that Joab had sent him for. [23]And the messenger said unto David, "Surely the men prevailed against us, and came out unto us into the field, and we were upon them even unto the entering of the gate. [24]And the shooters shot

David and Bathsheba *by Theodoros Poulakis*

Chapter 11

from off the wall upon thy servants; and some of the king's servants be dead, and thy servant Uriah the Hittite is dead also."

[25]Then David said unto the messenger, "Thus shalt thou say unto Joab, 'Let not this thing displease thee, for the sword devoureth one as well as another: make thy battle more strong against the city, and overthrow it': and encourage thou him."

[26]And when the wife of Uriah heard that Uriah her husband was dead, she mourned for her husband. [27]And when the mourning was past, David sent and fetched her to his house, and she became his wife, and bare him a son. But the thing that David had done displeased the LORD.

NATHAN REBUKES DAVID

Chapter 12

AND THE LORD SENT NATHAN UNTO DAVID. AND he came unto him, and said unto him, "There were two men in one city; the one rich, and the other poor. [2]The rich man had exceeding many flocks and herds: [3]but the poor man had nothing, save one little ewe lamb, which he had bought and nourished up: and it grew up together with him, and with his children; it did eat of his own meat, and drank of his own cup, and lay in his bosom, and was unto him as a daughter.

[4]"And there came a traveller unto the rich man, and he spared to take of his own flock and of his own herd, to dress for the wayfaring man that was come unto him; but took the poor man's lamb, and dressed it for the man that was come to him."

[5]And David's anger was greatly kindled against the man; and he said to Nathan, "As the LORD liveth, the man that hath done this thing shall surely die: [6]and he shall restore the lamb fourfold, because he did this thing, and because he had no pity."

[7]And Nathan said to David, "Thou art the man. Thus saith the LORD God of Israel, 'I anointed thee king over Israel, and I delivered thee out of the hand of Saul; [8]and I

gave thee thy master's house, and thy master's wives into thy bosom, and gave thee the house of Israel and of Judah; and if that had been too little, I would moreover have given unto thee such and such things. [9]Wherefore hast thou despised the commandment of the LORD, to do evil in his sight? Thou hast killed Uriah the Hittite with the sword, and hast taken his wife to be thy wife, and hast slain him with the sword of the children of Ammon. [10]Now therefore the sword shall never depart from thine house; because thou hast despised me, and hast taken the wife of Uriah the Hittite to be thy wife.'

[11]"Thus saith the LORD, 'Behold, I will raise up evil against thee out of thine own house, and I will take thy wives before thine eyes, and give them unto thy neighbour, and he shall lie with thy wives in the sight of this sun. [12]For thou didst it secretly: but I will do this thing before all Israel, and before the sun.'"

[13]And David said unto Nathan, "I have sinned against the LORD."

And Nathan said unto David, "The LORD also hath put away thy sin; thou shalt not die. [14]Howbeit, because by this deed thou hast given great occasion to the enemies of the LORD to blaspheme, the child also that is born unto thee shall surely die."

[15]And Nathan departed unto his house. And the LORD struck the child that Uriah's wife bare unto David, and it was very sick. [16]David therefore besought God for the child; and David fasted, and went in, and lay all night upon the earth. [17]And the elders of his house arose, and went to him, to raise him up from the earth: but he would not, neither did he eat bread with them.

[18]And it came to pass on the seventh day, that the child died. And the servants of David feared to tell him that the child was dead: for they said, "Behold, while the child was yet alive, we spake unto him, and he would not hearken unto our voice: how will he then vex himself, if we tell him that the child is dead?"

[19]But when David saw that his servants whispered, David perceived that the child was dead: therefore David said unto his servants, "Is the child dead?"

And they said, "He is dead."

[20]Then David arose from the earth, and washed, and

anointed himself, and changed his apparel, and came into the house of the LORD, and worshipped: then he came to his own house; and when he required, they set bread before him, and he did eat.

[21]Then said his servants unto him, "What thing is this that thou hast done? Thou didst fast and weep for the child, while it was alive; but when the child was dead, thou didst rise and eat bread."

[22]And he said, "While the child was yet alive, I fasted and wept: for I said, 'Who can tell whether God will be gracious to me, that the child may live?' [23]But now he is dead, wherefore should I fast? Can I bring him back again? I shall go to him, but he shall not return to me."

[24]And David comforted Bathsheba his wife, and went in unto her, and lay with her: and she bare him a son, and he called his name Solomon: and the LORD loved him.

SOLOMON AND THE QUEEN OF SHEBA *by Frans Francken the Younger*

Chapters & Verses
FROM
THE FIRST & SECOND BOOKS OF THE KINGS

DAVID'S CHARGE TO SOLOMON • SOLOMON'S CHOICE OF WISDOM • SOLOMON BUILDS THE TEMPLE • SOLOMON DEDICATES THE TEMPLE • THE QUEEN OF SHEBA VISITS SOLOMON • SOLOMON'S MANY WIVES • JEROBOAM'S REVOLT • THE DIVISION OF THE KINGDOM • JEROBOAM TURNS TO IDOLATRY • ASA KING OF JUDAH • AHAB AND ELIJAH • THE TRIAL ON MOUNT CARMEL • THE LORD APPEARS TO ELIJAH • NABOTH'S VINEYARD • THE DEATH OF AHAB • ELIJAH TAKEN UP TO HEAVEN • NAAMAN HEALED OF LEPROSY • JEHU ANOINTED KING OF ISRAEL • JEHU AVENGES NABOTH • ISRAEL EXILED BECAUSE OF SIN • THE IDOLATRY OF SAMARIA • JERUSALEM BESIEGED

David's Charge to Solomon

Chapter 2

NOW THE DAYS OF DAVID DREW NIGH THAT HE should die; and he charged Solomon his son, saying, [2]"I go the way of all the earth: be thou strong therefore, and shew thyself a man; [3]and keep the charge of the LORD thy God, to walk in his ways, to keep his statutes, and his commandments, and his judgments, and his testimonies, as it is written in the law of Moses, that thou mayest prosper in all that thou doest, and whithersoever thou turnest thyself: [4]that the LORD may continue his word which he spake concerning me, saying, 'If thy children take heed to their way, to walk before me in truth with all their heart and with all their soul, there shall not fail thee' (said he) 'a man on the throne of Israel.'" . . .

[10]So David slept with his fathers and was buried in the city of David. [11]And the days that David reigned over Israel were forty years: seven years reigned he in Hebron, and thirty and three years reigned he in Jerusalem. Then sat Solomon upon the throne of David his father; and his kingdom was established greatly.

Solomon's Choice of Wisdom

Chapter 3

AND SOLOMON MADE AFFINITY WITH PHARAOH king of Egypt, and took Pharaoh's daughter, and brought her into the city of David, until he had made an end of building his own house, and the house of the LORD, and the wall of Jerusalem round about. [2]Only the people sacrificed in high places, because there was no house built unto the name of the LORD, until those days. [3]And Solomon loved

the LORD, walking in the statutes of David his father: only he sacrificed and burnt incense in high places.

[4]And the king went to Gibeon to sacrifice there; for that was the great high place: a thousand burnt offerings did Solomon offer upon that altar. [5]In Gibeon the LORD appeared to Solomon in a dream by night: and God said, "Ask what I shall give thee."

[6]And Solomon said, "Thou hast shewed unto thy servant David my father great mercy, according as he walked before thee in truth, and in righteousness, and in uprightness of heart with thee; and thou hast kept for him this great kindness, that thou hast given him a son to sit on his throne, as it is this day.

[7]"And now, O LORD my God, thou hast made thy servant king instead of David my father: and I am but a little child: I know not how to go out or come in. [8]And thy servant is in the midst of thy people which thou hast chosen, a great people, that cannot be numbered nor counted for multitude. [9]Give therefore thy servant an understanding heart to judge thy people, that I may discern between good and bad: for who is able to judge this thy so great a people?"

[10]And the speech pleased the Lord, that Solomon had asked this thing. [11]And God said unto him, "Because thou hast asked this thing, and hast not asked for thyself long life; neither hast asked riches for thyself, nor hast asked the life of thine enemies; but hast asked for thyself understanding to discern judgment; [12]behold, I have done according to thy words: lo, I have given thee a wise and an understanding heart; so that there was none like thee before thee, neither after thee shall any arise like unto thee. [13]And I have also given thee that which thou hast not asked, both riches, and honour: so that there shall not be any among the kings like unto thee all thy days. [14]And if thou wilt walk in my ways, to keep my statutes and my commandments, as thy father David did walk, then I will lengthen thy days." [15]And Solomon awoke; and, behold, it was a dream.

And he came to Jerusalem, and stood before the ark of the covenant of the LORD, and offered up burnt offerings, and offered peace offerings, and made a feast to all his servants.

THE JUDGMENT OF SOLOMON *by Giorgio Giorgione*

Chapter 3

[16]Then came there two women, that were harlots, unto the king, and stood before him. [17]And the one woman said, "O my lord, I and this woman dwell in one house; and I was delivered of a child with her in the house. [18]And it came to pass the third day after that I was delivered, that this woman was delivered also: and we were together; there was no stranger with us in the house, save we two in the house.

[19]"And this woman's child died in the night; because she overlaid it. [20]And she arose at midnight, and took my son from beside me, while thine handmaid slept, and laid it in

Chapter 3

her bosom, and laid her dead child in my bosom. [21]And when I rose in the morning to give my child suck, behold, it was dead: but when I had considered it in the morning, behold, it was not my son, which I did bear."

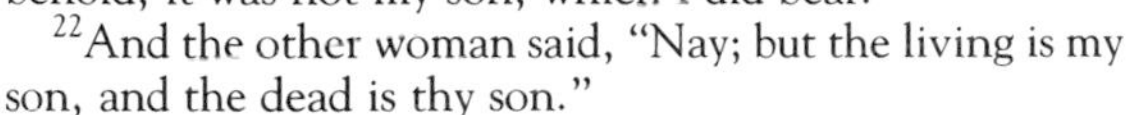

[22]And the other woman said, "Nay; but the living is my son, and the dead is thy son."

And this said, "No; but the dead is thy son, and the living is my son." Thus they spake before the king.

[23]Then said the king, "The one saith, 'This is my son that liveth, and thy son is the dead': and the other saith, 'Nay; but thy son is the dead, and my son is the living.'"

[24]And the king said, "Bring me a sword." And they brought a sword before the king. [25]And the king said, "Divide the living child in two, and give half to the one and half to the other."

[26]Then spake the woman whose the living child was unto the king, for her bowels yearned upon her son, and she said, "O my lord, give her the living child, and in no wise slay it."

But the other said, "Let it be neither mine nor thine, but divide it."

[27]Then the king answered and said, "Give her the living child, and in no wise slay it: she is the mother thereof."

[28]And all Israel heard of the judgment which the king had judged; and they feared for the king: for they saw that the wisdom of God was in him, to do judgment.

Solomon Builds the Temple

Chapter 5

AND THE LORD GAVE SOLOMON WISDOM, AS HE promised him: and there was peace between Hiram and Solomon; and they two made a league together.

[13]And king Solomon raised a levy out of all Israel; and the levy was thirty thousand men. [14]And he sent them to Lebanon, ten thousand a month by courses: a month they were in Lebanon, and two months at home: and Adoniram was over the levy. [15]And Solomon had threescore and ten thousand that bare burdens, and

Chapter 5

fourscore thousand hewers in the mountains; [16]beside the chief of Solomon's officers which were over the work, three thousand and three hundred, which ruled over the people that wrought in the work. [17]And the king commanded, and they brought great stones, costly stones, and hewed stones, to lay the foundation of the house. [18]And Solomon's builders and Hiram's builders did hew them, and the stonesquarers: so they prepared timber and stones to build the house.

Chapter 6

AND IT CAME TO PASS IN THE FOUR HUNDRED AND EIGHTieth year after the children of Israel were come out of the land of Egypt, in the fourth year of Solomon's reign over Israel, in the month Zif, which is the second month, that he began to build the house of the LORD . . .

[11]And the word of the LORD came to Solomon, saying, [12]"Concerning this house which thou art in building, if thou wilt walk in my statutes, and execute my judgments, and keep all my commandments to walk in them; then will I perform my word with thee, which I spake unto David thy father: [13]and I will dwell among the children of Israel, and will not forsake my people Israel."

[14]So Solomon built the house, and finished it. [15]And he built the walls of the house within with boards of cedar, both the floor of the house, and the walls of the ceiling: and he covered them on the inside with wood, and covered the floor of the house with planks of fir. [16]And he built twenty cubits on the sides of the house, both the floor and the walls with boards of cedar: he even built them for it within, even for the oracle, even for the most holy place. [17]And the house, that is, the temple before it, was forty cubits long. [18]And the cedar of the house within was carved with knops and open flowers: all was cedar; there was no stone seen.

[19]And the oracle he prepared in the house within, to set there the ark of the covenant of the LORD. [20]And the oracle

Chapter 6

in the forepart was twenty cubits in length, and twenty cubits in breadth, and twenty cubits in the height thereof: and he overlaid it with pure gold; and so covered the altar which was of cedar. [21]So Solomon overlaid the house within with pure gold: and he made a partition by the chains of gold before the oracle; and he overlaid it with gold. [22]And the whole house he overlaid with gold, until he had finished all the house: also the whole altar that was by the oracle he overlaid with gold.

Solomon Dedicates the Temple

Chapter 7

So was ended all the work that king Solomon made for the house of the Lord. And Solomon brought in the things which David his father had dedicated; even the silver, and the gold, and the vessels, did he put among the treasures of the house of the Lord.

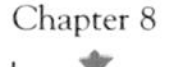

Chapter 8

Then Solomon assembled the elders of Israel, and all the heads of the tribes, the chief of the fathers of the children of Israel, unto king Solomon in Jerusalem, that they might bring up the ark of the covenant of the Lord out of the city of David, which is Zion. [2]And all the men of Israel assembled themselves unto king Solomon at the feast in the month Ethanim, which is the seventh month.

[3]And all the elders of Israel came, and the priests took up the ark. [4]And they brought up the ark of the Lord, and the tabernacle of the congregation, and all the holy vessels that were in the tabernacle, even those did the priests and the Levites bring up. [5]And king Solomon, and all the congregation of Israel, that were assembled unto him, were with him before the ark, sacrificing sheep and oxen, that could not be told nor numbered for multitude.

[6]And the priests brought in the ark of the covenant of the Lord unto his place, into the oracle of the house, to

the most holy place, even under the wings of the cherubims. [7]For the cherubims spread forth their two wings over the place of the ark, and the cherubims covered the ark and the staves thereof above. [8]And they drew out the staves, that the ends of the staves were seen out in the holy place before the oracle, and they were not seen without: and there they are unto this day. [9]There was nothing in the ark save the two tables of stone, which Moses put there at Horeb, when the LORD made a covenant with the children of Israel, when they came out of the land of Egypt.

[10]And it came to pass, when the priests were come out of the holy place, that the cloud filled the house of the LORD, [11]so that the priests could not stand to minister because of the cloud: for the glory of the LORD had filled the house of the LORD.

[12]Then spake Solomon, "The LORD said that he would dwell in the thick darkness. [13]I have surely built thee an house to dwell in, a settled place for thee to abide in for ever."

[14]And the king turned his face about, and blessed all the congregation of Israel: (and all the congregation of Israel stood;) [15]and he said,

"Blessed be the LORD God of Israel, which spake with his mouth unto David my father, and hath with his hand fulfilled it, saying, [16]'Since the day that I brought forth my people Israel out of Egypt, I chose no city out of all the tribes of Israel to build an house, that my name might be therein; but I chose David to be over my people Israel.'

[17]"And it was in the heart of David my father to build an house for the name of the LORD God of Israel. [18]And the LORD said unto David my father, 'Whereas it was in thine heart to build an house unto my name, thou didst well that it was in thine heart. [19]Nevertheless thou shalt not build the house; but thy son that shall come forth out of thy loins, he shall build the house unto my name.'

[20]"And the LORD hath performed his word that he spake, and I am risen up in the room of David my father, and sit on the throne of Israel, as the LORD promised, and have built an house for the name of the LORD God of Israel. [21]And I have set there a place for the ark, wherein is the covenant

THE TEMPLE OF SOLOMON, *Illuminated manuscript*

of the LORD, which he made with our fathers, when he brought them out of the land of Egypt."

[22]And Solomon stood before the altar of the LORD in the presence of all the congregation of Israel, and spread forth his hands toward heaven: [23]and he said,

"LORD God of Israel, there is no God like thee, in heaven above, or on earth beneath, who keepest covenant and mercy with thy servants that walk before thee with all their heart: [24]who hast kept with thy servant David my father that thou promisedst him: thou spakest also with thy mouth, and hast fulfilled it with thine hand, as it is this day.

[25]"Therefore now, LORD God of Israel, keep with thy servant David my father that thou promisedst him, saying, 'There shall not fail thee a man in my sight to sit on the throne of Israel; so that thy children take heed to their way, that they walk before me as thou hast walked before me.'

Chapter 8

[26]And now, O God of Israel, let thy word, I pray thee, be verified, which thou spakest unto thy servant David my father.

[27]"But will God indeed dwell on the earth? Behold, the heaven and heaven of heavens cannot contain thee; how much less this house that I have builded? [28]Yet have thou respect unto the prayer of thy servant, and to his supplication, O Lord my God, to hearken unto the cry and to the prayer, which thy servant prayeth before thee to day: [29]that thine eyes may be open toward this house night and day, even toward the place of which thou hast said, 'My name shall be there': that thou mayest hearken unto the prayer which thy servant shall make toward this place. [30]And hearken thou to the supplication of thy servant, and of thy people Israel, when they shall pray toward this place: and hear thou in heaven thy dwelling place: and when thou hearest, forgive."

The Queen of Sheba Visits Solomon

Chapter 10

And when the queen of Sheba heard of the fame of Solomon concerning the name of the Lord, she came to prove him with hard questions. [2]And she came to Jerusalem with a very great train, with camels that bare spices, and very much gold, and precious stones: and when she was come to Solomon, she communed with him of all that was in her heart. [3]And Solomon told her all her questions; there was not any thing hid from the king, which he told her not. [4]And when the queen of Sheba had seen all Solomon's wisdom, and the house that he had built, [5]and the meat of his table, and the sitting of his servants, and the attendance of his ministers, and their apparel, and his cupbearers, and his ascent by which he went up unto the house of the Lord; there was no more spirit in her.

[6]And she said to the king, "It was a true report that I heard in mine own land of thy acts and of thy wisdom. [7]Howbeit I believed not the words, until I came, and mine eyes had seen it: and, behold, the half was not told me: thy

Chapter 10

wisdom and prosperity exceedeth the fame which I heard. [8]Happy are thy men, happy are these thy servants, which stand continually before thee, and that hear thy wisdom. [9]Blessed be the LORD thy God, which delighted in thee, to set thee on the throne of Israel: because the LORD loved Israel for ever, therefore made he thee king, to do judgment and justice."

[10]And she gave the king an hundred and twenty talents of gold, and of spices very great store, and precious stones: there came no more such abundance of spices as these which the queen of Sheba gave to king Solomon.

[11]And the navy also of Hiram, that brought gold from Ophir, brought in from Ophir great plenty of almug trees, and precious stones. [12]And the king made of the almug trees pillars for the house of the LORD, and for the king's house, harps also and psalteries for singers: there came no such almug trees, nor were seen unto this day.

[13]And king Solomon gave unto the queen of Sheba all her desire, whatsoever she asked, beside that which Solomon gave her of his royal bounty. So she turned and went to her own country, she and her servants.

Solomon's Many Wives

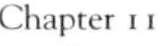

Chapter 11

BUT KING SOLOMON LOVED MANY STRANGE women, together with the daughter of Pharaoh, women of the Moabites, Ammonites, Edomites, Zidonians, and Hittites; [2]of the nations concerning which the LORD said unto the children of Israel, "Ye shall not go in to them, neither shall they come in unto you: for surely they will turn away your heart after their gods": Solomon clave unto these in love. [3]And he had seven hundred wives, princesses, and three hundred concubines: and his wives turned away his heart. [4]For it came to pass, when Solomon was old, that his wives turned away his heart after other gods: and his heart was not perfect with the LORD his God, as was the heart of David his father. [5]For Solomon went after Ashtoreth the goddess of the Zidonians, and after

SOLOMON WORSHIPPING FALSE GODS *by Pompeo Batoni*

Milcom the abomination of the Ammonites. [6]And Solomon did evil in the sight of the LORD, and went not fully after the LORD, as did David his father.

[7]Then did Solomon build an high place for Chemosh, the abomination of Moab, in the hill that is before Jerusalem, and for Molech, the abomination of the children of Ammon. [8]And likewise did he for all his strange wives, which burnt incense and sacrificed unto their gods.

Chapter 11

[9]And the LORD was angry with Solomon, because his heart was turned from the LORD God of Israel, which had appeared unto him twice, [10]and had commanded him concerning this thing, that he should not go after other gods: but he kept not that which the LORD commanded. [11]Wherefore the LORD said unto Solomon, "Forasmuch as this is done of thee, and thou hast not kept my covenant and my statutes, which I have commanded thee, I will surely rend the kingdom from thee, and will give it to thy servant. [12]Notwithstanding in thy days I will not do it for David thy father's sake: but I will rend it out of the hand of thy son. [13]Howbeit I will not rend away all the kingdom; but will give one tribe to thy son for David my servant's sake, and for Jerusalem's sake which I have chosen."

JEROBOAM'S REVOLT

Chapter 11

AND JEROBOAM THE SON OF NEBAT, AN EPHRATHITE of Zereda, Solomon's servant, whose mother's name was Zeruah, a widow woman, even he lifted up his hand against the king. [27]And this was the cause that he lifted up his hand against the king: Solomon built Millo, and repaired the breaches of the city of David his father. [28]And the man Jeroboam was a mighty man of valour: and Solomon seeing the young man that he was industrious, he made him ruler over all the charge of the house of Joseph. [29]And it came to pass at that time when Jeroboam went out of Jerusalem, that the prophet Ahijah the Shilonite found him in the way; and he had clad himself with a new garment; and they two were alone in the field: [30]and Ahijah caught the new garment that was on him, and rent it in twelve pieces: [31]and he said to Jeroboam, "Take thee ten pieces: for thus saith the LORD, the God of Israel, 'Behold, I will rend the kingdom out of the hand of Solomon, and will give ten tribes to thee: [32](but he shall have one tribe for my servant David's sake, and for Jerusalem's sake, the city which I have chosen out of all the tribes of Israel:) [33]because that they have forsaken me, and

Chapter 11

have worshipped Ashtoreth the goddess of the Zidonians, Chemosh the god of the Moabites, and Milcom the god of the children of Ammon, and have not walked in my ways, to do that which is right in mine eyes, and to keep my statutes and my judgments, as did David his father.

[34]"'Howbeit I will not take the whole kingdom out of his hand: but I will make him prince all the days of his life for David my servant's sake, whom I chose, because he kept my commandment and my statutes: [35]but I will take the kingdom out of his son's hand, and will give it unto thee, even ten tribes. [36]And unto his son will I give one tribe, that David my servant may have a light alway before me in Jerusalem, the city which I have chosen me to put my name there. [37]And I will take thee, and thou shalt reign according to all that thy soul desireth, and shalt be king over Israel. [38]And it shall be, if thou wilt hearken unto all that I command thee, and wilt walk in my ways, and do that is right in my sight, to keep my statutes and my commandments, as David my servant did; that I will be with thee, and build thee a sure house, as I built for David, and will give Israel unto thee. [39]And I will for this afflict the seed of David, but not for ever.'"

[40]Solomon sought therefore to kill Jeroboam. And Jeroboam arose, and fled into Egypt, unto Shishak king of Egypt, and was in Egypt until the death of Solomon.

[41]And the rest of the acts of Solomon, and all that he did, and his wisdom, are they not written in the book of the acts of Solomon? [42]And the time that Solomon reigned in Jerusalem over all Israel was forty years. [43]And Solomon slept with his fathers, and was buried in the city of David his father: and Rehoboam his son reigned in his stead.

The Division of the Kingdom

Chapter 12

And Rehoboam went to Shechem: for all Israel were come to Shechem to make him king. [2]And it came to pass, when Jeroboam the son of Nebat, who was yet in Egypt, heard of it, (for he was fled from the presence of king

Solomon, and Jeroboam dwelt in Egypt;) [3]that they sent and called him. And Jeroboam and all the congregation of Israel came, and spake unto Rehoboam, saying, [4]"Thy father made our yoke grievous: now therefore make thou the grievous service of thy father, and his heavy yoke which he put upon us, lighter, and we will serve thee."

[5]And he said unto them, "Depart yet for three days, then come again to me." And the people departed.

[6]And king Rehoboam consulted with the old men, that stood before Solomon his father while he yet lived, and said, "How do ye advise that I may answer this people?"

[7]And they spake unto him, saying, "If thou wilt be a servant unto this people this day, and wilt serve them, and answer them, and speak good words to them, then they will be thy servants for ever."

[8]But he forsook the counsel of the old men, which they had given him, and consulted with the young men that were grown up with him, and which stood before him: [9]and he said unto them, "What counsel give ye that we may answer this people, who have spoken to me, saying, 'Make the yoke which thy father did put upon us lighter'?"

[10]And the young men that were grown up with him spake unto him, saying, "Thus shalt thou speak unto this people that spake unto thee, saying, 'Thy father made our yoke heavy, but make thou it lighter unto us'; thus shalt thou say unto them, 'My little finger shall be thicker than my father's loins. [11]And now whereas my father did lade you with a heavy yoke, I will add to your yoke: my father hath chastised you with whips, but I will chastise you with scorpions.'"

[12]So Jeroboam and all the people came to Rehoboam the third day, as the king had appointed, saying, "Come to me again the third day." [13]And the king answered the people roughly, and forsook the old men's counsel that they gave him; [14]and spake to them after the counsel of the young men, saying, "My father made your yoke heavy, and I will add to your yoke: my father also chastised you with whips, but I will chastise you with scorpions." [15]Wherefore the king hearkened not unto the people; for the cause was from the LORD, that he might perform his saying, which the LORD spake by Ahijah the Shilonite unto Jeroboam the son of Nebat.

Chapter 12

THE DIVISION OF THE PROMISED LAND, *School of Raphael*

Chapter 12

[16]So when all Israel saw that the king hearkened not unto them, the people answered the king, saying, "What portion have we in David? neither have we inheritance in the son of Jesse: to your tents, O Israel: now see to thine own house, David." So Israel departed unto their tents. [17]But as for the children of Israel which dwelt in the cities of Judah, Rehoboam reigned over them.

[18]Then king Rehoboam sent Adoram, who was over the tribute; and all Israel stoned him with stones, that he died. Therefore king Rehoboam made speed to get him up to his chariot, to flee to Jerusalem. [19]So Israel rebelled against the house of David unto this day.

[20]And it came to pass, when all Israel heard that Jeroboam was come again, that they sent and called him unto the congregation, and made him king over all Israel: there was none that followed the house of David, but the tribe of Judah only.

Jeroboam Turns to Idolatry

Chapter 12

AND JEROBOAM SAID IN HIS HEART "NOW SHALL the kingdom return to the house of David: [27]if this people go up to do sacrifice in the house of the LORD at Jerusalem, then shall the heart of this people turn again unto their lord, even unto Rehoboam king of Judah, and they shall kill me, and go again to Rehoboam king of Judah."

[28]Whereupon the king took counsel, and made two calves of gold, and said unto them, "It is too much for you to go up to Jerusalem: behold thy gods, O Israel, which brought thee up out of the land of Egypt." [29]And he set the

JEROBOAM SACRIFICING TO AN IDOL *by J.H. Fragonard*

Chapter 12

one in Bethel, and the other put he in Dan. [30]And this thing became a sin: for the people went to worship before the one, even unto Dan.

[31]And he made an house of high places, and made priests of the lowest of the people, which were not of the sons of Levi. [32]And Jeroboam ordained a feast in the eighth

Chapter 12

month, on the fifteenth day of the month, like unto the feast that is in Judah, and he offered upon the altar. So did he in Bethel, sacrificing unto the calves that he had made: and he placed in Bethel the priests of the high places which he had made. [33]So he offered upon the altar which he had made in Bethel the fifteenth day of the eighth month, even in the month which he had devised of his own heart; and ordained a feast unto the children of Israel: and he offered upon the altar, and burnt incense.

Asa King of Judah

Chapter 15

AND IN THE TWENTIETH YEAR OF JEROBOAM KING of Israel reigned Asa over Judah. [10]And forty and one years reigned he in Jerusalem. And his mother's name was Maachah, the daughter of Abishalom.

[11]And Asa did that which was right in the eyes of the LORD, as did David his father. [12]And he took away the sodomites out of the land, and removed all the idols that his fathers had made. [13]And also Maachah his mother, even her he removed from being queen, because she had made an idol in a grove; and Asa destroyed her idol, and burnt it by the brook Kidron. [14]But the high places were not removed: nevertheless Asa's heart was perfect with the LORD all his days.

Ahab and Elijah

Chapter 16

AND IN THE THIRTY AND EIGHTH YEAR OF ASA KING of Judah began Ahab the son of Omri to reign over Israel: and Ahab the son of Omri reigned over Israel in Samaria twenty and two years. [30]And Ahab the son of Omri did evil in the sight of the LORD above all that were before him. [31]And it came to pass, as if it had been a light thing for him to walk

Chapter 16

in the sins of Jeroboam the son of Nebat, that he took to wife Jezebel the daughter of Ethbaal king of the Zidonians, and went and served Baal, and worshipped him. [32]And he reared up an altar for Baal in the house of Baal, which he had built in Samaria. [33]And Ahab made a grove; and Ahab did more to provoke the LORD God of Israel to anger than all the kings of Israel that were before him.

[34]In his days did Hiel the Bethelite build Jericho: he laid the foundation thereof in Abiram his firstborn, and set up the gates thereof in his youngest son Segub, according to the word of the LORD, which he spake by Joshua the son of Nun.

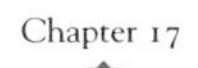

Chapter 17

AND ELIJAH THE TISHBITE, WHO WAS OF THE INHABITANTS of Gilead, said unto Ahab, "As the LORD God of Israel liveth, before whom I stand, there shall not be dew nor rain these years, but according to my word."

[2]And the word of the LORD came unto him, saying, [3]"Get thee hence, and turn thee eastward, and hide thyself by the brook Cherith, that is before Jordan. [4]And it shall be, that thou shalt drink of the brook; and I have commanded the ravens to feed thee there."

[5]So he went and did according unto the word of the LORD: for he went and dwelt by the brook Cherith, that is before Jordan. [6]And the ravens brought him bread and flesh in the morning, and bread and flesh in the evening; and he drank of the brook.

[7]And it came to pass after a while, that the brook dried up, because there had been no rain in the land. [8]And the word of the LORD came unto him, saying, [9]"Arise, get thee to Zarephath, which belongeth to Zidon, and dwell there: behold, I have commanded a widow woman there to sustain thee." [10]So he arose and went to Zarephath. And when he came to the gate of the city, behold, the widow woman was there gathering of sticks: and he called to her, and said, "Fetch me, I pray thee, a little water in a vessel, that I may drink." [11]And as she was going to fetch it, he called to her, and said, "Bring me, I pray thee, a morsel of bread in thine hand."

[12]And she said, "As the LORD thy God liveth, I have not a cake, but an handful of meal in a barrel, and a little oil in a cruse: and, behold, I am gathering two sticks, that I may go in and dress it for me and my son, that we may eat it, and die."

[13]And Elijah said unto her, "Fear not; go and do as thou hast said: but make me thereof a little cake first, and bring it unto me, and after make for thee and for thy son. [14]For thus saith the LORD God of Israel, 'The barrel of meal shall not waste, neither shall the cruse of oil fail, until the day that the LORD sendeth rain upon the earth.'"

[15]And she went and did according to the saying of Elijah: and she, and he, and her house, did eat many days. [16]And the barrel of meal wasted not, neither did the cruse of oil fail, according to the word of the LORD, which he spake by Elijah.

[17]And it came to pass after these things, that the son of the woman, the mistress of the house, fell sick; and his sickness was so sore, that there was no breath left in him. [18]And she said unto Elijah, "What have I to do with thee, O thou man of God? Art thou come unto me to call my sin to remembrance, and to slay my son?"

[19]And he said unto her, "Give me thy son." And he took him out of her bosom, and carried him up into a loft, where he abode, and laid him upon his own bed. [20]And he cried unto the LORD, and said, "O LORD my God, hast thou also brought evil upon the widow with whom I sojourn, by slaying her son?" [21]And he stretched himself upon the child three times, and cried unto the LORD, and said, "O LORD my God, I pray thee, let this child's soul come into him again."

[22]And the LORD heard the voice of Elijah; and the soul of the child came into him again, and he revived. [23]And Elijah took the child, and brought him down out of the chamber into the house, and delivered him unto his mother: and Elijah said, "See, thy son liveth."

[24]And the woman said to Elijah, "Now by this I know that thou art a man of God, and that the word of the LORD in thy mouth is truth."

AND IT CAME TO PASS AFTER MANY DAYS, THAT THE WORD of the LORD came to Elijah in the third year, saying, "Go, shew thyself unto Ahab; and I will send rain upon the earth." And Elijah went to shew himself unto Ahab. And there was a sore famine in Samaria.

Chapter 18

THE TRIAL ON MOUNT CARMEL

AND IT CAME TO PASS, WHEN AHAB SAW ELIJAH, that Ahab said unto him, "Art thou he that troubleth Israel?"

[18]And he answered, "I have not troubled Israel; but thou, and thy father's house, in that ye have forsaken the commandments of the LORD, and thou hast followed Baalim. [19]Now therefore send, and gather to me all Israel unto mount Carmel, and the prophets of Baal four hundred and fifty, and the prophets of the groves four hundred, which eat at Jezebel's table."

Chapter 18

THE SACRIFICE OF ELIJAH *by D. Fetti*

[20]So Ahab sent unto all the children of Israel, and gathered the prophets together unto mount Carmel. [21]And Elijah came unto all the people, and said, "How long halt ye between two opinions? If the LORD be God, follow him: but if Baal, then follow him."

And the people answered him not a word.

[22]Then said Elijah unto the people, "I, even I only, remain a prophet of the LORD; but Baal's prophets are four hundred and fifty men. [23]Let them therefore give us two bullocks; and let them choose one bullock for themselves, and cut it in pieces, and lay it on wood, and put no fire under: and I will dress the other bullock, and lay it on wood, and put no fire under: [24]and call ye on the name of your gods, and I will call on the name of the LORD: and the God that answereth by fire, let him be God."

And all the people answered and said, "It is well spoken."

[25]And Elijah said unto the prophets of Baal, "Choose you one bullock for yourselves, and dress it first; for ye are many; and call on the name of your gods, but put no fire under."

[26]And they took the bullock which was given them, and they dressed it, and called on the name of Baal from morning even until noon, saying, "O Baal, hear us." But there was no voice, nor any that answered. And they leaped upon the altar which was made.

[27]And it came to pass at noon, that Elijah mocked them, and said, "Cry aloud: for he is a god; either he is talking, or he is pursuing, or he is in a journey, or peradventure he sleepeth, and must be awaked." [28]And they cried aloud, and cut themselves after their manner with knives and lancets, till the blood gushed out upon them. [29]And it came to pass, when midday was past, and they prophesied until the time of the offering of the evening sacrifice, that there was neither voice, nor any to answer, nor any that regarded.

[30]And Elijah said unto all the people, "Come near unto me." And all the people came near unto him. And he repaired the altar of the LORD that was broken down. [31]And Elijah took twelve stones, according to the number of the tribes of the sons of Jacob, unto whom the word of the LORD came, saying, "Israel shall be thy name": [32]and with the stones he built an altar in the name of the LORD: and he

made a trench about the altar, as great as would contain two measures of seed. [33]And he put the wood in order, and cut the bullock in pieces, and laid him on the wood, and said, "Fill four barrels with water, and pour it on the burnt sacrifice, and on the wood."

[34]And he said, "Do it the second time." And they did it the second time.

And he said, "Do it the third time." And they did it the third time. [35]And the water ran round about the altar; and he filled the trench also with water.

[36]And it came to pass at the time of the offering of the evening sacrifice, that Elijah the prophet came near, and said, "LORD God of Abraham, Isaac, and of Israel, let it be known this day that thou art God in Israel, and that I am thy servant, and that I have done all these things at thy word. [37]Hear me, O LORD, hear me, that this people may know that thou art the LORD God, and that thou hast turned their heart back again."

[38]Then the fire of the LORD fell, and consumed the burnt sacrifice, and the wood, and the stones, and the dust, and licked up the water that was in the trench.

[39]And when all the people saw it, they fell on their faces: and they said, "The LORD, he is the God; the LORD, he is the God."

[40]And Elijah said unto them, "Take the prophets of Baal; let not one of them escape." And they took them: and Elijah brought them down to the brook Kishon, and slew them there.

[41]And Elijah said unto Ahab, "Get thee up, eat and drink; for there is a sound of abundance of rain." [42]So Ahab went up to eat and to drink. And Elijah went up to the top of Carmel; and he cast himself down upon the earth, and put his face between his knees, [43]and said to his servant, "Go up now, look toward the sea."

And he went up, and looked, and said, "There is nothing."

And he said, "Go again seven times."

[44]And it came to pass at the seventh time, that he said, "Behold, there ariseth a little cloud out of the sea, like a man's hand."

And he said, "Go up, say unto Ahab, 'Prepare thy chariot, and get thee down, that the rain stop thee not.'"

Chapter 18

[45]And it came to pass in the mean while, that the heaven was black with clouds and wind, and there was a great rain. And Ahab rode, and went to Jezreel. [46]And the hand of the LORD was on Elijah; and he girded up his loins, and ran before Ahab to the entrance of Jezreel.

THE LORD APPEARS TO ELIJAH

Chapter 19

AND AHAB TOLD JEZEBEL ALL THAT ELIJAH HAD done, and withal how he had slain all the prophets with the sword. [2]Then Jezebel sent a messenger unto Elijah, saying, "So let the gods do to me, and more also, if I make not thy life as the life of one of them by to morrow about this time."

[3]And when he saw that, he arose, and went for his life, and came to Beersheba, which belongeth to Judah, and left his servant there. [4]But he himself went a day's journey into the wilderness, and came and sat down under a juniper tree: and he requested for himself that he might die; and said, "It is enough; now, O LORD, take away my life; for I am not better than my fathers."

[5]And as he lay and slept under a juniper tree, behold, then an angel touched him, and said unto him, "Arise and eat." [6]And he looked, and, behold, there was a cake baken on the coals, and a cruse of water at his head. And he did eat and drink, and laid him down again.

[7]And the angel of the LORD came again the second time, and touched him, and said, "Arise and eat; because the journey is too great for thee." [8]And he arose, and did eat and drink, and went in the strength of that meat forty days and forty nights unto Horeb the mount of God.

[9]And he came thither unto a cave, and lodged there; and, behold, the word of the LORD came to him, and he said unto him, "What doest thou here, Elijah?"

[10]And he said, "I have been very jealous for the LORD God of hosts: for the children of Israel have forsaken their covenant, thrown down thine altars, and slain thy prophets with the sword; and I, even I only, am left; and they seek my life, to take it away."

Chapter 19

Elijah Visited by an Angel *by Dirck Bouts*

Chapter 19

[11]And he said, "Go forth, and stand upon the mount before the Lord."

And, behold, the Lord passed by, and a great and strong wind rent the mountains, and brake in pieces the rocks before the Lord; but the Lord was not in the wind: and after the wind an earthquake; but the Lord was not in the earthquake: [12]and after the earthquake a fire; but the Lord was not in the fire: and after the fire a still small voice. [13]And it was so, when Elijah heard it, that he wrapped his face in his mantle, and went out, and stood in the entering in of the cave. And, behold, there came a voice unto him, and said, "What doest thou here, Elijah?"

Chapter 19

[14]And he said, "I have been very jealous for the LORD God of hosts: because the children of Israel have forsaken thy covenant, thrown down thine altars, and slain thy prophets with the sword; and I, even I only, am left; and they seek my life, to take it away."

[15]And the LORD said unto him, "Go, return on thy way to the wilderness of Damascus: and when thou comest, anoint Hazael to be king over Syria: [16]and Jehu the son of Nimshi shalt thou anoint to be king over Israel: and Elisha the son of Shaphat of Abel-meholah shalt thou anoint to be prophet in thy room. [17]And it shall come to pass, that him that escapeth the sword of Hazael shall Jehu slay: and him that escapeth from the sword of Jehu shall Elisha slay. [18]Yet I have left me seven thousand in Israel, all the knees which have not bowed unto Baal, and every mouth which hath not kissed him."

NABOTH'S VINEYARD

Chapter 21

AND IT CAME TO PASS AFTER THESE THINGS, THAT Naboth the Jezreelite had a vineyard, which was in Jezreel, hard by the palace of Ahab king of Samaria. [2]And Ahab spake unto Naboth, saying, "Give me thy vineyard, that I may have it for a garden of herbs, because it is near unto my house: and I will give thee for it a better vineyard than it; or, if it seem good to thee, I will give thee the worth of it in money."

[3]And Naboth said to Ahab, "The LORD forbid it me, that I should give the inheritance of my fathers unto thee."

[4]And Ahab came into his house heavy and displeased because of the word which Naboth the Jezreelite had spoken to him: for he had said, "I will not give thee the inheritance of my fathers." And he laid him down upon his bed, and turned away his face, and would eat no bread.

[5]But Jezebel his wife came to him, and said unto him, "Why is thy spirit so sad, that thou eatest no bread?"

[6]And he said unto her, "Because I spake unto Naboth the Jezreelite, and said unto him, 'Give me thy vineyard for

money; or else, if it please thee, I will give thee another vineyard for it': and he answered, 'I will not give thee my vineyard.'"

[7]And Jezebel his wife said unto him, "Dost thou now govern the kingdom of Israel? Arise, and eat bread, and let thine heart be merry: I will give thee the vineyard of Naboth the Jezreelite."

[8]So she wrote letters in Ahab's name, and sealed them with his seal, and sent the letters unto the elders and to the nobles that were in his city, dwelling with Naboth. [9]And she wrote in the letters, saying, "Proclaim a fast, and set Naboth on high among the people: [10]and set two men, sons of Belial, before him, to bear witness against him, saying, 'Thou didst blaspheme God and the king.' And then carry him out, and stone him, that he may die."

[11]And the men of his city, even the elders and the nobles who were the inhabitants in his city, did as Jezebel had sent unto them, and as it was written in the letters which she had sent unto them. [12]They proclaimed a fast, and set Naboth on high among the people. [13]And there came in two men, children of Belial, and sat before him: and the men of Belial witnessed against him, even against Naboth, in the presence of the people, saying, "Naboth did blaspheme God and the king." Then they carried him forth out of the city, and stoned him with stones, that he died. [14]Then they sent to Jezebel, saying, "Naboth is stoned, and is dead."

[15]And it came to pass, when Jezebel heard that Naboth was stoned, and was dead, that Jezebel said to Ahab, "Arise, take possession of the vineyard of Naboth the Jezreelite, which he refused to give thee for money: for Naboth is not alive, but dead." [16]And it came to pass, when Ahab heard that Naboth was dead, that Ahab rose up to go down to the vineyard of Naboth the Jezreelite, to take possession of it.

[17]And the word of the LORD came to Elijah the Tishbite, saying, [18]"Arise, go down to meet Ahab king of Israel, which is in Samaria: behold, he is in the vineyard of Naboth, whither he is gone down to possess it. [19]And thou shalt speak unto him, saying, 'Thus saith the LORD, Hast thou killed, and also taken possession?' And thou shalt speak unto him, saying, 'Thus saith the LORD, In the place

Chapter 21

where dogs licked the blood of Naboth shall dogs lick thy blood, even thine.'"

[20]And Ahab said to Elijah, "Hast thou found me, O mine enemy?"

And he answered, "I have found thee: because thou hast sold thyself to work evil in the sight of the LORD."

THE DEATH OF AHAB

Chapter 22

AND THEY CONTINUED THREE YEARS WITHOUT war between Syria and Israel. [2]And it came to pass in the third year, that Jehoshaphat the king of Judah came down to the king of Israel. [3]And the king of Israel said unto his servants, "Know ye that Ramoth in Gilead is ours, and we be still, and take it not out of the hand of the king of Syria?"

[4]And he said unto Jehoshaphat, "Wilt thou go with me to battle to Ramoth-gilead?"

And Jehoshaphat said to the king of Israel, "I am as thou art, my people as thy people, my horses as thy horses." [5]And Jehoshaphat said unto the king of Israel, "Inquire, I pray thee, at the word of the LORD to day."

[6]Then the king of Israel gathered the prophets together, about four hundred men, and said unto them, "Shall I go against Ramoth-gilead to battle, or shall I forbear?"

And they said, "Go up; for the Lord shall deliver it into the hand of the king."

[7]And Jehoshaphat said, "Is there not here a prophet of the LORD besides, that we might inquire of him?"

[8]And the king of Israel said unto Jehoshaphat, "There is yet one man, Micaiah the son of Imlah, by whom we may inquire of the LORD: but I hate him; for he doth not prophesy good concerning me, but evil."

And Jehoshaphat said, "Let not the king say so."

[9]Then the king of Israel called an officer, and said, "Hasten hither Micaiah the son of Imlah."

[10]And the king of Israel and Jehoshaphat the king of Judah sat each on his throne, having put on their robes, in a void place in the entrance of the gate of Samaria; and all

the prophets prophesied before them. [11]And Zedekiah the son of Chenaanah made him horns of iron: and he said, "Thus saith the LORD, 'With these shalt thou push the Syrians, until thou have consumed them.'"

[12]And all the prophets prophesied so, saying, "Go up to Ramoth-gilead, and prosper: for the LORD shall deliver it into the king's hand."

[13]And the messenger that was gone to call Micaiah spake unto him, saying, "Behold now, the words of the prophets declare good unto the king with one mouth: let thy word, I pray thee, be like the word of one of them, and speak that which is good."

[14]And Micaiah said, "As the LORD liveth, what the LORD saith unto me, that will I speak."

[15]So he came to the king. And the king said unto him, "Micaiah, shall we go against Ramoth-gilead to battle, or shall we forbear?"

And he answered him, "Go, and prosper: for the LORD shall deliver it into the hand of the king."

[16]And the king said unto him, "How many times shall I adjure thee that thou tell me nothing but that which is true in the name of the LORD?"

[17]And he said, "I saw all Israel scattered upon the hills, as sheep that have not a shepherd: and the LORD said, 'These have no master: let them return every man to his house in peace.'"

[18]And the king of Israel said unto Jehoshaphat, "Did I not tell thee that he would prophesy no good concerning me, but evil?"

[19]And he said, "Hear thou therefore the word of the LORD: I saw the LORD sitting on his throne, and all the host of heaven standing by him on his right hand and on his left. [20]And the LORD said, 'Who shall persuade Ahab, that he may go up and fall at Ramoth-gilead?' And one said on this manner, and another said on that manner.

[21]"And there came forth a spirit, and stood before the LORD, and said, 'I will persuade him.'

[22]"And the LORD said unto him, 'Wherewith?'

"And he said, 'I will go forth, and I will be a lying spirit in the mouth of all his prophets.'

"And he said, 'Thou shalt persuade him, and prevail also: go forth, and do so.'

[23]"Now therefore, behold, the LORD hath put a lying spirit in the mouth of all these thy prophets, and the LORD hath spoken evil concerning thee."

[24]But Zedekiah the son of Chenaanah went near, and smote Micaiah on the cheek, and said, "Which way went the spirit of the LORD from me to speak unto thee?"

[25]And Micaiah said, "Behold, thou shalt see in that day, when thou shalt go into an inner chamber to hide thyself."

[26]And the king of Israel said, "Take Micaiah, and carry him back unto Amon the governor of the city, and to Joash the king's son; [27]and say, 'Thus saith the king, Put this fellow in the prison, and feed him with bread of affliction and with water of affliction, until I come in peace.'"

[28]And Micaiah said, "If thou return at all in peace, the LORD hath not spoken by me." And he said, "Hearken, O people, every one of you."

[29]So the king of Israel and Jehoshaphat the king of Judah went up to Ramoth-gilead. [30]And the king of Israel said unto Jehoshaphat, "I will disguise myself, and enter into the battle; but put thou on thy robes." And the king of Israel disguised himself, and went into the battle.

[31]But the king of Syria commanded his thirty and two captains that had rule over his chariots, saying, "Fight neither with small nor great, save only with the king of Israel." [32]And it came to pass, when the captains of the chariots saw Jehoshaphat, that they said, "Surely it is the king of Israel." And they turned aside to fight against him: and Jehoshaphat cried out. [33]And it came to pass, when the captains of the chariots perceived that it was not the king of Israel, that they turned back from pursuing him.

[34]And a certain man drew a bow at a venture, and smote the king of Israel between the joints of the harness: wherefore he said unto the driver of his chariot, "Turn thine hand, and carry me out of the host; for I am wounded." [35]And the battle increased that day: and the king was stayed up in his chariot against the Syrians, and died at even: and the blood ran out of the wound into the midst of the chariot. [36]And there went a proclamation throughout the host about the going down of the sun, saying, "Every man to his city, and every man to his own country."

Chapter 22

[37]So the king died, and was brought to Samaria; and they buried the king in Samaria. [38]And one washed the chariot in the pool of Samaria; and the dogs licked up his blood; and they washed his armour; according unto the word of the LORD which he spake.

THE SECOND BOOK OF THE KINGS

ELIJAH TAKEN UP TO HEAVEN

Chapter 2

AND IT CAME TO PASS, WHEN THE LORD WOULD take up Elijah into heaven by a whirlwind, that Elijah went with Elisha from Gilgal. [2]And Elijah said unto Elisha, "Tarry here, I pray thee; for the LORD hath sent me to Bethel."

And Elisha said unto him, "As the LORD liveth, and as thy soul liveth, I will not leave thee." So they went down to Bethel.

[3]And the sons of the prophets that were at Bethel came forth to Elisha, and said unto him, "Knowest thou that the LORD will take away thy master from thy head to day?"

And he said, "Yea, I know it; hold ye your peace."

[4]And Elijah said unto him, "Elisha, tarry here, I pray thee; for the LORD hath sent me to Jericho."

And he said, "As the LORD liveth, and as thy soul liveth, I will not leave thee." So they came to Jericho.

[5]And the sons of the prophets that were at Jericho came to Elisha, and said unto him, "Knowest thou that the LORD will take away thy master from thy head to day?"

And he answered, "Yea, I know it; hold ye your peace."

[6]And Elijah said unto him, "Tarry, I pray thee, here; for the LORD hath sent me to Jordan."

Elijah Taken up in a Chariot of Fire *by G. B. Piazetta*

And he said, "As the Lord liveth, and as thy soul liveth, I will not leave thee." And they two went on.

[7]And fifty men of the sons of the prophets went, and stood to view afar off: and they two stood by Jordan. And Elijah took his mantle, and wrapped it together, and smote the waters, and they were divided hither and thither, so that they two went over on dry ground.

[9]And it came to pass, when they were gone over, that Elijah said unto Elisha, "Ask what I shall do for thee, before I be taken away from thee."

And Elisha said, "I pray thee, let a double portion of thy spirit be upon me."

[10]And he said, "Thou hast asked a hard thing: nevertheless, if thou see me when I am taken from thee, it shall be so unto thee; but if not, it shall not be so."

[11]And it came to pass, as they still went on, and talked, that, behold, there appeared a chariot of fire, and horses of fire, and parted them both asunder; and Elijah went up by a whirlwind into heaven. [12]And Elisha saw it, and he cried, "My father, my father, the chariot of Israel, and the horsemen thereof." And he saw him no more: and he took hold of his own clothes, and rent them in two pieces.

[13]He took up also the mantle of Elijah that fell from him, and went back, and stood by the bank of Jordan; [14]and he

took the mantle of Elijah that fell from him, and smote the waters, and said, "Where is the LORD God of Elijah?" And when he also had smitten the waters, they parted hither and thither: and Elisha went over.

[15]And when the sons of the prophets which were to view at Jericho saw him, they said, "The spirit of Elijah doth rest on Elisha." And they came to meet him, and bowed themselves to the ground before him.

Chapter 2

NAAMAN HEALED OF LEPROSY

Chapter 5

NOW NAAMAN, CAPTAIN OF THE HOST OF THE king of Syria, was a great man with his master, and honourable, because by him the LORD had given deliverance unto Syria: he was also a mighty man in valour, but he was a leper.

[2]And the Syrians had gone out by companies, and had brought away captive out of the land of Israel a little maid; and she waited on Naaman's wife. [3]And she said unto her mistress, "Would God my lord were with the prophet that is in Samaria! for he would recover him of his leprosy."

[4]And one went in, and told his lord, saying, "Thus and thus said the maid that is of the land of Israel."

ELIJAH VISITED BY AN ANGEL *by Alessandro Bonvicino Moretto*

[5]And the king of Syria said, "Go to, go, and I will send a letter unto the king of Israel." And he departed, and took with him ten talents of silver, and six thousand pieces of gold, and ten changes of raiment. [6]And he brought the letter to the king of Israel, saying, "Now when this letter is come unto thee, behold, I have therewith sent Naaman my servant to thee, that thou mayest recover him of his leprosy."

[7]And it came to pass, when the king of Israel had read the letter, that he rent his clothes, and said, "Am I God, to kill and to make alive, that this man doth send unto me to recover a man of his leprosy? wherefore consider, I pray you, and see how he seeketh a quarrel against me."

[8]And it was so, when Elisha the man of God had heard that the king of Israel had rent his clothes, that he sent to the king, saying, "Wherefore hast thou rent thy clothes? Let him come now to me, and he shall know that there is a prophet in Israel." [9]So Naaman came with his horses and with his chariot, and stood at the door of the house of Elisha. [10]And Elisha sent a messenger unto him, saying, "Go and wash in Jordan seven times, and thy flesh shall come again to thee, and thou shalt be clean."

[11]But Naaman was wroth, and went away, and said, "Behold, I thought, 'He will surely come out to me, and stand, and call on the name of the Lord his God, and strike his hand over the place, and recover the leper.' [12]Are not Abana and Pharpar, rivers of Damascus, better than all the waters of Israel? May I not wash in them, and be clean?" So he turned and went away in a rage.

[13]And his servants came near, and spake unto him, and said, "My father, if the prophet had bid thee do some great thing, wouldest thou not have done it? How much rather then, when he saith to thee, 'Wash, and be clean'?" [14]Then went he down, and dipped himself seven times in Jordan, according to the saying of the man of God: and his flesh came again like unto the flesh of a little child, and he was clean.

[15]And he returned to the man of God, he and all his company, and came, and stood before him: and he said, "Behold, now I know that there is no God in all the earth, but in Israel: now therefore, I pray thee, take a blessing of thy servant."

[16]But he said, "As the LORD liveth, before whom I stand, I will receive none." And he urged him to take it; but he refused.

[17]And Naaman said, "Shall there not then, I pray thee, be given to thy servant two mules' burden of earth? for thy servant will henceforth offer neither burnt offering nor sacrifice unto other gods, but unto the LORD. [18]In this thing the LORD pardon thy servant, that when my master goeth into the house of Rimmon to worship there, and he leaneth on my hand, and I bow myself in the house of Rimmon: when I bow down myself in the house of Rimmon, the LORD pardon thy servant in this thing."

[19]And he said unto him, "Go in peace." So he departed from him a little way. But Gehazi, the servant of Elisha the man of God, said, "Behold, my master hath spared Naaman this Syrian, in not receiving at his hands that which he brought: but, as the LORD liveth, I will run after him, and take somewhat of him."

[21]So Gehazi followed after Naaman. And when Naaman saw him running after him, he lighted down from the chariot to meet him, and said, "Is all well?"

[22]And he said, "All is well. My master hath sent me, saying, 'Behold, even now there be come to me from mount Ephraim two young men of the sons of the prophets: give them, I pray thee, a talent of silver, and two changes of garments.'"

[23]And Naaman said, "Be content, take two talents." And he urged him, and bound two talents of silver in two bags, with two changes of garments, and laid them upon two of his servants; and they bare them before him. [24]And when he came to the tower, he took them from their hand, and bestowed them in the house: and he let the men go, and they departed. [25]But he went in, and stood before his master.

And Elisha said unto him, "Whence comest thou, Gehazi?"

And he said, "Thy servant went no whither."

[26]And he said unto him, "Went not mine heart with thee, when the man turned again from his chariot to meet thee? Is it a time to receive money, and to receive garments, and oliveyards, and vineyards, and sheep, and oxen, and menservants, and maidservants? [27]The leprosy

Chapter 5

therefore of Naaman shall cleave unto thee, and unto thy seed for ever." And he went out from his presence a leper as white as snow.

JEHU ANOINTED KING OF ISRAEL

Chapter 8

IN THE TWELFTH YEAR OF JORAM THE SON OF AHAB king of Israel did Ahaziah the son of Jehoram king of Judah begin to reign. [26]Two and twenty years old was Ahaziah when he began to reign; and he reigned one year in Jerusalem. And his mother's name was Athaliah, the daughter of Omri king of Israel. [27]And he walked in the way of the house of Ahab, and did evil in the sight of the LORD, as did the house of Ahab: for he was the son in law of the house of Ahab.

[28]And he went with Joram the son of Ahab to the war against Hazael king of Syria in Ramoth-gilead; and the Syrians wounded Joram. [29]And King Joram went back to be healed in Jezreel of the wounds which the Syrians had given him at Ramah, when he fought against Hazael king of Syria.

And Ahaziah the son of Jehoram king of Judah went down to see Joram the son of Ahab in Jezreel, because he was sick.

Chapter 9

AND ELISHA THE PROPHET CALLED ONE OF THE CHILDREN OF the prophets, and said unto him, "Gird up thy loins, and take this box of oil in thine hand, and go to Ramoth-gilead: [2]and when thou comest thither, look out there Jehu the son of Jehoshaphat the son of Nimshi, and go in, and make him arise up from among his brethren, and carry him to an inner chamber; [3]then take the box of oil, and pour it on his head, and say, 'Thus saith the LORD, I have anointed thee king over Israel.' Then open the door, and flee, and tarry not."

[4]So the young man, even the young man the prophet, went to Ramoth-gilead. [5]And when he came, behold, the

captains of the host were sitting; and he said, "I have an errand to thee, O captain."

And Jehu said, "Unto which of all us?"

And he said, "To thee, O captain."

[6]And he arose, and went into the house; and he poured the oil on his head, and said unto him, "Thus saith the LORD God of Israel, 'I have anointed thee king over the

THE ENTRY OF JEHU INTO JEZREEL *by E.H.Courbould*

Chapter 9

people of the LORD, even over Israel. [7]And thou shalt smite the house of Ahab thy master, that I may avenge the blood of my servants the prophets, and the blood of all the servants of the LORD, at the hand of Jezebel.'"

JEHU AVENGES NABOTH

Chapter 9

SO JEHU THE SON OF JEHOSHAPHAT THE SON OF Nimshi conspired against Joram. (Now Joram had kept Ramoth-gilead, he and all Israel, because of Hazael king of Syria. [15]But king Joram was returned to be healed in Jezreel of the wounds which the Syrians had given him, when he fought with Hazael king of Syria.) And Jehu said, "If it be your minds, then let none go forth nor escape out of the city to go to tell it in Jezreel." [16]So Jehu rode in a chariot, and went to Jezreel; for Joram lay there. And Ahaziah king of Judah was come down to see Joram.

[17]And there stood a watchman on the tower in Jezreel, and he spied the company of Jehu as he came, and said, "I see a company."

And Joram said, "Take an horseman, and send to meet them, and let him say, 'Is it peace?'"

[18]So there went one on horseback to meet him, and said, "Thus saith the king, 'Is it peace?'"

And Jehu said, "What hast thou to do with peace? Turn thee behind me."

And the watchman told, saying, "The messenger came to them, but he cometh not again."

[19]Then he sent out a second on horseback, which came to them, and said, "Thus saith the king, 'Is it peace?'"

And Jehu answered, "What hast thou to do with peace? Turn thee behind me."

[20]And the watchman told, saying, "He came even unto them, and cometh not again: and the driving is like the driving of Jehu the son of Nimshi; for he driveth furiously."

[21]And Joram said, "Make ready." And his chariot was made ready. And Joram king of Israel and Ahaziah king of Judah went out, each in his chariot, and they went out

against Jehu, and met him in the portion of Naboth the Jezreelite. [22]And it came to pass, when Joram saw Jehu, that he said, "Is it peace, Jehu?"

And he answered, "What peace, so long as the whoredoms of thy mother Jezebel and her witchcrafts are so many?"

[23]And Joram turned his hands, and fled, and said to Ahaziah, "There is treachery, O Ahaziah."

[24]And Jehu drew a bow with his full strength, and smote Jehoram between his arms, and the arrow went out at his heart, and he sunk down in his chariot. [25]Then said Jehu to Bidkar his captain, "Take up, and cast him in the portion of the field of Naboth the Jezreelite: for remember how that, when I and thou rode together after Ahab his father, the LORD laid this burden upon him; [26]'Surely I have seen yesterday the blood of Naboth, and the blood of his sons, saith the LORD; and I will requite thee in this plat, saith the LORD.' Now therefore take and cast him into the plat of ground, according to the word of the LORD."

[27]But when Ahaziah the king of Judah saw this, he fled by the way of the garden house. And Jehu followed after him, and said, "Smite him also in the chariot." And they did so at the going up to Gur, which is by Ibleam. And he fled to Megiddo, and died there. [28]And his servants carried him in a chariot to Jerusalem, and buried him in his sepulchre with his fathers in the city of David. [29]And in the eleventh year of Joram the son of Ahab began Ahaziah to reign over Judah.

[30]And when Jehu was come to Jezreel, Jezebel heard of it; and she painted her face, and tired her head, and looked out at a window. [31]And as Jehu entered in at the gate, she said, "Had Zimri peace, who slew his master?"

[32]And he lifted up his face to the window, and said, "Who is on my side? who?" And there looked out to him two or three eunuchs. [33]And he said, "Throw her down." So they threw her down: and some of her blood was sprinkled on the wall, and on the horses: and he trode her under foot.

[34]And when he was come in, he did eat and drink, and said, "Go, see now this cursed woman, and bury her: for she is a king's daughter." [35]And they went to bury her: but they found no more of her than the skull, and the feet, and

Chapter 9

the palms of her hands. [36]Wherefore they came again, and told him. And he said, "This is the word of the LORD, which he spake by his servant Elijah the Tishbite, saying, 'In the portion of Jezreel shall dogs eat the flesh of Jezebel: [37]and the carcase of Jezebel shall be as dung upon the face of the field in the portion of Jezreel; so that they shall not say, This is Jezebel.'"

Chapter 10

. . . AND THE LORD SAID UNTO JEHU, "BECAUSE THOU HAST done well in executing that which is right in mine eyes, and hast done unto the house of Ahab according to all that was in mine heart, thy children of the fourth generation shall sit on the throne of Israel." [31]But Jehu took no heed to walk in the law of the LORD God of Israel with all his heart: for he departed not from the sins of Jeroboam, which made Israel to sin.

ISRAEL EXILED BECAUSE OF SIN

Chapter 17

IN THE TWELFTH YEAR OF AHAZ KING OF JUDAH BEGAN Hoshea the son of Elah to reign in Samaria over Israel nine years. [2]And he did that which was evil in the sight of the LORD, but not as the kings of Israel that were before him.

[3]Against him came up Shalmaneser king of Assyria; and Hoshea became his servant, and gave him presents. [4]And the king of Assyria found conspiracy in Hoshea: for he had sent messengers to So king of Egypt, and brought no present to the king of Assyria, as he had done year by year: therefore the king of Assyria shut him up, and bound him in prison. [5]Then the king of Assyria came up throughout all the land, and went up to Samaria, and besieged it three years. [6]In the ninth year of Hoshea the king of Assyria took Samaria, and carried Israel away into Assyria, and placed them in Halah and in Habor by the river of Gozan, and in the cities of the Medes.

[7]For so it was, that the children of Israel had sinned against the LORD their God, which had brought them up out of the land of Egypt, from under the hand of Pharaoh king of Egypt, and had feared other gods, [8]and walked in the statutes of the heathen, whom the LORD cast out from before the children of Israel, and of the kings of Israel, which they had made. [9]And the children of Israel did secretly those things that were not right against the LORD their God, and they built them high places in all their cities, from the tower of the watchmen to the fenced city. [10]And they set them up images and groves in every high hill, and under every green tree: [11]and there they burnt incense in all the high places, as did the heathen whom the LORD carried away before them; and wrought wicked things to provoke the LORD to anger: [12]for they served idols, whereof the LORD had said unto them, "Ye shall not do this thing." [13]Yet the LORD testified against Israel, and against Judah, by all the prophets, and by all the seers, saying, "Turn ye from your evil ways, and keep my commandments and my statutes, according to all the law which I commanded your fathers, and which I sent to you by my servants the prophets."

[14]Notwithstanding they would not hear, but hardened their necks, like to the neck of their fathers, that did not believe in the LORD their God. [15]And they rejected his statutes, and his covenant that he made with their fathers, and his testimonies which he testified against them; and they followed vanity, and became vain, and went after the heathen that were round about them, concerning whom the LORD had charged them, that they should not do like them.

[16]And they left all the commandments of the LORD their God, and made them molten images, even two calves, and made a grove, and worshipped all the host of heaven, and served Baal. [17]And they caused their sons and their daughters to pass through the fire, and used divination and enchantments, and sold themselves to do evil in the sight of the LORD, to provoke him to anger.

[18]Therefore the LORD was very angry with Israel, and removed them out of his sight: there was none left but the tribe of Judah only. [19]Also Judah kept not the commandments of the LORD their God, but walked in the statutes of

Chapter 17

Israel which they made. [20]And the LORD rejected all the seed of Israel, and afflicted them, and delivered them into the hand of spoilers, until he had cast them out of his sight.

THE IDOLATRY OF SAMARIA

Chapter 17

AND THE KING OF ASSYRIA BROUGHT MEN FROM Babylon, and from Cuthah, and from Ava, and from Hamath, and from Sepharvaim, and placed them in the cities of Samaria instead of the children of Israel: and they possessed Samaria, and dwelt in the cities thereof. [25]And so it was at the beginning of their dwelling there, that they feared not the LORD: therefore the LORD sent lions among them, which slew some of them. [26]Wherefore they spake to the king of Assyria, saying, "The nations which thou hast removed, and placed in the cities of Samaria, know not the manner of the God of the land: therefore he hath sent lions among them, and, behold, they slay them, because they know not the manner of the God of the land."

[27]Then the king of Assyria commanded, saying, "Carry thither one of the priests whom ye brought from thence; and let them go and dwell there, and let him teach them the manner of the God of the land." [28]Then one of the priests whom they had carried away from Samaria came and dwelt in Bethel, and taught them how they should fear the LORD.

[29]Howbeit every nation made gods of their own, and put them in the houses of the high places which the Samaritans had made, every nation in their cities wherein they dwelt . . .

Chapter 17

[34]Unto this day they do after the former manners: they fear not the LORD, neither do they after their statutes, or after their ordinances, or after the law and commandment which the LORD commanded the children of Jacob, whom

Chapter 17

he named Israel; [35]with whom the LORD had made a covenant, and charged them, saying, "Ye shall not fear other gods, nor bow yourselves to them, nor serve them, nor sacrifice to them: [36]but the LORD, who brought you up out of the land of Egypt with great power and a stretched out arm, him shall ye fear, and him shall ye worship, and to him shall ye do sacrifice. [37]And the statutes, and the ordinances, and the law, and the commandment, which he wrote for you, ye shall observe to do for evermore; and ye shall not fear other gods. [38]And the covenant that I have made with you ye shall not forget; neither shall ye fear other gods. [39]But the LORD your God ye shall fear; and he shall deliver you out of the hand of all your enemies."

[40]Howbeit they did not hearken, but they did after their former manner. [41]So these nations feared the LORD, and served their graven images, both their children, and their children's children: as did their fathers, so do they unto this day.

JERUSALEM BESIEGED

Chapter 18

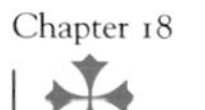

NOW IT CAME TO PASS IN THE THIRD YEAR OF Hoshea son of Elah king of Israel, that Hezekiah the son of Ahaz king of Judah began to reign. [2]Twenty and five years old was he when he began to reign; and he reigned twenty and nine years in Jerusalem. His mother's name also was Abi, the daughter of Zachariah. [3]And he did that which was right in the sight of the LORD, according to all that David his father did. [4]He removed the high places, and brake the images, and cut down the groves, and brake in pieces the brasen serpent that Moses had made: for unto those days the children of Israel did burn incense to it: and he called it Nehushtan.

[5]He trusted in the LORD God of Israel; so that after him was none like him among all the kings of Judah, nor any that were before him. [6]For he clave to the LORD, and departed not from following him, but kept his commandments, which the LORD commanded Moses. [7]And the

Chapter 18 LORD was with him; and he prospered whithersoever he went forth: and he rebelled against the king of Assyria, and served him not . . .

[17]And the king of Assyria sent Tartan and Rabsaris and Rab-shakeh from Lachish to king Hezekiah with a great host against Jerusalem. And they went up and came to Jerusalem. And when they were come up, they came and stood by the conduit of the upper pool, which is in the highway of the fuller's field. [18]And when they had called to the king, there came out to them Eliakim the son of Hilkiah, which was over the household, and Shebna the scribe, and Joah the son of Asaph the recorder. [19]And Rab-shakeh said unto them, "Speak ye now to Hezekiah,

"Thus saith the great king, the king of Assyria, 'What confidence is this wherein thou trustest? [20]Thou sayest, (but they are but vain words,) "I have counsel and strength for the war." Now on whom dost thou trust, that thou rebellest against me? [21]Now, behold, thou trustest upon the staff of this bruised reed, even upon Egypt, on which if a man lean, it will go into his hand, and pierce it: so is Pharaoh king of Egypt unto all that trust on him. [22]But if ye say unto me, "We trust in the LORD our God": is not that he, whose

THE FALL OF JERUSALEM, *Flemish School*

high places and whose altars Hezekiah hath taken away, and hath said to Judah and Jerusalem, "Ye shall worship before this altar in Jerusalem"?

[23]"'Now therefore, I pray thee, give pledges to my lord the king of Assyria, and I will deliver thee two thousand horses, if thou be able on thy part to set riders upon them. [24]How then wilt thou turn away the face of one captain of the least of my master's servants, and put thy trust on Egypt for chariots and for horsemen? [25]Am I now come up without the LORD against this place to destroy it? The LORD said to me, "Go up against this land, and destroy it."'". . .

AND IT CAME TO PASS, WHEN KING HEZEKIAH HEARD IT, that he rent his clothes and covered himself with sackcloth, and went into the house of the LORD. [2]And he sent Eliakim, which was over the household, and Shebna the scribe, and the elders of the priests, covered with sackcloth, to Isaiah the prophet the son of Amoz. [3]And they said unto him, "Thus saith Hezekiah, 'This day is a day of trouble, and of rebuke, and blasphemy: for the children are come to the birth, and there is not strength to bring forth. [4]It may be the LORD thy God will hear all the words of Rabshakeh, whom the king of Assyria his master hath sent to reproach the living God; and will reprove the words which the LORD thy God hath heard: wherefore lift up thy prayer for the remnant that are left.'" . . .

[15]And Hezekiah prayed before the LORD, and said, "O LORD God of Israel, which dwellest between the cherubims, thou art the God, even thou alone, of all the kingdoms of the earth; thou hast made heaven and earth. [16]LORD, bow down thine ear, and hear: open, LORD, thine eyes, and see: and hear the words of Sennacherib, which hath sent him to reproach the living God.

[17]"Of a truth, LORD, the kings of Assyria have destroyed the nations and their lands, [18]and have cast their gods into

Chapter 19 the fire: for they were no gods, but the work of men's hands, wood and stone: therefore they have destroyed them. [19]Now therefore, O LORD our God, I beseech thee, save thou us out of his hand, that all the kingdoms of the earth may know that thou art the LORD God, even thou only." . . .

[35]And it came to pass that night, that the angel of the LORD went out, and smote in the camp of the Assyrians an hundred fourscore and five thousand: and when they arose early in the morning, behold, they were all dead corpses. [36]So Sennacherib king of Assyria departed, and went and returned, and dwelt at Nineveh.

[37]And it came to pass, as he was worshipping in the house of Nisroch his god, that Adrammelech and Sharezer his sons smote him with the sword: and they escaped into the land of Armenia. And Esarhaddon his son reigned in his stead.

Chapters & Verses
FROM
THE SECOND BOOK
OF THE

CHRONICLES
&
E Z R A
& THE BOOKS OF
# NEHEMIAH
# & J O B

✠

MANASSEH KING OF JUDAH • THE BOOK OF THE LAW FOUND • THE DEATH OF JOSIAH • THE LAST KINGS OF JUDAH • THE FALL OF JERUSALEM • THE RETURN FROM BABYLON • THE DEDICATION OF THE TEMPLE • EZRA READS THE LAW • JOB'S TRIALS • JOB'S OUTBURST • JOB LAMENTS THE BREVITY OF LIFE • THE LORD ANSWERS JOB • JOB HUMBLES HIMSELF TO GOD • JOB'S BLESSINGS

THE SECOND BOOK OF THE CHRONICLES

Manasseh King of Judah

Chapter 32

NOW THE REST OF THE ACTS OF HEZEKIAH, AND his goodness, behold, they are written in the vision of Isaiah the prophet, the son of Amoz, and in the book of the kings of Judah and Israel. [33]And Hezekiah slept with his fathers, and they buried him in the chiefest of the sepulchres of the sons of David: and all Judah and the inhabitants of Jerusalem did him honour at his death. And Manasseh his son reigned in his stead.

Chapter 33

MANASSEH WAS TWELVE YEARS OLD WHEN HE BEGAN TO reign, and he reigned fifty and five years in Jerusalem: [2]but did that which was evil in the sight of the LORD, like unto the abominations of the heathen, whom the LORD had cast out before the children of Israel. [3]For he built again the high places which Hezekiah his father had broken down, and he reared up altars for Baalim, and made groves, and worshipped all the host of heaven, and served them. [4]Also he built altars in the house of the LORD, whereof the LORD had said, "In Jerusalem shall my name be for ever." [5]And he built altars for all the host of heaven in the two courts of the house of the LORD. [6]And he caused his children to pass through the fire in the valley of the son of Hinnom: also he observed times, and used enchantments, and used witchcraft, and dealt with a familiar spirit, and with wizards: he wrought much evil in the sight of the LORD, to provoke him to anger.

[7]And he set a carved image, the idol which he had made, in the house of God, of which God had said to David and to Solomon his son, "In this house, and in Jerusalem, which I have chosen before all the tribes of Israel, will I put my name for ever: [8]neither will I any more remove the foot of Israel from out of the land which I have appointed for your fathers; so that they will take heed to do all that I have commanded them, according to the whole law and the statutes and the ordinances by the hand of Moses." [9]So Manasseh made Judah and the inhabitants of Jerusalem to err, and to do worse than the heathen, whom the LORD had destroyed before the children of Israel.

[10]And the LORD spake to Manasseh, and to his people: but they would not hearken. [11]Wherefore the LORD brought upon them the captains of the host of the king of Assyria, which took Manasseh among the thorns, and bound him with fetters, and carried him to Babylon. [12]And when he was in affliction, he besought the LORD his God, and humbled himself greatly before the God of his fathers, [13]and prayed unto him: and he was entreated of him, and heard his supplication, and brought him again to Jerusalem into his kingdom. Then Manasseh knew that the LORD he was God.

GOD CREATING HEAVEN AND EARTH *by Michelangelo*

Chapter 33

[14]Now after this he built a wall without the city of David, on the west side of Gihon, in the valley, even to the entering in at the fish gate, and compassed about Ophel, and raised it up a very great height, and put captains of war in all the fenced cities of Judah.

[15]And he took away the strange gods, and the idol out of the house of the LORD, and all the altars that he had built in the mount of the house of the LORD, and in Jerusalem, and cast them out of the city. [16]And he repaired the altar of the LORD, and sacrificed thereon peace offerings and thank offerings, and commanded Judah to serve the LORD God of Israel. [17]Nevertheless the people did sacrifice still in the high places, yet unto the LORD their God only.

[18]Now the rest of the acts of Manasseh, and his prayer unto his God, and the words of the seers that spake to him in the name of the LORD God of Israel, behold, they are written in the book of the kings of Israel. [19]His prayer also, and how God was entreated of him, and all his sin, and his trespass, and the places wherein he built high places, and set up groves and graven images, before he was humbled: behold, they are written among the sayings of the seers. [20]So Manasseh slept with his fathers, and they buried him in his own house: and Amon his son reigned in his stead.

THE BOOK OF THE LAW FOUND

Chapter 33

AMON WAS TWO AND TWENTY YEARS OLD WHEN HE began to reign, and reigned two years in Jerusalem. [22]But he did that which was evil in the sight of the LORD, as did Manasseh his father: for Amon sacrificed unto all the carved images which Manasseh his father had made, and served them: [23]and humbled not himself before the LORD, as Manasseh his father had humbled himself; but Amon trespassed more and more.

[24]And his servants conspired against him, and slew him in his own house. [25]But the people of the land slew all them that had conspired against king Amon; and the people of the land made Josiah his son king in his stead.

Chapter 34

JOSIAH WAS EIGHT YEARS OLD WHEN HE BEGAN TO REIGN, and he reigned in Jerusalem one and thirty years. [2]And he did that which was right in the sight of the LORD, and walked in the ways of David his father, and declined neither to the right hand, nor to the left.

[3]For in the eighth year of his reign, while he was yet young, he began to seek after the God of David his father: and in the twelfth year he began to purge Judah and Jerusalem from the high places, and the groves, and the carved images, and the molten images. [4]And they brake down the altars of Baalim in his presence; and the images, that were on high above them, he cut down; and the groves, and the carved images, and the molten images, he brake in pieces, and made dust of them, and strowed it upon the graves of them that had sacrificed unto them. [5]And he burnt the bones of the priests upon their altars, and cleansed Judah and Jerusalem. [6]And so did he in the cities of Manasseh, and Ephraim, and Simeon, even unto Naphtali, with their mattocks round about. [7]And when he had broken down the altars and the groves, and had beaten the graven images into powder, and cut down all the idols throughout all the land of Israel, he returned to Jerusalem.

[8]Now in the eighteenth year of his reign, when he had purged the land, and the house, he sent Shaphan the son of Azaliah, and Maaseiah the governor of the city, and Joah the son of Joahaz the recorder, to repair the house of the LORD his God.

[9]And when they came to Hilkiah the high priest, they delivered the money that was brought into the house of God, which the Levites that kept the doors had gathered of the hand of Manasseh and Ephraim, and of all the remnant of Israel, and of all Judah and Benjamin; and they returned to Jerusalem. [10]And they put it in the hand of the workmen that had the oversight of the house of the LORD, and they gave it to the workmen that wrought in the house of the LORD, to repair and amend the house: [11]even to the artificers and builders gave they it, to buy hewn stone, and timber for couplings, and to floor the houses which the kings of Judah had destroyed.

[12]And the men did the work faithfully: and the overseers of them were Jahath and Obadiah, the Levites, of the sons of Merari; and Zechariah and Meshullam, of the sons of the

Kohathites, to set it forward; and other of the Levites, all that could skill of instruments of musick. [13]Also they were over the bearers of burdens, and were overseers of all that wrought the work in any manner of service: and of the Levites there were scribes, and officers, and porters.

[14]And when they brought out the money that was brought into the house of the LORD, Hilkiah the priest found a book of the law of the LORD given by Moses. [15]And Hilkiah answered and said to Shaphan the scribe, "I have found the book of the law in the house of the LORD." And Hilkiah delivered the book to Shaphan.

[16]And Shaphan carried the book to the king, and brought the king word back again, saying, "All that was committed to thy servants, they do it. [17]And they have gathered together the money that was found in the house of the LORD, and have delivered it into the hand of the overseers, and to the hand of the workmen." [18]Then Shaphan the scribe told the king, saying, "Hilkiah the priest hath given me a book." And Shaphan read it before the king.

[19]And it came to pass, when the king had heard the words of the law, that he rent his clothes. [20]And the king commanded Hilkiah, and Akiham the son of Shaphan, and Abdon the son of Micah, and Shaphan the scribe, and Asaiah a servant of the king's, saying, [21]"Go, inquire of the LORD for me, and for them that are left in Israel and in Judah, concerning the words of the book that is found: for great is the wrath of the LORD that is poured out upon us, because our fathers have not kept the word of the LORD, to do after all that is written in this book."

[22]And Hilkiah, and they that the king had appointed, went to Huldah the prophetess, the wife of Shallum the son of Tikvath, the son of Hasrah, keeper of the wardrobe; (now she dwelt in Jerusalem in the college:) and they spake to her to that effect.

[23]And she answered them, "Thus saith the LORD God of Israel, Tell ye the man that sent you to me, [24]'Thus saith the LORD, Behold, I will bring evil upon this place, and upon the inhabitants thereof, even all the curses that are written in the book which they have read before the king of Judah: [25]because they have forsaken me, and have burned incense unto other gods, that they might provoke me to anger with all the works of their hands; therefore my wrath

Chapter 34

Moses and the Tablets of Law *by Rembrandt*

Chapter 34

shall be poured out upon this place, and shall not be quenched.' [26]And as for the king of Judah, who sent you to inquire of the Lord, so shall ye say unto him, 'Thus saith the Lord God of Israel concerning the words which thou hast heard; [27]because thine heart was tender, and thou didst humble thyself before God, when thou heardest his words against this place, and against the inhabitants thereof, and humbledst thyself before me, and didst rend thy clothes, and weep before me; I have even heard thee also, saith the Lord. [28]Behold, I will gather thee to thy fathers, and thou shalt be gathered to thy grave in peace,

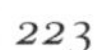

Chapter 34

neither shall thine eyes see all the evil that I will bring upon this place, and upon the inhabitants of the same.'"

So they brought the king word again.

[29]Then the king sent and gathered together all the elders of Judah and Jerusalem. [30]And the king went up into the house of the LORD, and all the men of Judah, and the inhabitants of Jerusalem, and the priests, and the Levites, and all the people, great and small: and he read in their ears all the words of the book of the covenant that was found in the house of the LORD. [31]And the king stood in his place, and made a covenant before the LORD, to walk after the LORD, and to keep his commandments, and his testimonies, and his statutes, with all his heart, and with all his soul, to perform the words of the covenant which are written in this book.

[32]And he caused all that were present in Jerusalem and Benjamin to stand to it. And the inhabitants of Jerusalem did according to the covenant of God, the God of their fathers.

[33]And Josiah took away all the abominations out of all the countries that pertained to the children of Israel, and made all that were present in Israel to serve, even to serve the LORD their God. And all his days they departed not from following the LORD, the God of their fathers.

THE DEATH OF JOSIAH

Chapter 35

AFTER ALL THIS, WHEN JOSIAH HAD PREPARED the temple, Necho king of Egypt came up to fight against Carchemish by Euphrates: and Josiah went out against him. [21]But he sent ambassadors to him, saying, "What have I to do with thee, thou king of Judah? I come not against thee this day, but against the house wherewith I have war: for God commanded me to make haste: forbear thee from meddling with God, who is with me, that he destroy thee not."

[22]Nevertheless Josiah would not turn his face from him, but disguised himself, that he might fight with him,

Chapter 35

and hearkened not unto the words of Necho from the mouth of God, and came to fight in the valley of Megiddo.
[23]And the archers shot at king Josiah; and the king said to his servants, "Have me away; for I am sore wounded." [24]His servants therefore took him out of that chariot, and put him in the second chariot that he had; and they brought him to Jerusalem, and he died, and was buried in one of the sepulchres of his fathers. And all Judah and Jerusalem mourned for Josiah.

The Last Kings of Judah

Chapter 36

THEN THE PEOPLE OF THE LAND TOOK JEHOAHAZ the son of Josiah, and made him king in his father's stead in Jerusalem.
[2]Jehoahaz was twenty and three years old when he began to reign, and he reigned three months in Jerusalem. [3]And the king of Egypt put him down at Jerusalem, and condemned the land in an hundred talents of silver and a talent of gold. [4]And the king of Egypt made Eliakim his brother king over Judah and Jerusalem, and turned his name to Jehoiakim. And Necho took Jehoahaz his brother, and carried him to Egypt.

[5]Jehoiakim was twenty and five years old when he began to reign, and he reigned eleven years in Jerusalem: and he did that which was evil in the sight of the LORD his God. [6]Against him came up Nebuchadnezzar king of Babylon, and bound him in fetters, to carry him to Babylon. [7]Nebuchadnezzar also carried of the vessels of the house of the LORD to Babylon, and put them in his temple at Babylon.

[8]Now the rest of the acts of Jehoiakim, and his abominations which he did, and that which was found in him, behold, they are written in the book of the kings of Israel and Judah: and Jehoiachin his son reigned in his stead.

[9]Jehoiachin was eight years old when he began to reign, and he reigned three months and ten days in Jerusalem: and he did that which was evil in the sight of the LORD.
And when the year was expired, king Nebuchadnezzar

Chapter 36

sent, and brought him to Babylon, with the goodly vessels of the house of the LORD, and made Zedekiah his brother king over Judah and Jerusalem.

[11]Zedekiah was one and twenty years old when he began to reign, and reigned eleven years in Jerusalem. [12]And he did that which was evil in the sight of the LORD his God, and humbled not himself before Jeremiah the prophet speaking from the mouth of the LORD. [13]And he also rebelled against king Nebuchadnezzar, who had made him swear by God: but he stiffened his neck, and hardened his heart from turning unto the LORD God of Israel. [14]Moreover all the chief of the priests, and the people, transgressed very much after all the abominations of the heathen; and polluted the house of the LORD which he had hallowed in Jerusalem.

THE FALL OF JERUSALEM

Chapter 36

AND THE LORD GOD OF THEIR FATHERS SENT TO them by his messengers, rising up betimes, and sending; because he had compassion on his people, and on his dwelling place: [16]but they mocked the messengers of God, and despised his words, and misused his prophets, until the wrath of the LORD arose against his people, till there was no remedy. [17]Therefore he brought upon them the king of the Chaldees, who slew their young men with the sword in the house of their sanctuary, and had no compassion upon young man or maiden, old man, or him that stooped for age: he gave them all into his hand. [18]And all the vessels of the house of God, great and small, and the treasures of the house of the LORD, and the treasures of the king, and of his princes; all these he brought to Babylon. [19]And they burnt the house of God, and brake down the wall of Jerusalem, and burnt all the palaces thereof with fire, and destroyed all the goodly vessels thereof.

[20]And them that had escaped from the sword carried he away to Babylon; where they were servants to him and his sons until the reign of the kingdom of Persia: [21]to fulfil t

word of the LORD by the mouth of Jeremiah, until the land had enjoyed her sabbaths: for as long as she lay desolate she kept sabbath, to fulfil threescore and ten years.

Chapter 36

E Z R A

THE RETURN FROM BABYLON

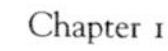

Chapter 1

NOW IN THE FIRST YEAR OF CYRUS KING OF Persia, that the word of the LORD by the mouth of Jeremiah might be fulfilled, the LORD stirred up the spirit of Cyrus king of Persia, that he made a proclamation throughout all his kingdom, and put it also in writing, saying,

2"Thus saith Cyrus king of Persia, 'The LORD God of heaven hath given me all the kingdoms of the earth; and he hath charged me to build him an house at Jerusalem, which is in Judah. 3Who is there among you of all his people? His God be with him, and let him go up to Jerusalem, which is in Judah, and build the house of the LORD God of Israel, (he is the God,) which is in Jerusalem. 4And whosoever remaineth in any place where he sojourneth, let the men of his place help him with silver, and with gold, and with goods, and with beasts, beside the freewill offering for the house of God that is in Jerusalem.'"

5Then rose up the chief of the fathers of Judah and Benjamin, and the priests, and the Levites, with all them whose spirit God had raised, to go up to build the house of the

Chapter 1

LORD which is in Jerusalem. [6]And all they that were about them strengthened their hands with vessels of silver, with gold, with goods, and with beasts, and with precious things, beside all that was willingly offered. [7]Also Cyrus the king brought forth the vessels of the house of the LORD, which Nebuchadnezzar had brought forth out of Jerusalem, and had put them in the house of his gods; [8]even those did Cyrus king of Persia bring forth by the hand of Mithredath the treasurer, and numbered them unto Sheshbazzar, the prince of Judah.

The Dedication of the Temple

Chapter 6

AND THE CHILDREN OF ISRAEL, THE PRIESTS, AND the Levites, and the rest of the children of the captivity, kept the dedication of this house of God with joy, [17]and offered at the dedication of this house of God an hundred bullocks, two hundred rams, four hundred lambs; and for a sin offering for all Israel, twelve he goats, according to the number of the tribes of Israel. [18]And they set the priests in their divisions, and the Levites in their courses, for the service of God, which is at Jerusalem; as it is written in the book of Moses.

[19]And the children of the captivity kept the passover upon the fourteenth day of the first month. [20]For the priests and the Levites were purified together, all of them were pure, and killed the passover for all the children of the captivity, and for their brethren the priests, and for themselves. [21]And the children of Israel, which were come again out of captivity, and all such as had separated themselves unto them from the filthiness of the heathen of the land, to seek the LORD God of Israel, did eat, [22]and kept the feast of unleavened bread seven days with joy: for the LORD had made them joyful, and turned the heart of the king of Assyria unto them, to strengthen their hands in the work of the house of God, the God of Israel.

NEHEMIAH

Ezra Reads the Law

Chapter 8

AND ALL THE PEOPLE GATHERED THEMSELVES together as one man into the street that was before the water gate; and they spake unto Ezra the scribe to bring the book of the law of Moses, which the LORD had commanded to Israel.

[2]And Ezra the priest brought the law before the congregation both of men and women, and all that could hear with understanding, upon the first day of the seventh month. [3]And he read therein before the street that was before the water gate from the morning until midday, before the men and the women, and those that could understand; and the ears of all the people were attentive unto the book of the law.

[4]And Ezra the scribe stood upon a pulpit of wood, which they had made for the purpose; and beside him stood Mattithiah, and Shema, and Anaiah, and Urijah, and Hilkiah, and Maaseiah, on his right hand; and on his left hand, Pedaiah, and Mishael, and Malchiah, and Hashum, and Hashbadana, Zechariah, and Meshullam.

[5]And Ezra opened the book in the sight of all the people; (for he was above all the people;) and when he opened it, all the people stood up: [6]and Ezra blessed the LORD, the great God. And all the people answered, "Amen, Amen," with lifting up their hands: and they bowed their heads, and worshipped the LORD with their faces to the ground.

[7]Also Jeshua, and Bani, and Sherebiah, Jamin, Akkub, Shabbethai, Hodijah, Maaseiah, Kelita, Azariah, Jozabad,

Chapter 8

Hanan, Pelaiah, and the Levites, caused the people to understand the law: and the people stood in their place. [8]So they read in the book in the law of God distinctly, and gave the sense, and caused them to understand the reading.

[9]And Nehemiah, which is the Tirshatha, and Ezra the priest the scribe, and the Levites that taught the people, said unto all the people, "This day is holy unto the LORD your God; mourn not, nor weep." For all the people wept, when they heard the words of the law.

[10]Then he said unto them, "Go your way, eat the fat, and drink the sweet, and send portions unto them for whom nothing is prepared: for this day is holy unto our Lord: neither be ye sorry; for the joy of the LORD is your strength."

[11]So the Levites stilled all the people, saying, "Hold your peace, for the day is holy; neither be ye grieved."

[12]And all the people went their way to eat, and to drink, and to send portions, and to make great mirth, because they had understood the words that were declared unto them.

JOB'S TRIALS

Chapter 1

THERE WAS A MAN IN THE LAND OF UZ, WHOSE name was Job; and that man was perfect and upright, and one that feared God, and eschewed evil. [2]And there were born unto him seven sons and three daughters. [3]His substance also was seven thousand sheep, and three thousand camels, and five hundred yoke of oxen, and five hundred she asses,

THE PROPHET JOB *by Fra Bartolommeo*

and a very great household; so that this man was the greatest of all the men of the east.

[4]And his sons went and feasted in their houses, every one his day; and sent and called for their three sisters to eat

and to drink with them. [5]And it was so, when the days of their feasting were gone about, that Job sent and sanctified them, and rose up early in the morning, and offered burnt offerings according to the number of them all: for Job said, "It may be that my sons have sinned, and cursed God in their hearts." Thus did Job continually.

[6]Now there was a day when the sons of God came to present themselves before the LORD, and Satan came also among them. [7]And the LORD said unto Satan, "Whence comest thou?"

Then Satan answered the LORD, and said, "From going to and fro in the earth, and from walking up and down in it."

[8]And the LORD said unto Satan, "Hast thou considered my servant Job, that there is none like him in the earth, a perfect and an upright man, one that feareth God, and escheweth evil?"

[9]Then Satan answered the LORD, and said, "Doth Job fear God for nought? [10]Hast not thou made an hedge about him, and about his house, and about all that he hath on every side? Thou hast blessed the work of his hands, and his substance is increased in the land. [11]But put forth thine hand now, and touch all that he hath, and he will curse thee to thy face."

[12]And the LORD said unto Satan, "Behold, all that he hath is in thy power: only upon himself put not forth thine hand."

So Satan went forth from the presence of the LORD.

[13]And there was a day when his sons and his daughters were eating and drinking wine in their eldest brother's house: [14]and there came a messenger unto Job, and said, "The oxen were plowing, and the asses feeding beside them: [15]and the Sabeans fell upon them, and took them away; yea, they have slain the servants with the edge of the sword; and I only am escaped alone to tell thee."

[16]While he was yet speaking, there came also another, and said, "The fire of God is fallen from heaven, and hath burned up the sheep, and the servants, and consumed them; and I only am escaped alone to tell thee."

[17]While he was yet speaking, there came also another, and said, "The Chaldeans made out three bands, and fell upon the camels, and have carried them away, yea, and

Chapter 1

slain the servants with the edge of the sword; and I only am escaped alone to tell thee."

[18]While he was yet speaking, there came also another, and said, "Thy sons and thy daughters were eating and drinking wine in their eldest brother's house: [19]and, behold, there came a great wind from the wilderness, and smote the four corners of the house, and it fell upon the young men, and they are dead; and I only am escaped alone to tell thee."

[20]Then Job arose, and rent his mantle, and shaved his head, and fell down upon the ground, and worshipped, [21]and said, "Naked came I out of my mother's womb, and naked shall I return thither: the LORD gave, and the LORD hath taken away; blessed be the name of the LORD."

[22]In all this Job sinned not, nor charged God foolishly.

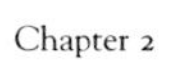

Chapter 2

AGAIN THERE WAS A DAY WHEN THE SONS OF GOD CAME TO present themselves before the LORD, and Satan came also among them to present himself before the LORD. [2]And the LORD said unto Satan, "From whence comest thou?"

And Satan answered the LORD, and said, "From going to and fro in the earth, and from walking up and down in it."

[3]And the LORD said unto Satan, "Hast thou considered my servant Job, that there is none like him in the earth, a perfect and an upright man, one that feareth God, and escheweth evil? And still he holdeth fast his integrity, although thou movedst me against him, to destroy him without cause."

[4]And Satan answered the LORD, and said, "Skin for skin, yea, all that a man hath will he give for his life. [5]But put forth thine hand now, and touch his bone and his flesh, and he will curse thee to thy face."

[6]And the LORD said unto Satan, "Behold, he is in thine hand; but save his life."

[7]So went Satan forth from the presence of the LORD, and smote Job with sore boils from the sole of his foot unto his crown. [8]And he took him a potsherd to scrape himself withal; and he sat down among the ashes.

JOB IN ADVERSITY *by Gaspard de Crayer*

[9]Then said his wife unto him, "Dost thou still retain thine integrity? Curse God, and die."

[10]But he said unto her, "Thou speakest as one of the foolish women speaketh. What? Shall we receive good at the hand of God, and shall we not receive evil?"

In all this did not Job sin with his lips.

Job's outburst

Chapter 2

NOW WHEN JOB'S THREE FRIENDS HEARD OF ALL this evil that was come upon him, they came every one from his own place; Eliphaz the Temanite, and Bildad the Shuhite, and Zophar the Naamathite: for they had made an appointment together to come to mourn with him and to comfort him. [12]And when they lifted up their eyes afar off, and knew him not, they lifted up their voice, and wept; and they rent every one his mantle, and sprinkled dust upon their heads toward heaven. [13]So they sat down with him upon the ground seven days and seven nights, and none spake a word unto him: for they saw that his grief was very great.

Chapter 3

AFTER THIS OPENED JOB HIS MOUTH, AND CURSED HIS DAY. [2]And Job spake, and said,

[3]"Let the day perish wherein I was born,
And the night in which it was said,
'There is a man child conceived.'
[4]Let that day be darkness;
Let not God regard it from above,
Neither let the light shine upon it.
[5]Let darkness and the shadow of death stain it;
Let a cloud dwell upon it;
Let the blackness of the day terrify it.
[6]As for that night, let darkness seize upon it;
Let it not be joined unto the days of the year,
Let it not come into the number of the months.
[7]Lo, let that night be solitary,
Let no joyful voice come therein.
[8]Let them curse it that curse the day,
Who are ready to raise up their mourning.
[9]Let the stars of the twilight thereof be dark;
Let it look for light, but have none;

Neither let it see the dawning of the day:
[10]Because it shut not up the doors of my mother's womb,
Nor hid sorrow from mine eyes.

[11]"Why died I not from the womb?
Why did I not give up the ghost when I came out of the belly?
[12]Why did the knees prevent me?
Or why the breasts that I should suck?
[13]For now should I have lain still and been quiet,
I should have slept: then had I been at rest,
[14]With kings and counsellors of the earth,
Which built desolate places for themselves;
[15]Or with princes that had gold,
Who filled their houses with silver:
[16]Or as an hidden untimely birth I had not been;
As infants which never saw light.
[17]There the wicked cease from troubling;
And there the weary be at rest.
[18]There the prisoners rest together;
They hear not the voice of the oppressor.
[19]The small and great are there;
And the servant is free from his master.

[20]"Wherefore is light given to him that is in misery,
And life unto the bitter in soul;
[21]Which long for death, but it cometh not;
and dig for it more than for hid treasures;
[22]Which rejoice exceedingly,
And are glad, when they can find the grave?
[23]Why is light given to a man whose way is hid,
And whom God hath hedged in?
[24]For my sighing cometh before I eat,
And my roarings are poured out like the waters.
[25]For the thing which I greatly feared is come upon me,
And that which I was afraid of is come unto me.
[26]I was not in safety, neither had I rest, neither was I quiet
Yet trouble came."

Job Laments the Brevity of Life

Chapter 14

"MAN THAT IS BORN OF A WOMAN
Is of few days, and full of trouble.
[2]He cometh forth like a flower, and is cut down:
He fleeth also as a shadow, and continueth not.
[3]And dost thou open thine eyes upon such an one,
And bringest me into judgment with thee?
[4]Who can bring a clean thing out of an unclean?
Not one.
[5]Seeing his days are determined,
The number of his months are with thee,
Thou hast appointed his bounds that he cannot pass;
[6]Turn from him, that he may rest,
Till he shall accomplish, as an hireling, his day.

[7]"For there is hope of a tree, if it be cut down, that it will sprout again,
And that the tender branch thereof will not cease.
[8]Though the root thereof wax old in the earth,
And the stock thereof die in the ground;
[9]Yet through the scent of water it will bud,
And bring forth boughs like a plant.
[10]But man dieth, and wasteth away:
Yea, man giveth up the ghost, and where is he?
[11]As the waters fail from the sea,
And the flood decayeth and drieth up:
[12]So man lieth down, and riseth not:
Till the heavens be no more, they shall not awake,
Nor be raised out of their sleep.

[13]"O that thou wouldest hide me in the grave,
That thou wouldest keep me secret, until thy wrath be past,
That thou wouldest appoint me a set time, and remember me!
[14]If a man die, shall he live again?
All the days of my appointed time will I wait,

Chapter 14 Till my change come.
[15]Thou shalt call, and I will answer thee:
Thou wilt have a desire to the work of thine hands.
[16]For now thou numberest my steps:
Dost thou not watch over my sin?
[17]My transgression is sealed up in a bag,
And thou sewest up mine iniquity.

[18]"And surely the mountain falling cometh to nought,
And the rock is removed out of his place.
[19]The waters wear the stones:
Thou washest away the things which grow out of the dust of the earth;
And thou destroyest the hope of man.
[20]Thou prevailest for ever against him, and he passeth:
Thou changest his countenance, and sendest him away.
[21]His sons come to honour, and he knoweth it not;
And they are brought low, but he perceiveth it not of them.
[22]But his flesh upon him shall have pain,
And his soul within him shall mourn."

Job, *Illuminated manuscript*

The Lord Answers Job

Chapter 38

Then the Lord answered Job out of the whirlwind, and said,

[2]"Who is this that darkeneth counsel
By words without knowledge?
[3]Gird up now thy loins like a man;
for I will demand of thee,
And answer thou me.

[4]"Where wast thou when I laid the foundations of the earth?
Declare if thou hast understanding,
[5]Who hath laid the measures thereof, if thou knowest?
Or who hath stretched the line upon it?
[6]Whereupon are the foundations thereof fastened?
Or who laid the corner stone thereof;
[7]When the morning stars sang together,
And all the sons of God shouted for joy?

[8]"Or who shut up the sea with doors,
When it brake forth, as if it had issued out of the womb?
[9]When I made the cloud the garment thereof,
And thick darkness a swaddlingband for it,
[10]And brake up for it my decreed place,
And set bars and doors,
[11]And said, 'Hitherto shalt thou come, but no further:
And here shall thy proud waves be stayed'?

[12]"Hast thou commanded the morning since thy days;
And caused the dayspring to know his place;
[13]That it might take hold of the ends of the earth,
That the wicked might be shaken out of it?
[14]It is turned as clay to the seal;
And they stand as a garment.
[15]And from the wicked their light is withholden,
And the high arm shall be broken.

[16]"Hast thou entered into the springs of the sea?
Or hast thou walked in the search of the depth?
[17]Have the gates of death been opened unto thee?
Or hast thou seen the doors of the shadow of death?
[18]Hast thou perceived the breadth of the earth?
Declare if thou knowest it all.

[19]"Where is the way where light dwelleth?
And as for darkness, where is the place thereof,
[20]That thou shouldest take it to the bound thereof,
And that thou shouldest know the paths to the house thereof?
[21]Knowest thou it, because thou wast then born?
Or because the number of thy days is great?

[22]"Hast thou entered into the treasures of the snow?
Or hast thou seen the treasures of the hail,
[23]Which I have reserved against the time of trouble,
Against the day of battle and war?
[24]By what way is the light parted,
Which scattereth the east wind upon the earth?
[25]Who hath divided a watercourse for the overflowing of waters,
Or a way for the lightning of thunder;
[26]To cause it to rain on the earth, where no man is;
On the wilderness, wherein there is no man;
[27]To satisfy the desolate and waste ground;
And to cause the bud of the tender herb to spring forth?
[28]Hath the rain a father?
Or who hath begotten the drops of dew?
[29]Out of whose womb came the ice?
And the hoary frost of heaven, who hath gendered it?
[30]The waters are hid as with a stone,
And the face of the deep is frozen.

[31]"Canst thou bind the sweet influences of Pleiades,
Or loose the bands of Orion?
[32]Canst thou bring forth Mazzaroth in his season?
Or canst thou guide Arcturus with his sons?
[33]Knowest thou the ordinances of heaven?
Canst thou set the dominion thereof in the earth?

Chapter 38

[34]"Canst thou lift up thy voice to the clouds,
That abundance of waters may cover thee?
[35]Canst thou send lightnings, that they may go,
And say unto thee, Here we are?
[36]Who hath put wisdom in the inward parts?
Or who hath given understanding to the heart?"

Job Humbles Himself to God

Chapter 42

THEN JOB ANSWERED THE LORD, AND SAID,

[2]"I know that thou canst do everything,
And that no thought can be withholden from thee.
[3]Who is he that hideth counsel without knowledge?
Therefore have I uttered that I understood not;
Things too wonderful for me, which I knew not.

[4]"Hear, I beseech thee, and I will speak:
I will demand of thee, and declare thou unto me.
[5]I have heard of thee by the hearing of the ear:
But now mine eye seeth thee.
[6]Wherefore I abhor myself, and repent
In dust and ashes."

Job's Blessings

Chapter 42

AND THE LORD TURNED THE CAPTIVITY OF JOB, when he prayed for his friends: also the LORD gave Job twice as much as he had before. [11]Then came there unto him all his brethren, and all his sisters, and all they that had been of his acquaintance before, and did eat bread with him in his house: and they bemoaned him, and comforted him over all the evil that the LORD had brought upon him:

JOB RESTORED *by the Master of the St Barbara Legend*

every man also gave him a piece of money, and every one an earring of gold.

[12]So the LORD blessed the latter end of Job more than his beginning: for he had fourteen thousand sheep, and six thousand camels, and a thousand yoke of oxen, and a thousand she asses. [13]He had also seven sons and three daughters. [14]And he called the name of the first, Jemima; and the name of the second, Kezia; and the name of the third, Keren-happuch. [15]And in all the land were no women found so fair as the daughters of Job: and their father gave them inheritance among their brethren.

[16]After this lived Job an hundred and forty years, and saw his sons, and his sons' sons, even four generations. [17]So Job died, being old and full of days.

Chapters & Verses
FROM
THE BOOK OF
PSALMS

PSALM 1 • PSALM 8 • PSALM 16 • PSALM 19 • PSALM 22 •
PSALM 23 • PSALM 24 • PSALM 27 • PSALM 46 • PSALM 51 •
PSALM 67 • PSALM 84 • PSALM 91 • PSALM 95 • PSALM 96 •
PSALM 100 • PSALM 103 • PSALM 116 • PSALM 118 • PSALM 121 •
PSALM 122 • PSALM 125 • PSALM 126 • PSALM 128 • PSALM 130 •
PSALM 131 • PSALM 134 • PSALM 139 • PSALM 148 •
PSALM 150

Psalm 1

BLESSED IS THE MAN
That walketh not in the counsel of the ungodly,
Nor standeth in the way of sinners,
Nor sitteth in the seat of the scornful.
[2]But his delight is in the law of the LORD;
And in his law doth he meditate day and night.
[3]And he shall be like a tree planted by the rivers of water,
That bringeth forth his fruit in his season;
His leaf also shall not wither;
And whatsoever he doeth shall prosper.

[4]The ungodly are not so:
But are like the chaff which the wind driveth away.
[5]Therefore the ungodly shall not stand in the judgment,
Nor sinners in the congregation of the righteous.

[6]For the LORD knoweth the way of the righteous:
But the way of the ungodly shall perish.

Psalm 8

To the chief Musician upon Gittith, A Psalm of David.

O LORD OUR LORD,
How excellent is thy name in all the earth!
Who hast set thy glory above the heavens.

[2]Out of the mouth of babes and sucklings
Hast thou ordained strength
Because of thine enemies,
That thou mightest still the enemy and the avenger.

[3]When I consider thy heavens, the work of thy fingers,
The moon and the stars, which thou hast ordained;
[4]What is man, that thou art mindful of him?
And the son of man, that thou visitest him?
[5]For thou hast made him a little lower than the angels,
And hast crowned him with glory and honour.

[6]Thou madest him to have dominion over the works of thy hands;

Psalm 8

Thou hast put all things under his feet:
[7]All sheep and oxen,
Yea, and the beasts of the field;
[8]The fowl of the air, and the fish of the sea,
And whatsoever passeth through the paths of the seas.

[9]O Lord our Lord,
How excellent is thy name in all the earth!

Psalm 16

PRESERVE ME, O GOD:
For in thee do I put my trust.

[2]O my soul, thou hast said unto the Lord,
"Thou art my Lord: my goodness extendeth not to thee;
[3]But to the saints that are in the earth,
And to the excellent, in whom is all my delight."
[4]Their sorrows shall be multiplied
That hasten after another god:
Their drink offerings of blood will I not offer,
Nor take up their names into my lips.

[5]The Lord is the portion of mine inheritance and of my cup:
Thou maintainest my lot.
[6]The lines are fallen unto me in pleasant places;
Yea, I have a goodly heritage.

[7]I will bless the Lord, who hath given me counsel:
My reins also instruct me in the night seasons.
[8]I have set the Lord always before me:
Because he is at my right hand, I shall not be moved.

[9]Therefore my heart is glad, and my glory rejoiceth:
My flesh also shall rest in hope.
[10]For thou wilt not leave my soul in hell;
Neither wilt thou suffer thy Holy One to see corruption.

Psalm 16

[11]Thou wilt show me the path of life:
In thy presence is fulness of joy;
At thy right hand there are pleasures for evermore.

Psalm 19

To the chief Musician, A Psalm of David.

THE HEAVENS DECLARE THE GLORY OF GOD;
And the firmament sheweth his handywork.
[2]Day unto day uttereth speech,
And night unto night sheweth knowledge.
[3]There is no speech nor language,
Where their voice is not heard.
[4]Their line is gone out through all the earth,
And their words to the end of the world.

In them hath he set a tabernacle for the sun,
[5]Which is as a bridegroom coming out of his chamber,
And rejoiceth as a strong man to run a race.
[6]His going forth is from the end of the heaven,
And his circuit unto the ends of it:
And there is nothing hid from the heat thereof.

[7]The law of the LORD is perfect, converting the soul:
The testimony of the LORD is sure, making wise the simple.
[8]The statutes of the LORD are right, rejoicing the heart:
The commandment of the LORD is pure, enlightening the eyes.
[9]The fear of the LORD is clean, enduring for ever:
The judgments of the LORD are true and righteous altogether.
[10]More to be desired are they than gold,
Yea, than much fine gold:
Sweeter also than honey and the honeycomb.
[11]Moreover by them is thy servant warned:
And in keeping of them there is great reward.

[12]Who can understand his errors?
Cleanse thou me from secret faults.

THE WEIGHING OF SOULS *by Rogier van der Weyden*

[13]Keep back thy servant also from presumptuous sins;
Let them not have dominion over me:
Then shall I be upright,
And I shall be innocent from the great transgression.

[14]Let the words of my mouth, and the meditation of my heart,
Be acceptable in thy sight,
O LORD, my strength, and my redeemer.

Psalm 22

To the chief Musician upon Aijeleth Shahar, A Psalm of David.

MY GOD, MY GOD, WHY HAST THOU forsaken me?
Why art thou so far from helping me,
And from the words of my roaring?
[2]O my God, I cry in the daytime, but thou hearest not;
And in the night season, and am not silent.

[3]But thou art holy,
O thou that inhabitest the praises of Israel.
[4]Our fathers trusted in thee:
They trusted, and thou didst deliver them.
[5]They cried unto thee, and were delivered:
They trusted in thee, and were not confounded.

[6]But I am a worm, and no man;
A reproach of men, and despised of the people.
[7]All they that see me laugh me to scorn:
They shoot out the lip, they shake the head, saying,
[8]"He trusted on the LORD that he would deliver him:
Let him deliver him, seeing he delighted in him."

[9]But thou art he that took me out of the womb:
Thou didst make me hope when I was upon my mother's breasts.
[10]I was cast upon thee from the womb:
Thou art my God from my mother's belly.
[11]Be not far from me;
For trouble is near;
For there is none to help.

[12]Many bulls have compassed me:
Strong bulls of Bashan have beset me round.
[13]They gaped upon me with their mouths,
As a ravening and a roaring lion.
[14]I am poured out like water,
And all my bones are out of joint:
My heart is like wax;
It is melted in the midst of my bowels.
[15]My strength is dried up like a potsherd;

And my tongue cleaveth to my jaws;
And thou hast brought me into the dust of death.
[16]For dogs have compassed me:
The assembly of the wicked have inclosed me:
They pierced my hands and my feet.
[17]I may tell all my bones:
They look and stare upon me.
[18]They part my garments among them,
And cast lots upon my vesture.

[19]But be not thou far from me, O LORD:
O my strength, haste thee to help me.
[20]Deliver my soul from the sword;
My darling from the power of the dog.
[21]Save me from the lion's mouth:
For thou hast heard me from the horns of the unicorns.

[22]I will declare thy name unto my brethren:
In the midst of the congregation will I praise thee.
[23]Ye that fear the LORD, praise him;
All ye the seed of Jacob, glorify him;
And fear him, all ye the seed of Israel.
[24]For he hath not despised nor abhorred
The affliction of the afflicted;
Neither hath he hid his face from him;
But when he cried unto him, he heard.

[25]My praise shall be of thee in the great congregation:
I will pay my vows before them that fear him.
[26]The meek shall eat and be satisfied:
They shall praise the LORD that seek him:
Your heart shall live for ever.
[27]All the ends of the world
Shall remember and turn unto the LORD:
And all the kindreds of the nations
Shall worship before thee.
[28]For the kingdom is the LORD's:
And he is the governor among the nations.

[29]All they that be fat upon earth shall eat and worship:
All they that go down to the dust shall bow before him:
And none can keep alive his own soul.

Psalm 22

[30]A seed shall serve him;
It shall be accounted to the LORD for a generation.
[31]They shall come, and shall declare his righteousness
Unto a people that shall be born,
That he hath done this.

THE GOOD SHEPHERD *by Abel Grimmer*

Psalm 23

THE LORD IS MY SHEPHERD; I SHALL NOT WANT.
[2]He maketh me to lie down in green pastures:
He leadeth me beside the still waters.
[3]He restoreth my soul:
He leadeth me in the paths of righteousness
For his name's sake.
[4]Yea, though I walk through the valley of the shadow of death,
I will fear no evil:

Psalm 23

For thou art with me;
Thy rod and thy staff they comfort me.

[5]Thou preparest a table before me in the presence of mine enemies:
Thou anointest my head with oil; my cup runneth over.
[6]Surely goodness and mercy shall follow me all the days of my life:
And I will dwell in the house of the LORD for ever.

Psalm 24

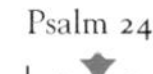

A Psalm of David

THE EARTH IS THE LORD'S, AND THE FULNESS thereof;
The world, and they that dwell therein.
[2]For he hath founded it upon the seas,
And established it upon the floods.

[3]Who shall ascend into the hill of the LORD?
Or who shall stand in his holy place?
[4]He that hath clean hands, and a pure heart;

JACOB BLESSING THE CHILDREN OF JOSEPH *by Rembrandt*

Psalm 24

Who hath not lifted up his soul unto vanity,
Nor sworn deceitfully.
[5]He shall receive the blessing from the LORD,
And righteousness from the God of his salvation.
[6]This is the generation of them that seek him,
That seek thy face, O Jacob. *Selah*

[7]Lift up your heads, O ye gates;
And be ye lift up, ye everlasting doors;
And the King of glory shall come in.
[8]Who is this King of glory?
The LORD strong and mighty,
The LORD mighty in battle.
[9]Lift up your heads, O ye gates;
Even lift them up, ye everlasting doors;
And the King of glory shall come in.
[10]Who is this King of glory?
The LORD of hosts, he is the King of glory. *Selah*

Psalm 27

A Psalm of David.

THE LORD IS MY LIGHT AND MY SALVATION;
Whom shall I fear?
The LORD is the strength of my life;
Of whom shall I be afraid?
[2]When the wicked, even mine enemies and my foes,
Came upon me to eat up my flesh,
They stumbled and fell.
[3]Though an host should encamp against me,
My heart shall not fear:
Though war should rise against me,
In this will I be confident.

[4]One thing have I desired of the LORD,
That will I seek after;
That I may dwell in the house of the LORD
All the days of my life,
To behold the beauty of the LORD,

And to inquire in his temple.
[5]For in the time of trouble he shall hide me in his pavilion:
In the secret of his tabernacle shall he hide me;
He shall set me up upon a rock.
[6]And now shall mine head be lifted up
Above mine enemies round about me:
Therefore will I offer in his tabernacle sacrifices of joy;
I will sing, yea, I will sing praises unto the LORD.

[7]Hear, O LORD, when I cry with my voice:
Have mercy also upon me, and answer me.
[8]When thou saidst, "Seek ye my face";
My heart said unto thee,
"Thy face, LORD, will I seek."
[9]Hide not thy face far from me;
Put not thy servant away in anger:
Thou hast been my help;
Leave me not, neither forsake me, O God of my salvation.
[10]When my father and my mother forsake me,
Then the LORD will take me up.
[11]Teach me thy way, O LORD,
And lead me in a plain path,
Because of mine enemies.
[12]Deliver me not over unto the will of mine enemies:
For false witnesses are risen up against me,
And such as breathe out cruelty.

[13]I had fainted, unless I had believed to see
The goodness of the LORD in the land of the living.
[14]Wait on the LORD:
Be of good courage, and he shall strengthen thine heart:
Wait, I say, on the LORD.

Psalm 46

KING DAVID *by Pietro Perugino*

Psalm 46

To the chief Musician for the sons of Korah, A Song upon Alamoth.

GOD IS OUR REFUGE AND STRENGTH,
A very present help in trouble.
[2]Therefore will not we fear, though the earth be removed,
And though the mountains be carried into the midst of the sea;
[3]Though the waters thereof roar and be troubled,
Though the mountains shake with the swelling thereof. *Selah*

[4]There is a river, the streams whereof shall make glad the city of God,
The holy place of the tabernacles of the most High.
[5]God is in the midst of her; she shall not be moved:
God shall help her, and that right early.

[6]The heathen raged, the kingdoms were moved:
He uttered his voice, the earth melted.

[7]The LORD of hosts is with us;
The God of Jacob is our refuge. *Selah*

[8]Come, behold the works of the LORD,
What desolations he hath made in the earth.
[9]He maketh wars to cease unto the end of the earth;
He breaketh the bow, and cutteth the spear in sunder;
He burneth the chariot in the fire.
[10]Be still, and know that I am God:
I will be exalted among the heathen,
I will be exalted in the earth.

[11]The LORD of hosts is with us;
The God of Jacob is our refuge. *Selah*

Psalm 51

To the chief Musician, A Psalm of David, when Nathan the prophet came unto him, after he had gone in to Bathsheba.

HAVE MERCY UPON ME, O GOD,
According to thy lovingkindness:
According unto the multitude of thy tender mercies
Blot out my transgressions.
[2]Wash me throughly from mine iniquity,
And cleanse me from my sin.

[3]For I acknowledge my transgressions:
and my sin is ever before me.
[4]Against thee, thee only, have I sinned,
And done this evil in thy sight:
That thou mightest be justified when thou speakest,
And be clear when thou judgest.
[5]Behold, I was shapen in iniquity;
And in sin did my mother conceive me.
[6]Behold, thou desirest truth in the inward parts:
And in the hidden part thou shalt make me to know wisdom.

Psalm 51

[7]Purge me with hyssop, and I shall be clean:
Wash me, and I shall be whiter than snow.
[8]Make me to hear joy and gladness;
That the bones which thou hast broken may rejoice.
[9]Hide thy face from my sins,
And blot out all mine iniquities.

[10]Create in me a clean heart, O God;
And renew a right spirit within me.
[11]Cast me not away from thy presence;
And take not thy holy spirit from me.
[12]Restore unto me the joy of thy salvation;
And uphold me with thy free spirit.
[13]Then will I teach transgressors thy ways;
And sinners shall be converted unto thee.
[14]Deliver me from bloodguiltiness, O God,
Thou God of my salvation:
And my tongue shall sing aloud of thy righteousness.
[15]O Lord, open thou my lips;
And my mouth shall shew forth thy praise.
[16]For thou desirest not sacrifice; else would I give it:
Thou delightest not in burnt offering.
[17]The sacrifices of God are a broken spirit:
A broken and a contrite heart,
O God, thou wilt not despise.

[18]Do good in thy good pleasure unto Zion:
Build thou the walls of Jerusalem.
[19]Then shalt thou be pleased with the sacrifices of righteousness,
With burnt offering and whole burnt offering:
Then shall they offer bullocks upon thine altar.

Psalm 67

To the chief Musician on Neginoth, A Psalm or Song.

GOD BE MERCIFUL UNTO US, AND BLESS US;
And cause his face to shine upon us; *Selah*
[2]That thy way may be known upon earth,
Thy saving health among all nations.

Psalm 67

[3]Let the people praise thee, O God;
Let all the people praise thee.
[4]O let the nations be glad and sing for joy:
For thou shalt judge the people righteously,
And govern the nations upon earth. *Selah*
[5]Let the people praise thee, O God;
Let all the people praise thee.

[6]Then shall the earth yield her increase;
And God, even our own God, shall bless us.
[7]God shall bless us;
And all the ends of the earth shall fear him.

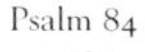

Psalm 84

To the chief Musician upon Gittith, A Psalm for the sons for Korah.

HOW AMIABLE ARE THY TABERNACLES,
O LORD of hosts!
[2]My soul longeth, yea, even fainteth
For the courts of the LORD:
My heart and my flesh crieth out
For the living God.

[3]Yea, the sparrow hath found an house,
And the swallow a nest for herself,
Where she may lay her young,
Even thine altars, O LORD of hosts,
My King, and my God.
[4]Blessed are they that dwell in thy house:
They will be still praising thee. *Selah*

[5]Blessed is the man whose strength is in thee;
In whose heart are the ways of them.
[6]Who passing through the valley of Baca make it a well;
The rain also filleth the pools.
[7]They go from strength to strength,
Every one of them in Zion appeareth before God.

[8]O LORD, God of hosts, hear my prayer:
Give ear, O God of Jacob. *Selah*

Psalm 84

9Behold, O God our shield,
And look upon the face of thine anointed.
10For a day in thy courts is better than a thousand.
I had rather be a doorkeeper in the house of my God,
Than to dwell in the tents of wickedness.
11For the LORD God is a sun and shield:
The LORD will give grace and glory:
No good thing will he withhold
From them that walk uprightly.

12O LORD of hosts,
Blessed is the man that trusteth in thee.

Psalm 91

HE THAT DWELLETH IN THE SECRET PLACE OF the most High
Shall abide under the shadow of the Almighty.
2I will say of the LORD, "He is my refuge and my fortress:
My God; in him will I trust."

3Surely he shall deliver thee from the snare of the fowler,
And from the noisome pestilence.
4He shall cover thee with his feathers,
And under his wings shalt thou trust:
His truth shall be thy shield and buckler.
5Thou shalt not be afraid for the terror by night;
Nor for the arrow that flieth by day;
6Nor for the pestilence that walketh in darkness;
Nor for the destruction that wasteth at noonday.
7A thousand shall fall at thy side,
And ten thousand at thy right hand;
But it shall not come nigh thee.
8Only with thine eyes shalt thou behold
And see the reward of the wicked.

9Because thou hast made the LORD, which is my refuge,
Even the most High, thy habitation;
10There shall no evil befall thee,

THE PROPHET DAVID *by the Master of Riofrio*

Neither shall any plague come nigh thy dwelling.
[11]For he shall give his angels charge over thee,
To keep thee in all thy ways.
[12]They shall bear thee up in their hands,
Lest thou dash thy foot against a stone.
[13]Thou shalt tread upon the lion and adder:
The young lion and the dragon shalt thou trample under
feet.

Psalm 91

[14]Because he hath set his love upon me, therefore will I deliver him;
I will set him on high, because he hath known my name.
[15]He shall call upon me, and I will answer him:
I will be with him in trouble;
I will deliver him, and honour him.
[16]With long life will I satisfy him,
And shew him my salvation.

Psalm 95

O COME, LET US SING UNTO THE LORD:
Let us make a joyful noise to the rock of our salvation.
[2]Let us come before his presence with thanksgiving,
And make a joyful noise unto him with psalms.

[3]For the LORD is a great God,
And a great King above all gods.
[4]In his hand are the deep places of the earth:
The strength of the hills is his also.
[5]The sea is his, and he made it:
And his hands formed the dry land.

[6]O come, let us worship and bow down:
Let us kneel before the LORD our maker.
[7]For he is our God;
And we are the people of his pasture,
And the sheep of his hand.

To day if ye will hear his voice,
[8]Harden not your heart, as in the provocation,
And as in the day of temptation in the wilderness:
[9]When your fathers tempted me,
Proved me, and saw my work.
[10]Forty years long was I grieved with this generation,
And said, "It is a people that do err in their heart,
And they have not known my ways":
[11]Unto whom I sware in my wrath
That they should not enter into my rest.

Psalm 96

O SING UNTO THE LORD A NEW SONG:
Sing unto the LORD, all the earth.
[2]Sing unto the LORD, bless his name;
Shew forth his salvation from day to day.
[3]Declare his glory among the heathen,
His wonders among all people.

[4]For the LORD is great, and greatly to be praised:
He is to be feared above all gods.
[5]For all the gods of the nations are idols:
But the LORD made the heavens.
[6]Honour and majesty are before him:
Strength and beauty are in his sanctuary.

[7]Give unto the LORD, O ye kindreds of the people,
Give unto the LORD glory and strength.
[8]Give unto the LORD the glory due unto his name:
Bring an offering, and come into his courts.
[9]O worship the LORD in the beauty of holiness:
Fear before him, all the earth.

[10]Say among the heathen that the LORD reigneth:
The world also shall be established that it shall not be moved:
He shall judge the people righteously.
[11]Let the heavens rejoice, and let the earth be glad;
Let the sea roar, and the fulness thereof.
[12]Let the field be joyful, and all that is therein:
Then shall all the trees of the wood rejoice
[13]Before the LORD: for he cometh,
For he cometh to judge the earth:
He shall judge the world with righteousness,
And the people with his truth.

Psalm 100

A Psalm of praise.

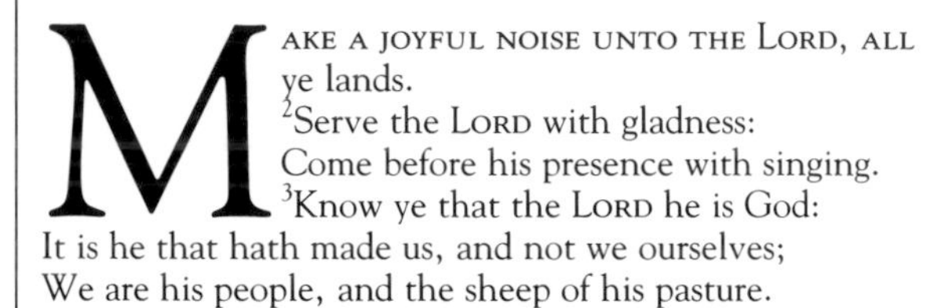

MAKE A JOYFUL NOISE UNTO THE LORD, ALL ye lands.
[2]Serve the LORD with gladness:
Come before his presence with singing.
[3]Know ye that the LORD he is God:
It is he that hath made us, and not we ourselves;
We are his people, and the sheep of his pasture.

[4]Enter into his gates with thanksgiving,
And into his courts with praise:
Be thankful unto him, and bless his name.
[5]For the LORD is good; his mercy is everlasting;
And his truth endureth to all generations.

Psalm 103

A Psalm of David.

BLESS THE LORD, O MY SOUL:
And all that is within me, bless his holy name.
[2]Bless the LORD, O my soul,
And forget not all his benefits:
[3]Who forgiveth all thine iniquities;
Who healeth all thy diseases;
[4]Who redeemeth thy life from destruction;
Who crowneth thee with lovingkindness and tender mercies;
[5]Who satisfieth thy mouth with good things;
So that thy youth is renewed like the eagle's.

[6]The LORD executeth righteousness
And judgment for all that are oppressed.

[7]He made known his ways unto Moses,
His acts unto the children of Israel.
[8]The LORD is merciful and gracious,
Slow to anger, and plenteous in mercy.
[9]He will not always chide:
Neither will he keep his anger for ever.

SCENES FROM THE LIFE OF MOSES *by Sandro Botticelli*

Psalm 103

[10]He hath not dealt with us after our sins;
Nor rewarded us according to our iniquities.
[11]For as the heaven is high above the earth,
So great is his mercy toward them that fear him.
[12]As far as the east is from the west,
So far hath he removed our transgressions from us.
[13]Like as a father pitieth his children,
So the LORD pitieth them that fear him.
[14]For he knoweth our frame;
He remembereth that we are dust.
[15]As for man, his days are as grass:
As a flower of the field, so he flourisheth.
[16]For the wind passeth over it, and it is gone;
And the place thereof shall know it no more.
[17]But the mercy of the LORD is from everlasting to everlasting
Upon them that fear him,
And his righteousness unto children's children;
[18]To such as keep his covenant,
And to those that remember his commandments to do them.

Psalm 103

[19]The LORD hath prepared his throne in the heavens;
And his kingdom ruleth over all.

[20]Bless the LORD, ye his angels,
That excel in strength, that do his commandments,
Hearkening unto the voice of his word.
[21]Bless ye the LORD, all ye his hosts;
Ye ministers of his, that do his pleasure.
[22]Bless the LORD, all his works
In all places of his dominion:
Bless the LORD, O my soul.

Psalm 116

I LOVE THE LORD, BECAUSE HE HATH HEARD
My voice and my supplications.
[2]Because he hath inclined his ear unto me,
Therefore will I call upon him as long as I live.

[3]The sorrows of death compassed me,
And the pains of hell gat hold upon me:
I found trouble and sorrow.
[4]Then called I upon the name of the LORD;
"O LORD, I beseech thee, deliver my soul."

[5]Gracious is the LORD, and righteous;
Yea, our God is merciful.
[6]The LORD preserveth the simple:
I was brought low, and he helped me.

[7]Return unto thy rest, O my soul;
For the LORD hath dealt bountifully with thee.

[8]For thou hast delivered my soul from death,
Mine eyes from tears, and my feet from falling.
[9]I will walk before the LORD
In the land of the living.
[10]I believed, therefore have I spoken:
I was greatly afflicted:
[11]I said in my haste,
"All men are liars."

Psalm 116

[12]What shall I render unto the LORD
For all his benefits toward me?
[13]I will take the cup of salvation,
And call upon the name of the LORD.
[14]I will pay my vows unto the LORD
Now in the presence of all his people.

[15]Precious in the sight of the LORD
Is the death of his saints.
[16]O LORD, truly I am thy servant;
I am thy servant, and the son of thine handmaid:
Thou hast loosed my bonds.

[17]I will offer to thee the sacrifice of thanksgiving,
And will call upon the name of the LORD.
[18]I will pay my vows unto the LORD
Now in the presence of all his people,
[19]In the courts of the LORD's house,
In the midst of thee, O Jerusalem.

Praise ye the LORD.

Psalm 118

O GIVE THANKS UNTO THE LORD; FOR HE IS good:
Because his mercy endureth for ever.

[2]Let Israel now say,
That his mercy endureth for ever.
[3]Let the house of Aaron now say,
That his mercy endureth for ever.
[4]Let them now that fear the LORD say,
That his mercy endureth for ever.

[5]I called upon the LORD in distress:
The LORD answered me, and set me in a large place.
[6]The LORD is on my side; I will not fear:
What can man do unto me?
[7]The LORD taketh my part with them that help me:
Therefore shall I see my desire upon them that hate me.

[8]It is better to trust in the LORD
Than to put confidence in man.
[9]It is better to trust in the LORD
Than to put confidence in princes.

[10]All nations compassed me about:
But in the name of the LORD will I destroy them.
[11]They compassed me about; yea, they compassed me about:
But in the name of the LORD will I destroy them.
[12]They compassed me about like bees;
They are quenched as the fire of thorns:
For in the name of the LORD I will destroy them.

[13]Thou hast thrust sore at me that I might fall:
But the LORD helped me.
[14]The LORD is my strength and song,
And is become my salvation.

[15]The voice of rejoicing and salvation
Is in the tabernacles of the righteous:
"The right hand of the LORD doeth valiantly.
[16]The right hand of the LORD is exalted:
The right hand of the LORD doeth valiantly."

[17]I shall not die, but live,
And declare the works of the LORD.
[18]The LORD hath chastened me sore:
But he hath not given me over unto death.

[19]Open to me the gates of righteousness:
I will go into them, and I will praise the LORD:
[20]This gate of the LORD,
Into which the righteous shall enter.
[21]I will praise thee: for thou hast heard me,
And art become my salvation.

[22]The stone which the builders refused
Is become the head stone of the corner.
[23]This is the LORD's doing;
It is marvellous in our eyes.
[24]This is the day which the LORD hath made;
We will rejoice and be glad in it.

Psalm 118

[25]Save now, I beseech thee, O LORD:
O LORD, I beseech thee, send now prosperity.
[26]Blessed be he that cometh in the name of the LORD:
We have blessed you out of the house of the LORD.
[27]God is the LORD, which hath shewed us light:
Bind the sacrifice with cords,
Even unto the horns of the altar.

[28]Thou art my God, and I will praise thee:
Thou art my God, I will exalt thee.

[29]O give thanks unto the LORD; for he is good:
For his mercy endureth for ever.

Psalm 121

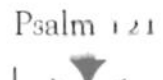

A Song of degrees.

I WILL LIFT UP MINE EYES UNTO THE HILLS,
From whence cometh my help.
[2]My help cometh from the LORD,
Which made heaven and earth.

Detail from THE AGONY IN THE GARDEN *by Andrea Mantegna*

Psalm 121

[3]He will not suffer thy foot to be moved:
He that keepeth thee will not slumber.
[4]Behold, he that keepeth Israel
Shall neither slumber nor sleep.

[5]The LORD is thy keeper:
The LORD is thy shade upon thy right hand.
[6]The sun shall not smite thee by day,
Nor the moon by night.

[7]The LORD shall preserve thee from all evil:
He shall preserve thy soul.
[8]The LORD shall preserve thy going out and thy coming in
From this time forth, and even for evermore.

Psalm 122

A Song of degrees of David

I WAS GLAD WHEN THEY SAID UNTO ME,
"Let us go into the house of the LORD."
[2]Our feet shall stand
Within thy gates, O Jerusalem.

[3]Jerusalem is builded
As a city that is compact together:
[4]Whither the tribes go up, the tribes of the LORD,
Unto the testimony of Israel,
To give thanks unto the name of the LORD.
[5]For there are set thrones of judgment,
The thrones of the house of David.

[6]Pray for the peace of Jerusalem:
They shall prosper that love thee.
[7]Peace be within thy walls,
And prosperity within thy palaces.
[8]For my brethren and companions' sakes,
I will now say, "Peace be within thee."
[9]Because of the house of the LORD our God
I will seek thy good.

Psalm 125

A Song of degrees

THEY THAT TRUST IN THE LORD SHALL BE AS mount Zion,
Which cannot be removed, but abideth for ever.
[2]As the mountains are round about Jerusalem,
So the LORD is round about his people
From henceforth even for ever.

[3]For the rod of the wicked shall not rest upon the lot of the righteous;
Lest the righteous put forth their hands unto iniquity.

[4]Do good, O LORD, unto those that be good,
And to them that are upright in their hearts.
[5]As for such as turn aside unto their crooked ways,
The LORD shall lead them forth with the workers of iniquity:
But peace shall be upon Israel.

Psalm 126

WHEN THE LORD TURNED AGAIN THE captivity of Zion,
We were like them that dream.
[2]Then was our mouth filled with laughter,
And our tongue with singing:
Then said they among the heathen,
"The LORD hath done great things for them."
[3]The LORD hath done great things for us;
Whereof we are glad.

[4]Turn again our captivity, O LORD,
As the streams in the south.
[5]They that sow in tears shall reap in joy.
[6]He that goeth forth and weepeth, bearing precious seed,
Shall doubtless come again with rejoicing,
Bringing his sheaves with him.

Psalm 128

A Song of degrees.

BLESSED IS EVERY ONE THAT FEARETH THE LORD;
That walketh in his ways.
[2]For thou shalt eat the labour of thine hands:
Happy shalt thou be, and it shall be well with thee.
[3]Thy wife shall be as a fruitful vine by the sides of thine house:
Thy children like olive plants round about thy table.
[4]Behold, that thus shall the man be blessed
That feareth the LORD.

[5]The LORD shall bless thee out of Zion:
And thou shalt see the good of Jerusalem
All the days of thy life.
[6]Yea, thou shalt see thy children's children,
And peace upon Israel.

Psalm 130

A Song of degrees.

OUT OF THE DEPTHS HAVE I CRIED UNTO THEE,
O LORD.
[2]Lord, hear my voice:
Let thine ears be attentive
To the voice of my supplications.

[3]If thou, LORD, shouldest mark iniquities,
O Lord, who shall stand?
[4]But there is forgiveness with thee,
That thou mayest be feared.

[5]I wait for the LORD, my soul doth wait,
And in his word do I hope.
[6]My soul waiteth for the Lord
More than they that watch for the morning:
I say, more than they that watch for the morning.

Psalm 130

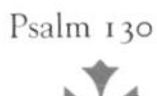

DAVID AS PSALMIST *after P. de Witte*

[7]Let Israel hope in the LORD:
For with the LORD there is mercy,
And with him is plenteous redemption.
[8]And he shall redeem Israel
From all his iniquities.

Psalm 130

Psalm 131

A Song of degrees of David.

LORD, MY HEART IS NOT HAUGHTY,
Nor mine eyes lofty:
Neither do I exercise myself in great matters,
Or in things too high for me.
[2]Surely I have behaved and quieted myself,
As a child that is weaned of his mother:
My soul is even as a weaned child.

[3]Let Israel hope in the LORD
From henceforth and for ever.

Psalm 134

A Song of degrees.

BEHOLD, BLESS YE THE LORD, ALL YE SERVANTS OF
the LORD,
Which by night stand in the house of the LORD.
[2]Lift up your hands in the sanctuary,
And bless the LORD.

[3]The LORD that made heaven and earth
Bless thee out of Zion.

Psalm 139

To the chief Musician, A Psalm of David.

O LORD, THOU HAST SEARCHED ME, AND
known me.
[2]Thou knowest my downsitting and mine
uprising,
Thou understandest my thought afar off.
[3]Thou compassest my path and my lying down,
And art acquainted with all my ways.
[4]For there is not a word in my tongue,
But, lo, O LORD, thou knowest it altogether.

[5]Thou hast beset me behind and before,
And laid thine hand upon me.
[6]Such knowledge is too wonderful for me;
It is high, I cannot attain unto it.

[7]Whither shall I go from thy spirit?
Or whither shall I flee from thy presence?
[8]If I ascend up into heaven, thou art there:
If I make my bed in hell, behold, thou art there.
[9]If I take the wings of the morning,
And dwell in the uttermost parts of the sea;
[10]Even there shall thy hand lead me,
And thy right hand shall hold me.

[11]If I say, "Surely the darkness shall cover me";
Even the night shall be light about me.
[12]Yea, the darkness hideth not from thee;
But the night shineth as the day:
The darkness and the light are both alike to thee.

[13]For thou hast possessed my reins:
Thou hast covered me in my mother's womb.
[14]I will praise thee; for I am fearfully and wonderfully made:
Marvellous are thy works;
And that my soul knoweth right well.
[15]My substance was not hid from thee,
When I was made in secret,
And curiously wrought in the lowest parts of the earth.
[16]Thine eyes did see my substance, yet being unperfect;
And in thy book all my members were written,
Which in continuance were fashioned,
When as yet there was none of them.

[17]How precious also are thy thoughts unto me, O God!
How great is the sum of them!
[18]If I should count them,
They are more in number than the sand:
When I awake, I am still with thee.

[19]Surely thou wilt slay the wicked, O God:
Depart from me therefore, ye bloody men.

Psalm 139

Detail of HEAVEN, FROM THE LAST JUDGMENT *by Fra Angelico*

Psalm 139

[20]For they speak against thee wickedly,
And thine enemies take thy name in vain.
[21]Do not I hate them, O LORD, that hate thee?
And am not I grieved with those that rise up against thee?
[22]I hate them with perfect hatred:
I count them mine enemies.

[23]Search me, O God, and know my heart:
Try me, and know my thoughts:
[24]And see if there be any wicked way in me,
And lead me in the way everlasting.

Psalm 148

PRAISE YE THE LORD.
Praise ye the LORD from the heavens:
Praise him in the heights.
2Praise ye him, all his angels:
Praise ye him, all his hosts.
3Praise ye him, sun and moon:
Praise him, all ye stars of light.
4Praise him, ye heavens of heavens,
And ye waters that be above the heavens.
5Let them praise the name of the LORD:

Detail from THE GARDEN OF PARADISE *by Roland Savery*

Psalm 148

For he commanded, and they were created.
[6]He hath also stablished them for ever and ever:
He hath made a decree which shall not pass.

[7]Praise the LORD from the earth,
Ye dragons, and all deeps:
[8]Fire, and hail; snow, and vapours;
Stormy wind fulfilling his word:
[9]Mountains, and all hills;
Fruitful trees, and all cedars:
[10]Beasts, and all cattle;
Creeping things, and flying fowl:
[11]Kings of the earth, and all people;
Princes, and all judges of the earth:
[12]Both young men, and maidens;
Old men, and children:
[13]Let them praise the name of the LORD:
For his name alone is excellent;
His glory is above the earth and heaven.
[14]He also exalteth the horn of his people,
The praise of all his saints;
Even of the children of Israel, a people near unto him.

Praise ye the LORD.

Psalm 150

PRAISE YE THE LORD.
Praise God in his sanctuary:
Praise him in the firmament of his power.
[2]Praise him for his mighty acts:
Praise him according to his excellent greatness.
[3]Praise him with the sound of the trumpet:
Praise him with the psaltery and harp.
[4]Praise him with the timbrel and dance:
Praise him with stringed instruments and organs.
[5]Praise him upon the loud cymbals:
Praise him upon the high sounding cymbals.
[6]Let every thing that hath breath praise the LORD.

Praise ye the LORD.

Chapters & Verses

FROM

THE

PROVERBS

&

ECCLESIASTES

OR

THE PREACHER

&

THE SONG OF

SOLOMON

THE BENEFITS OF WISDOM • THE WIFE OF NOBLE CHARACTER • "ALL IS VANITY" • TIMES AND SEASONS • THE BELOVED SPEAKS • THE BEAUTY OF THE LOVER • "LOVE IS STRONG AS DEATH"

PROVERBS

The Benefits of Wisdom

Chapter 3

HAPPY IS THE MAN THAT FINDETH WISDOM,
And the man that getteth understanding.
[14]For the merchandise of it is better than the merchandise of silver,
And the gain thereof than fine gold.
[15]She is more precious than rubies:
And all the things thou canst desire are not to be compared unto her.
[16]Length of days is in her right hand;
And in her left hand riches and honour.
[17]Her ways are ways of pleasantness,
And all her paths are peace.
[18]She is a tree of life to them that lay hold upon her:
And happy is every one that retaineth her.

[19]The LORD by wisdom hath founded the earth;
By understanding hath he established the heavens.
[20]By his knowledge the depths are broken up,
And the clouds drop down the dew.

[21]My son, let not them depart from thine eyes:
Keep sound wisdom and discretion:
[22]So shall they be life unto thy soul,
And grace to thy neck.
[23]Then shalt thou walk in thy way safely,
And thy foot shall not stumble.
[24]When thou liest down, thou shalt not be afraid:
Yea, thou shalt lie down, and thy sleep shall be sweet.

PERSONIFICATION OF WISDOM *by Nicholas Regnier*

[25]Be not afraid of sudden fear,
Neither of the desolation of the wicked when it cometh.
[26]For the LORD shall be thy confidence,
And shall keep thy foot from being taken.

Chapter 3

The Wife of Noble Character

Chapter 31

WHO CAN FIND A VIRTUOUS WOMAN?
For her price is far above rubies.
[11]The heart of her husband doth safely trust in her,
So that he shall have no need of spoil.
[12]She will do him good and not evil
All the days of her life.
[13]She seeketh wool, and flax,
And worketh willingly with her hands.
[14]She is like the merchants' ships;
She bringeth her food from afar.
[15]She riseth also while it is yet night,
And giveth meat to her household,
And a portion to her maidens.
[16]She considereth a field, and buyeth it:
With the fruit of her hands she planteth a vineyard.
[17]She girdeth her loins with strength,
And strengtheneth her arms.
[18]She perceiveth that her merchandise is good:
Her candle goeth not out by night.
[19]She layeth her hands to the spindle,
And her hands hold the distaff.
[20]She stretcheth out her hand to the poor;
Yea, she reacheth forth her hands to the needy.
[21]She is not afraid of the snow for her household:
For all her household are clothed with scarlet.
[22]She maketh herself coverings of tapestry;
Her clothing is silk and purple.
[23]Her husband is known in the gates,
When he sitteth among the elders of the land.
[24]She maketh fine linen, and selleth it;
And delivereth girdles unto the merchant.
[25]Strength and honour are her clothing;
And she shall rejoice in time to come.
[26]She openeth her mouth with wisdom;
And in her tongue is the law of kindness.
[27]She looketh well to the ways of her household,
And eateth not the bread of idleness.

[28]Her children arise up, and call her blessed;
Her husband also, and he praiseth her.
[29]"Many daughters have done virtuously,
But thou excellest them all."
[30]Favour is deceitful, and beauty is vain:
But a woman that feareth the LORD, she shall be praised.
[31]Give her of the fruit of her hands;
And let her own works praise her in the gates.

ECCLESIASTES

"ALL IS VANITY"

Chapter 1

THE WORDS OF THE PREACHER, THE SON OF David, king in Jerusalem.

[2]"Vanity of vanities," saith the Preacher,
"Vanity of vanities; all is vanity."

[3]What profit hath a man of all his labour
Which he taketh under the sun?
[4]One generation passeth away, and another generation cometh:
But the earth abideth for ever.
[5]The sun also ariseth, and the sun goeth down,
And hasteth to his place where he arose.
[6]The wind goeth toward the south,
And turneth about unto the north;
It whirleth about continually,
And the wind returneth again according to his circuits.
[7]All the rivers run into the sea;
Yet the sea is not full;

Chapter 1

Unto the place from whence the rivers come,
Thither they return again.
[8]All things are full of labour;
Man cannot utter it:
The eye is not satisfied with seeing,
Nor the ear filled with hearing.
[9]The thing that hath been, it is that which shall be;
And that which is done is that which shall be done:
And there is no new thing under the sun.
[10]Is there any thing whereof it may be said,
"See, this is new?"
It hath been already of old time,
Which was before us.
[11]There is no remembrance of former things;
Neither shall there be any remembrance
Of things that are to come
With those that shall come after.

Times and Seasons

Chapter 3

To every thing there is a season, and a time to every purpose under the heaven:

[2]A time to be born, and a time to die;
A time to plant, and a time to pluck up that which is planted;
[3]A time to kill, and a time to heal;
A time to break down, and a time to build up;
[4]A time to weep, and a time to laugh;
A time to mourn, and a time to dance;
[5]A time to cast away stones, and a time to gather stones together;
A time to embrace, and a time to refrain from embracing;
[6]A time to get, and a time to lose;
A time to keep, and a time to cast away;
[7]A time to rend, and a time to sew;
A time to keep silence, and a time to speak;
[8]A time to love, and a time to hate;
A time of war, and a time of peace.

Les Très Riches Heures du Duc de Berry *by Limbourg Brothers*

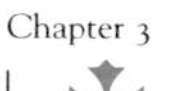

[9]What profit hath he that worketh in that wherein he laboureth? [10]I have seen the travail, which God hath given to the sons of men to be exercised in it. [11]He hath made every thing beautiful in his time: also he hath set the world in their heart, so that no man can find out the work that God maketh from the beginning to the end. [12]I know that there is no good in them, but for a man to rejoice, and to do good in his life. [13]And also that every man should eat and drink, and enjoy the good of all his labour, it is the gift of God. [14]I know that, whatsoever God doeth, it shall be for ever: nothing can be put to it, nor any thing taken from it: and God doeth it, that men should fear before him. [15]That which hath been is now; and that which is to be hath already been; and God requireth that which is past.

Chapter 3

[16]And moreover I saw under the sun the place of judgment, that wickedness was there; and the place of righteousness, that iniquity was there. [17]I said in mine heart, "God shall judge the righteous and the wicked: for there is a time there for every purpose and for every work."

THE SONG OF SOLOMON

The Beloved Speaks

Chapter 2

AS THE APPLE TREE AMONG THE TREES OF THE wood,
So is my beloved among the sons.
I sat down under his shadow with great delight,
And his fruit was sweet to my taste.
[4]He brought me to the banqueting house,
And his banner over me was love.
[5]Stay me with flagons, comfort me with apples:
For I am sick of love.
[6]His left hand is under my head,
And his right hand doth embrace me.
[7]I charge you, O ye daughters of Jerusalem,
By the roes, and by the hinds of the field,
That ye stir not up, nor awake my love,
Till he please.

[8]The voice of my beloved! Behold, he cometh
Leaping upon the mountains, skipping upon the hills.
[9]My beloved is like a roe or a young hart:
Behold, he standeth behind our wall,
He looketh forth at the windows,
Shewing himself through the lattice.

Chapter 2

[10]My beloved spake, and said unto me,
"Rise up, my love, my fair one, and come away.
[11]For, lo, the winter is past,
The rain is over and gone;
[12]The flowers appear on the earth;
The time of the singing of birds is come,
And the voice of the turtle is heard in our land;
[13]The fig tree putteth forth her green figs,
And the vines with the tender grape give a good smell.
Arise, my love, my fair one, and come away.
[14]O my dove, that art in the clefts of the rock,
In the secret places of the stairs,
Let me see thy countenance, let me hear thy voice;
For sweet is thy voice, and thy countenance is comely."

The Beauty of the Lover

Chapter 5

MY BELOVED IS WHITE AND RUDDY,
The chiefest among ten thousand.
[11]His head is as the most fine gold,
His locks are bushy, and black as a raven.
[12]His eyes are as the eyes of doves by the rivers of waters,
Washed with milk, and fitly set.
[13]His cheeks are as a bed of spices, as sweet flowers:
His lips like lilies, dropping sweet smelling myrrh.
[14]His hands are as gold rings set with the beryl:
His belly is as bright ivory overlaid with sapphires.
[15]His legs are as pillars of marble, set upon sockets of fine gold:
His countenance is as Lebanon, excellent as the cedars.
[16]His mouth is most sweet: yea, he is altogether lovely.
This is my beloved, and this is my friend,
O daughters of Jerusalem.

Chapter 6

WHITHER IS THY BELOVED GONE,
O thou fairest among women?
Whither is thy beloved turned aside?
That we may seek him with thee.

[2]My beloved is gone down into his garden,
To the beds of spices,
To feed in the gardens, and to gather lilies.
[3]I am my beloved's, and my beloved is mine:
He feedeth among the lilies.

"LOVE IS STRONG AS DEATH"

Chapter 8

SET ME AS A SEAL UPON THINE HEART,
As a seal upon thine arm:
For love is strong as death;
Jealousy is cruel as the grave:
The coals thereof are coals of fire,
Which hath a most vehement flame.
[7]Many waters cannot quench love,
Neither can the floods drown it:
If a man would give all the substance of his house for love,
It would utterly be contemned.

SOLOMON DICTATES THE PROVERBS, *illuminated manuscript*

Chapters & Verses
FROM
THE BOOK OF THE PROPHET
ISAIAH

A REBELLIOUS NATION • THE SONG OF THE VINEYARD • ISAIAH'S VISION • THE SIGN OF IMMANUEL • THE PRINCE OF PEACE • A BRANCH FROM JESSE • A PROPHECY AGAINST BABYLON • PRAISE FOR GOD'S SALVATION • THE LORD'S GRACIOUSNESS • THE JOY OF THE REDEEMED • COMFORT FOR GOD'S PEOPLE • THE SERVANT OF THE LORD • ISRAEL'S ONLY SAVIOUR • THE SERVANT'S COMMISSION • "AWAKE, AWAKE, ZION" • THE SUFFERING SERVANT • "SEEK YE THE LORD" • THE GLORY OF ZION • THE LORD'S ANOINTED • NEW HEAVENS AND A NEW EARTH

A Rebellious Nation

Chapter 1

"TO WHAT PURPOSE IS THE MULTITUDE
Of your sacrifices unto me?" saith the
LORD:
"I am full of the burnt offerings of rams,
And the fat of fed beasts;
And I delight not in the blood of bullocks,
Or of lambs, or of he goats.
[12]When ye come to appear before me,
Who hath required this at your hand, to tread my courts?
[13]Bring no more vain oblations;
Incense is an abomination unto me;
The new moons and sabbaths, the calling of assemblies,
I cannot away with; it is iniquity, even the solemn
meeting.
[14]Your new moons and your appointed feasts
My soul hateth:
They are a trouble unto me;
I am weary to bear them.
[15]And when ye spread forth your hands,
I will hide mine eyes from you:
Yea, when ye make many prayers, I will not hear:
Your hands are full of blood.
[16]Wash you, make you clean;
Put away the evil of your doings from before mine eyes;
Cease to do evil; [17]learn to do well;
Seek judgment, relieve the oppressed,
Judge the fatherless, plead for the widow.

[18]"Come now, and let us reason together," saith the
LORD:
"Though your sins be as scarlet, they shall be as white as
snow;
Though they be red like crimson, they shall be as wool.
[19]If ye be willing and obedient,
Ye shall eat the good of the land:
[20]But if ye refuse and rebel,
Ye shall be devoured with the sword":
For the mouth of the LORD hath spoken it.

The Song of the Vineyard

Chapter 5

NOW WILL I SING TO MY WELLBELOVED
A song of my beloved touching his vineyard.
My wellbeloved hath a vineyard in a very fruitful hill:
[2]And he fenced it, and gathered out the stones thereof,
And planted it with the choicest vine,
And built a tower in the midst of it,
And also made a winepress therein:
And he looked that it should bring forth grapes,
And it brought forth wild grapes.

[3]And now, O inhabitants of Jerusalem, and men of Judah,
Judge, I pray you, betwixt me and my vineyard.
[4]What could have been done more to my vineyard,
That I have not done in it?
Wherefore, when I looked that it should bring forth grapes,
Brought it forth wild grapes?
[5]And now go to;
I will tell you what I will do to my vineyard:
I will take away the hedge thereof, and it shall be eaten up;
And break down the wall thereof, and it shall be trodden down:
[6]And I will lay it waste:
It shall not be pruned, nor digged;
But there shall come up briers and thorns:
I will also command the clouds
That they rain no rain upon it.

[7]For the vineyard of the LORD of hosts is the house of Israel,
And the men of Judah his pleasant plant:
And he looked for judgment, but behold oppression;
For righteousness, but behold a cry.

Isaiah's Vision

Chapter 6

In the year that king Uzziah died I saw also the Lord sitting upon a throne, high and lifted up, and his train filled the temple. [2]Above it stood the seraphims: each one had six wings; with twain he covered his face, and with twain he covered his feet, and with twain he did fly. [3]And one cried unto another, and said, "Holy, holy, holy, is the Lord of hosts: the whole earth is full of his glory." [4]And the posts of the door moved at the voice of him that cried, and the house was filled with smoke.

[5]Then said I, "Woe is me! for I am undone; because I am a man of unclean lips, and I dwell in the midst of a people of unclean lips: for mine eyes have seen the King, the Lord of hosts."

Isaiah Prophesies the Death of Hiskia the King *by J. de Backer*

Chapter 6

[6]Then flew one of the seraphims unto me, having a live coal in his hand, which he had taken with the tongs from off the altar: [7]and he laid it upon my mouth, and said, "Lo, this hath touched thy lips; and thine iniquity is taken away, and thy sin purged."

[8]Also I heard the voice of the Lord, saying, "Whom shall I send, and who will go for us?"

Then said I, "Here am I; send me."

[9]And he said, "Go, and tell this people, 'Hear ye indeed, but understand not; and see ye indeed, but perceive not.' [10]Make the heart of this people fat, and make their ears heavy, and shut their eyes; lest they see with their eyes, and hear with their ears, and understand with their heart, and convert, and be healed."

[11]Then said I, "Lord, how long?"

And he answered, "Until the cities be wasted without inhabitant, and the houses without man, and the land be utterly desolate, [12]and the LORD have removed men far away, and there be a great forsaking in the midst of the land. [13]But yet in it shall be a tenth, and it shall return, and shall be eaten: as a teil tree, and as an oak, whose substance is in them, when they cast their leaves: so the holy seed shall be the substance thereof."

THE SIGN OF IMMANUEL

Chapter 7

AND IT CAME TO PASS IN THE DAYS OF AHAZ THE son of Jotham, the son of Uzziah, king of Judah, that Rezin the king of Syria, and Pekah the son of Remaliah, king of Israel, went up toward Jerusalem to war against it, but could not prevail against it.

[2]And it was told the house of David, saying, "Syria is confederate with Ephraim." And his heart was moved, and the heart of his people, as the trees of the wood are moved with the wind.

[3]Then said the LORD unto Isaiah, "Go forth now to meet Ahaz, thou, and Shear-jashub thy son, at the end of the conduit of the upper pool in the highway of the fuller's

Chapter 7

field; [4]and say unto him, 'Take heed, and be quiet; fear not, neither be fainthearted for the two tails of these smoking firebrands, for the fierce anger of Rezin with Syria, and of the son of Remaliah. [5]Because Syria, Ephraim, and the son of Remaliah, have taken evil counsel against thee, saying, [6]"Let us go up against Judah, and vex it, and let us make a breach therein for us, and set a king in the midst of it, even the son of Tabeal": [7]thus saith the Lord God, It shall not stand, neither shall it come to pass. [8]For the head of Syria is Damascus, and the head of Damascus is Rezin; and within threescore and five years shall Ephraim be broken, that it be not a people. [9]And the head of Ephraim is Samaria, and the head of Samaria is Remaliah's son. If ye will not believe, surely ye shall not be established.'"

[10]Moreover the Lord spake again unto Ahaz, saying, [11]"Ask thee a sign of the Lord thy God; ask it either in the depth, or in the height above."

[12]But Ahaz said, "I will not ask, neither will I tempt the Lord."

[13]And he said, "Hear ye now, O house of David; Is it a small thing for you to weary men, but will ye weary my God also? [14]Therefore the Lord himself shall give you a sign; Behold, a virgin shall conceive, and bear a son, and shall call his name Immanuel. [15]Butter and honey shall he eat, that he may know to refuse the evil, and choose the good. [16]For before the child shall know to refuse the evil, and choose the good, the land that thou abhorrest shall be forsaken of both her kings. [17]The Lord shall bring upon thee, and upon thy people, and upon thy father's house, days that have not come, from the day that Ephraim departed from Judah; even the king of Assyria."

The Prince of Peace

Chapter 9

The people that walked in darkness
Have seen a great light:
They that dwell in the land of the shadow of death,
Upon them hath the light shined.

[3]Thou hast multiplied the nation,
And not increased the joy:
They joy before thee according to the joy in harvest,
And as men rejoice when they divide the spoil.
[4]For thou hast broken
The yoke of his burden, and the staff of his shoulder,
The rod of his oppressor, as in the day of Midian.
[5]For every battle of the warrior
Is with confused noise, and garments rolled in blood;
But this shall be with burning and fuel of fire.
[6]For unto us a child is born,
Unto us a son is given:
And the government shall be upon his shoulder:
And his name shall be called
Wonderful, Counsellor, The mighty God,
The everlasting Father, The Prince of Peace.
[7]Of the increase of his government and peace
There shall be no end,
Upon the throne of David, and upon his kingdom;
To order it, and to establish it
With judgment and with justice
From henceforth even for ever.
The zeal of the LORD of hosts will perform this.

A BRANCH FROM JESSE

AND THERE SHALL COME FORTH A ROD OUT OF THE stem of Jesse,
And a Branch shall grow out of his roots:
[2]And the spirit of the LORD shall rest upon him,
The spirit of wisdom and understanding,
The spirit of counsel and might,
The spirit of knowledge and of the fear of the LORD;
[3]And shall make him of quick understanding in the fear of the LORD:
And he shall not judge after the sight of his eyes,
Neither reprove after the hearing of his ears:
[4]But with righteousness shall he judge the poor,

Chapter 11

And reprove with equity for the meek of the earth:
And he shall smite the earth with the rod of his mouth,
And with the breath of his lips shall he slay the wicked.
[5]And righteousness shall be the girdle of his loins,
And faithfulness the girdle of his reins.

[6]The wolf also shall dwell with the lamb,
And the leopard shall lie down with the kid;
And the calf and the young lion and the fatling together;
And a little child shall lead them.
[7]And the cow and the bear shall feed;
Their young ones shall lie down together:
And the lion shall eat straw like the ox.
[8]And the suckling child shall play on the hole of the asp,
And the weaned child shall put his hand on the cockatrice' den.
[9]They shall not hurt nor destroy in all my holy mountain:
For the earth shall be full of the knowledge of the LORD,
As the waters cover the sea.

[10]And in that day there shall be a root of Jesse,
Which shall stand for an ensign of the people;
To it shall the Gentiles seek:
And his rest shall be glorious.

A PROPHECY AGAINST BABYLON

Chapter 14

HOW ART THOU FALLEN FROM HEAVEN,
O Lucifer, son of the morning!
How art thou cut down to the ground,
Which didst weaken the nations!
[13]For thou hast said in thine heart,
"I will ascend into heaven,
I will exalt my throne above the stars of God:
I will sit also upon the mount of the congregation,
In the sides of the north:
[14]I will ascend above the heights of the clouds;
I will be like the most High."
[15]Yet thou shalt be brought down to hell,
To the sides of the pit.

The Wicked Led Off to Hell *by Rogier van der Weyden*

Chapter 14

[16]They that see thee shall narrowly look upon thee,
And consider thee, saying,
"Is this the man that made the earth to tremble,
That did shake kingdoms;
[17]That made the world as a wilderness,
And destroyed the cities thereof;
That opened not the house of his prisoners?"

[18]All the kings of the nations, even all of them,
Lie in glory, every one in his own house.
[19]But thou art cast out of thy grave
Like an abominable branch,
And as the raiment of those that are slain,
Thrust through with a sword,
That go down to the stones of the pit;
As a carcase trodden under feet.
[20]Thou shalt not be joined with them in burial,
Because thou hast destroyed thy land, and slain thy people:
The seed of evildoers shall never be renowned.
[21]Prepare slaughter for his children
For the iniquity of their fathers;
That they do not rise, nor possess the land,
Nor fill the face of the world with cities.

[22]"For I will rise up against them," saith the LORD of hosts,
"And cut off from Babylon the name, and remnant,
And son, and nephew," saith the LORD.
[23]"I will also make it a possession for the bittern,
And pools of water:
And I will sweep it with the besom of destruction,"
Saith the LORD of hosts.

PRAISE FOR GOD'S SALVATION

Chapter 25

O LORD, THOU ART MY GOD;
I will exalt thee, I will praise thy name;
For thou hast done wonderful things;
Thy counsels of old are faithfulness and truth.

[2]For thou hast made of a city an heap;
Of a defenced city a ruin:
A palace of strangers to be no city;
It shall never be built.
[3]Therefore shall the strong people glorify thee,
The city of the terrible nations shall fear thee.
[4]For thou hast been a strength to the poor,
A strength to the needy in his distress,
A refuge from the storm, a shadow from the heat,
When the blast of the terrible ones is as a storm against the wall.
[5]Thou shalt bring down the noise of strangers,
As the heat in a dry place;
Even the heat with the shadow of a cloud:
The branch of the terrible ones shall be brought low.

[6]And in this mountain shall the LORD of hosts
Make unto all people a feast of fat things,
A feast of wines on the lees,
Of fat things full of marrow,
Of wines on the lees well refined.
[7]And he will destroy in this mountain
The face of the covering cast over all people,
And the veil that is spread over all nations.
[8]He will swallow up death in victory;
And the Lord GOD will wipe away tears from off all faces;
And the rebuke of his people shall he take away
From off all the earth:
For the LORD hath spoken it.

[9]And it shall be said in that day,
"Lo, this is our God;
We have waited for him, and he will save us:
This is the LORD; we have waited for him,
We will be glad and rejoice in his salvation."

The Lord's Graciousness

Chapter 30

FOR THUS SAITH THE LORD GOD, THE HOLY ONE OF Israel; "In returning and rest shall ye be saved; in quietness and in confidence shall be your strength: and ye would not. [16]But ye said, 'No; for we will flee upon horses'; therefore shall ye flee: and, 'We will ride upon the swift'; therefore shall they that pursue you be swift. [17]One thousand shall flee at the rebuke of one; at the rebuke of five shall ye flee: till ye be left as a beacon upon the top of a mountain, and as an ensign on an hill."

[18]And therefore will the LORD wait, that he may be gracious unto you, and therefore will he be exalted, that he may have mercy upon you: for the LORD is a God of judgment: blessed are all they that wait for him.

[19]For the people shall dwell in Zion at Jerusalem: thou shalt weep no more: he will be very gracious unto thee at the voice of thy cry; when he shall hear it, he will answer thee. [20]And though the Lord give you the bread of adversity, and the water of affliction, yet shall not thy teachers be removed into a corner any more, but thine eyes shall see

IMAGINARY VIEW OF JERUSALEM *by Desiderio Monsu*

thy teachers: [21]and thine ears shall hear a word behind thee, saying, "This is the way, walk ye in it," when ye turn to the right hand, and when ye turn to the left.

The Joy of the Redeemed

THE WILDERNESS AND THE SOLITARY PLACE shall be glad for them;
And the desert shall rejoice, and blossom as the rose.
[2]It shall blossom abundantly, and rejoice
Even with joy and singing:
The glory of Lebanon shall be given unto it,
The excellency of Carmel and Sharon,
They shall see the glory of the LORD,
And the excellency of our God.

[3]Strengthen ye the weak hands,
And confirm the feeble knees.
[4]Say to them that are of a fearful heart,
"Be strong, fear not:
Behold, your God will come with vengeance,
Even God with a recompence;
He will come and save you."

[5]Then the eyes of the blind shall be opened,
And the ears of the deaf shall be unstopped.
[6]Then shall the lame man leap as an hart,
And the tongue of the dumb sing:
For in the wilderness shall waters break out,
And streams in the desert.
[7]And the parched ground shall become a pool,
And the thirsty land springs of water:
In the habitation of dragons, where each lay,
Shall be grass with reeds and rushes.

[8]And an highway shall be there, and a way,
And it shall be called the way of holiness;
The unclean shall not pass over it; but it shall be for those:

Chapter 35

The wayfaring men, though fools, shall not err therein.
[9]No lion shall be there,
Nor any ravenous beast shall go up thereon,
It shall not be found there;
But the redeemed shall walk there:
[10]And the ransomed of the LORD shall return,
And come to Zion with songs
And everlasting joy upon their heads:
They shall obtain joy and gladness,
And sorrow and sighing shall flee away.

COMFORT FOR GOD'S PEOPLE

Chapter 40

COMFORT YE, COMFORT YE MY PEOPLE, SAITH
your God.
[2]Speak ye comfortably to Jerusalem,
And cry unto her,
That her warfare is accomplished,
That her iniquity is pardoned:
For she hath received of the LORD's hand
Double for all her sins.

[3]The voice of him that crieth in the wilderness,
"Prepare ye the way of the LORD,
Make straight in the desert a highway for our God.
[4]Every valley shall be exalted,
And every mountain and hill shall be made low:
And the crooked shall be made straight,
And the rough places plain:
[5]And the glory of the LORD shall be revealed,
And all flesh shall see it together":
For the mouth of the LORD hath spoken it.

[6]The voice said, "Cry."
And he said, "What shall I cry?"
"All flesh is grass,
And all the goodliness thereof is as the flower of the field:
[7]The grass withereth, the flower fadeth:
Because the spirit of the LORD bloweth upon it:

Chapter 40

Surely the people is grass.
[8]The grass withereth, the flower fadeth:
But the word of our God shall stand for ever."

[9]O Zion, that bringest good tidings,
Get thee up into the high mountain;
O Jerusalem, that bringest good tidings,
Lift up thy voice with strength;
Lift it up, be not afraid;
Say unto the cities of Judah,
"Behold your God!"
[10]Behold, the Lord God will come with strong hand,
And his arm shall rule for him:
Behold, his reward is with him,
And his work before him.
[11]He shall feed his flock like a shepherd:
He shall gather the lambs with his arm;
And carry them in his bosom,
And shall gently lead those that are with young.

The Servant of the Lord

Chapter 42

BEHOLD MY SERVANT, WHOM I UPHOLD;
Mine elect, in whom my soul delighteth;
I have put my spirit upon him:
He shall bring forth judgment to the Gentiles.
[2]He shall not cry, nor lift up,
Nor cause his voice to be heard in the street.
[3]A bruised reed shall he not break,
And the smoking flax shall he not quench:
He shall bring forth judgment unto truth.
[4]He shall not fail nor be discouraged,
Till he have set judgment in the earth:
And the isles shall wait for his law.

[5]Thus saith God the Lord,
He that created the heavens, and stretched them out;
He that spread forth the earth, and that which cometh out of it;

Chapter 42

He that giveth breath unto the people upon it,
And spirit to them that walk therein:
[6]"I the LORD have called thee in righteousness,
And will hold thine hand, and will keep thee,
And will give thee for a covenant of the people,
For a light of the Gentiles;
[7]To open the blind eyes,
To bring out the prisoners from the prison,
And them that sit in darkness out of the prison house."

ISRAEL'S ONLY SAVIOUR

Chapter 43

BUT NOW THUS SAITH THE LORD
That created thee, O Jacob,
And he that formed thee, O Israel,
"Fear not: for I have redeemed thee,
I have called thee by thy name; thou art mine.
[2]When thou passest through the waters, I will be with thee;
And through the rivers, they shall not overflow thee:
When thou walkest through the fire, thou shalt not be burned;
Neither shall the flame kindle upon thee.
[3]For I am the LORD thy God,
The Holy One of Israel, thy Saviour:
I gave Egypt for thy ransom,
Ethiopia and Seba for thee.
[4]Since thou wast precious in my sight,
Thou hast been honourable, and I have loved thee:
Therefore will I give men for thee,
And people for thy life.
[5]Fear not: for I am with thee:
I will bring thy seed from the east,
And gather thee from the west;
[6]I will say to the north, 'Give up';
And to the south, 'Keep not back':
Bring my sons from far,
And my daughters from the ends of the earth;
[7]Even every one that is called by my name:
For I have created him for my glory,

THE PROPHET ISAIAH *by Pietro Perugino*

Chapter 43

I have formed him; yea, I have made him."
[8]Bring forth the blind people that have eyes,
And the deaf that have ears.
[9]Let all the nations be gathered together,
And let the people be assembled:
Who among them can declare this,
And shew us former things?
Let them bring forth their witnesses, that they may be justified:
Or let them hear, and say, "It is truth."
[10]"Ye are my witnesses," saith the LORD,
"And my servant whom I have chosen:
That ye may know and believe me,
And understand that I am he:
Before me there was no God formed,
Neither shall there be after me.
[11]I, even I, am the LORD;
And beside me there is no saviour."

The Servant's Commission

Chapter 49

LISTEN, O ISLES, UNTO ME;
And hearken, ye people, from far;
The LORD hath called me from the womb;
From the bowels of my mother hath he made mention of my name.
[2]And he hath made my mouth like a sharp sword;
In the shadow of his hand hath he hid me,
And made me a polished shaft;
In his quiver hath he hid me;
[3]And said unto me, "Thou art my servant,
O Israel, in whom I will be glorified."
[4]Then I said, "I have laboured in vain,
I have spent my strength for nought, and in vain:
Yet surely my judgment is with the LORD,
And my work with my God."

[5]And now, saith the LORD
That formed me from the womb to be his servant,
To bring Jacob again to him,
Though Israel be not gathered,
Yet shall I be glorious in the eyes of the LORD,
And my God shall be my strength.
[6]And he said,
"It is a light thing that thou shouldest be my servant
To raise up the tribes of Jacob,
And to restore the preserved of Israel:
I will also give thee for a light to the Gentiles,
That thou mayest be my salvation unto the end of the earth."

[7]Thus saith the LORD,
The Redeemer of Israel, and his Holy One,
To him whom man despiseth,
To him whom the nation abhorreth,
To a servant of rulers,
"Kings shall see and arise,
Princes also shall worship,
Because of the LORD that is faithful,
And the Holy One of Israel, and he shall choose thee."

Chapter 49

[8]Thus saith the LORD,
"In an acceptable time have I heard thee,
And in a day of salvation have I helped thee:
And I will preserve thee, and give thee
For a covenant of the people,
To establish the earth,
To cause to inherit the desolate heritages;
[9]That thou mayest say to the prisoners, 'Go forth';
To them that are in darkness, 'Shew yourselves.'

"They shall feed in the ways,
And their pastures shall be in all high places.
[10]They shall not hunger nor thirst;
Neither shall the heat nor sun smite them:
For he that hath mercy on them shall lead them,
Even by the springs of water shall he guide them.
[11]And I will make all my mountains a way,
And my highways shall be exalted.
[12]Behold, these shall come from far:
And, lo, these from the north and from the west;
and these from the land of Sinim."

[13]Sing, O heavens; and be joyful, O earth;
And break forth into singing, O mountains:
For the LORD hath comforted his people,
And will have mercy upon his afflicted.

"AWAKE, AWAKE, ZION"

Chapter 52

AWAKE, AWAKE; PUT ON THY STRENGTH, O ZION;
Put on thy beautiful garments,
O Jerusalem, the holy city:
For henceforth there shall no more come into thee
The uncircumcised and the unclean.
[2]Shake thyself from the dust;
Arise, and sit down, O Jerusalem:
Loose thyself from the bands of thy neck,

O captive daughter of Zion.
[3]For thus saith the LORD,
"Ye have sold yourselves for nought;
And ye shall be redeemed without money."

[4]For thus saith the Lord GOD,
"My people went down aforetime into Egypt to sojourn there;
And the Assyrian oppressed them without cause.
[5]Now therefore, what have I here," saith the LORD,
"That my people is taken away for nought?
They that rule over them make them to howl," saith the LORD;
"And my name continually every day is blasphemed.
[6]Therefore my people shall know my name:
Therefore they shall know in that day
That I am he that doth speak:
Behold, it is I."

[7]How beautiful upon the mountains
Are the feet of him that bringeth good tidings,
That publisheth peace;
That bringeth good tidings of good,
That publisheth salvation;
That saith unto Zion,
"Thy God reigneth!"
[8]Thy watchmen shall lift up the voice;
With the voice together shall they sing:
For they shall see eye to eye,
When the LORD shall bring again Zion.
[9]Break forth into joy, sing together,
Ye waste places of Jerusalem:
For the LORD hath comforted his people,
He hath redeemed Jerusalem.
[10]The LORD hath made bare his holy arm
In the eyes of all the nations;
And all the ends of the earth shall see
The salvation of our God.

The Suffering Servant

Chapter 52

BEHOLD, MY SERVANT SHALL DEAL PRUDENTLY,
He shall be exalted and extolled, and be very high.
[14]As many were astonied at thee;
His visage was so marred more than any man,
And his form more than the sons of men:
[15]So shall he sprinkle many nations;
The kings shall shut their mouths at him:
For that which had not been told them shall they see;
And that which they had not heard shall they consider.

Prophet Isaiah *by Michelangelo*

Chapter 53

WHO HATH BELIEVED OUR REPORT?
And to whom is the arm of the LORD revealed?
[2]For he shall grow up before him as a tender plant,
And as a root out of a dry ground:
He hath no form nor comeliness;
And when we shall see him, there is no beauty that we should desire him.
[3]He is despised and rejected of men;
A man of sorrows, and acquainted with grief:
And we hid as it were our faces from him;
He was despised, and we esteemed him not.

[4]Surely he hath borne our griefs, and carried our sorrows:
Yet we did esteem him stricken,
Smitten of God, and afflicted.
[5]But he was wounded for our transgressions,
He was bruised for our iniquities:
The chastisement of our peace was upon him;
And with his stripes we are healed.
[6]All we like sheep have gone astray;
We have turned every one to his own way;
And the LORD hath laid on him
The iniquity of us all.

[7]He was oppressed, and he was afflicted,
Yet he opened not his mouth:
He is brought as a lamb to the slaughter,
And as a sheep before her shearers is dumb,
So he openeth not his mouth.
[8]He was taken from prison and from judgment:
And who shall declare his generation?
For he was cut off out of the land of the living:
For the transgression of my people was he stricken.
[9]And he made his grave with the wicked,
And with the rich in his death;
Because he had done no violence,
Neither was any deceit in his mouth.

[10]Yet it pleased the LORD to bruise him; he hath put him to grief:
When thou shalt make his soul an offering for sin,
He shall see his seed, he shall prolong his days,

Chapter 53

And the pleasure of the LORD shall prosper in his hand.
[11]He shall see of the travail of his soul, and shall be satisfied:
By his knowledge shall my righteous servant justify many;
For he shall bear their iniquities.
[12]Therefore will I divide him a portion with the great,
And he shall divide the spoil with the strong;
Because he hath poured out his soul unto death:
And he was numbered with the transgressors;
And he bare the sin of many,
And made intercession for the transgressors.

"SEEK YE THE LORD"

Chapter 55

"HO, EVERY ONE THAT THIRSTETH,
Come ye to the waters,
And he that hath no money;
Come ye, buy, and eat;
Yea, come, buy wine and milk
Without money and without price.
[2]Wherefore do ye spend money for that which is not bread?
And your labour for that which satisfieth not?
Hearken diligently unto me, and eat ye that which is good,
And let your soul delight itself in fatness.
[3]Incline your ear, and come unto me:
Hear, and your soul shall live;
And I will make an everlasting covenant with you,
Even the sure mercies of David.
[4]Behold, I have given him for a witness to the people,
A leader and commander to the people.
[5]Behold, thou shalt call a nation that thou knowest not,
And nations that knew not thee shall run unto thee
Because of the LORD thy God,
And for the Holy One of Israel;
For he hath glorified thee."

[6]Seek ye the LORD while he may be found,
Call ye upon him while he is near.
[7]Let the wicked forsake his way,
And the unrighteous man his thoughts:

Chapter 55

And let him return unto the LORD, and he will have mercy upon him;
And to our God, for he will abundantly pardon.

[8]"For my thoughts are not your thoughts,
Neither are your ways my ways," saith the LORD.
[9]"For as the heavens are higher than the earth,
So are my ways higher than your ways,
And my thoughts than your thoughts.
[10]For as the rain cometh down, and the snow from heaven,
And returneth not thither, but watereth the earth,
And maketh it bring forth and bud,
That it may give seed to the sower, and bread to the eater:
[11]So shall my word be that goeth forth out of my mouth:
It shall not return unto me void,
But it shall accomplish that which I please,
And it shall prosper in the thing whereto I sent it.
[12]For ye shall go out with joy, and be led forth with peace:
The mountains and the hills shall break forth before you into singing,
And all the trees of the field shall clap their hands.
[13]Instead of the thorn shall come up the fir tree,
And instead of the brier shall come up the myrtle tree:
And it shall be to the LORD for a name,
For an everlasting sign that shall not be cut off."

THE GLORY OF ZION

Chapter 60

ARISE, SHINE; FOR THY LIGHT IS COME,
And the glory of the LORD is risen upon thee.
[2]For, behold, the darkness shall cover the earth,
And gross darkness the people:
But the LORD shall arise upon thee,
And his glory shall be seen upon thee.
[3]And the Gentiles shall come to thy light,
And kings to the brightness of thy rising.

THE ADORATION OF THE KINGS *by Joos van Cleve*

[4]Lift up thine eyes round about, and see:
All they gather themselves together, they come to thee:
Thy sons shall come from far,
And thy daughters shall be nursed at thy side.
[5]Then thou shalt see, and flow together;
And thine heart shall fear, and be enlarged;
Because the abundance of the sea shall be converted unto
thee,

Chapter 60

Chapter 60

The forces of the Gentiles shall come unto thee.
[6]The multitude of camels shall cover thee,
The dromedaries of Midian and Ephah;
All they from Sheba shall come:
They shall bring gold and incense;
And they shall shew forth the praises of the LORD.
[7]All the flocks of Kedar shall be gathered together unto thee,
The rams of Nebaioth shall minister unto thee:
They shall come up with acceptance on mine altar,
And I will glorify the house of my glory.

[8]Who are these that fly as a cloud,
And as the doves to their windows?
[9]Surely the isles shall wait for me,
And the ships of Tarshish first,
To bring thy sons from far,
Their silver and their gold with them,
Unto the name of the LORD thy God,
And to the Holy One of Israel,
Because he hath glorified thee.

THE LORD'S ANOINTED

Chapter 61

THE SPIRIT OF THE LORD GOD IS UPON ME;
Because the LORD hath anointed me
To preach good tidings unto the meek;
He hath sent me to bind up the brokenhearted,
To proclaim liberty to the captives,
And the opening of the prison to them that are bound;
[2]To proclaim the acceptable year of the LORD,
And the day of vengeance of our God;
To comfort all that mourn;
[3]To appoint unto them that mourn in Zion,
To give unto them beauty for ashes,
The oil of joy for mourning,

Chapter 61

The garment of praise for the spirit of heaviness;
That they might be called trees of righteousness,
The planting of the LORD, that he might be glorified.

NEW HEAVENS AND A NEW EARTH

Chapter 65

"FOR, BEHOLD, I CREATE
New heavens and a new earth:
And the former shall not be remembered,
Nor come into mind.
[18]But be ye glad and rejoice for ever
In that which I create:
For, behold, I create Jerusalem a rejoicing,
And her people a joy.
[19]And I will rejoice in Jerusalem,
And joy in my people:
And the voice of weeping shall be no more heard in her,
Nor the voice of crying.

[20]"There shall be no more thence an infant of days,
Nor an old man that hath not filled his days:
For the child shall die an hundred years old;
But the sinner being an hundred years old shall be accursed.
[21]And they shall build houses, and inhabit them;
And they shall plant vineyards, and eat the fruit of them.
[22]They shall not build, and another inhabit;
They shall not plant, and another eat:
For as the days of a tree are the days of my people,
And mine elect shall long enjoy the work of their hands.
[23]They shall not labour in vain, nor bring forth for trouble;
For they are the seed of the blessed of the LORD,
And their offspring with them.
[24]And it shall come to pass, that before they call, I will answer;
And while they are yet speaking, I will hear.
[25]The wolf and the lamb shall feed together,

Chapter 65

PROPHET ISAIAH *by Fra Bartolommeo*

Chapter 65

And the lion shall eat straw like the bullock:
And dust shall be the serpent's meat.
They shall not hurt nor destroy
In all my holy mountain," saith the LORD.

Chapters & Verses

FROM

THE BOOK OF THE PROPHET

JEREMIAH

THE

LAMENTATIONS

OF JEREMIAH

&

THE BOOK OF THE PROPHET

EZEKIEL

THE CALL OF JEREMIAH • THE PROPHET'S SORROW • TRUST IN THE LORD • THE RIGHTEOUS BRANCH • THE RESTORATION OF ISRAEL • THE NEW COVENANT • THE PROPHET'S AFFLICTION AND HOPE • THE VALLEY OF DRY BONES

JEREMIAH

The Call of Jeremiah

Chapter 1

THE WORDS OF JEREMIAH THE SON OF HILKIAH, of the priests that were in Anathoth in the land of Benjamin: [2]to whom the words of the LORD came in the days of Josiah the son of Amon king of Judah, in the thirteenth year of his reign. [3]It came also in the days of Jehoiakim the son of Josiah king of Judah, unto the end of the eleventh year of Zedekiah the son of Josiah king of Judah, unto the carrying away of Jerusalem captive in the fifth month.

[4]Then the word of the LORD came unto me, saying, [5]"Before I formed thee in the belly I knew thee, and before thou camest forth out of the womb I sanctified thee, and I ordained thee a prophet unto the nations."

[6]Then said I, "Ah, Lord GOD! behold, I cannot speak: for I am a child."

[7]But the LORD said unto me, "Say not, 'I am a child': for thou shalt go to all that I shall send thee, and whatsoever I command thee thou shalt speak. [8]Be not afraid of their faces: for I am with thee to deliver thee, saith the LORD."

[9]Then the LORD put forth his hand, and touched my mouth. And the LORD said unto me, "Behold, I have put my words in thy mouth. [10]See, I have this day set thee over the nations and over the kingdoms, to root out, and to pull down, and to destroy, and to throw down, to build, and to plant."

The Prophet's Sorrow

Chapter 8

WHEN I WOULD COMFORT MYSELF AGAINST sorrow,
My heart is faint in me.
[19]Behold the voice of the cry of the daughter of my people
Because of them that dwell in a far country:
"Is not the LORD in Zion?
Is not her king in her?"
Why have they provoked me to anger with their graven images,
And with strange vanities?
[20]"The harvest is past, the summer is ended,
And we are not saved."
[21]For the hurt of the daughter of my people am I hurt;
I am black; astonishment hath taken hold on me.

[22]Is there no balm in Gilead;
Is there no physician there?
Why then is not the health
Of the daughter of my people recovered?

Chapter 9

OH THAT MY HEAD WERE WATERS,
And mine eyes a fountain of tears,
That I might weep day and night
For the slain of the daughter of my people!
[2]Oh that I had in the wilderness
A lodging place of wayfaring men;
That I might leave my people, and go from them!
For they be all adulterers, an assembly of treacherous men.
[3]And they bend their tongues like their bow for lies:
But they are not valiant for the truth upon the earth;
For they proceed from evil to evil,
And they know not me, saith the LORD.

Trust in the Lord

Chapter 17

THUS SAITH THE LORD;
"Cursed be the man that trusteth in man,
And maketh flesh his arm,
And whose heart departeth from the LORD.
[6]For he shall be like the heath in the desert,
And shall not see when good cometh;
But shall inhabit the parched places in the wilderness,
In a salt land and not inhabited.

[7]"Blessed is the man that trusteth in the LORD,
And whose hope the LORD is.
[8]For he shall be as a tree planted by the waters,
And that spreadeth out her roots by the river,
And shall not see when heat cometh,
But her leaf shall be green;
And shall not be careful in the year of drought,
Neither shall cease from yielding fruit."

[9]The heart is deceitful above all things,
And desperately wicked: who can know it?
[10]"I the LORD search the heart, I try the reins,
Even to give every man according to his ways,
And according to the fruit of his doings."

The Righteous Branch

Chapter 23

"WOE BE UNTO THE PASTORS THAT DESTROY and scatter the sheep of my pasture!" saith the LORD. [2]Therefore thus saith the LORD God of Israel against the pastors that feed my people; "Ye have scattered my flock, and driven them away, and have not visited them: behold, I will visit upon you the evil of your doings," saith the LORD. [3]"And I will gather the remnant of my flock out of all countries whither

The Righteous Branch

Chapter 23

Chapter 23

I have driven them, and will bring them again to their folds; and they shall be fruitful and increase. [4]And I will set up shepherds over them which shall feed them: and they shall fear no more, nor be dismayed, neither shall they be lacking," saith the LORD.

[5]"Behold, the days come," saith the LORD, "that I will raise unto David a righteous Branch, and a King shall reign and prosper, and shall execute judgment and justice in the earth. [6]In his days Judah shall be saved, and Israel shall dwell safely: and this is his name whereby he shall be called, THE LORD OUR RIGHTEOUSNESS.

[7]"Therefore, behold, the days come," saith the LORD, "that they shall no more say, 'The LORD liveth, which brought up the children of Israel out of the land of Egypt'; [8]but, 'The LORD liveth, which brought up and which led the seed of the house of Israel out of the north country,' and from all countries whither I had driven them; and they shall dwell in their own land."

THE RESTORATION OF ISRAEL

Chapter 31

THE LORD HATH APPEARED OF OLD UNTO ME, saying,
"Yea, I have loved thee with an everlasting love:
Therefore with lovingkindness have I drawn thee.
[4]Again I will build thee,
And thou shalt be built, O virgin of Israel:
Thou shalt again be adorned with thy tabrets,
And shalt go forth in the dances of them that make merry.
[5]Thou shalt yet plant vines
Upon the mountains of Samaria:
The planters shall plant,
And shall eat them as common things.
[6]For there shall be a day, that the watchmen
Upon the mount Ephraim shall cry,
'Arise ye, and let us go up to Zion
Unto the LORD our God.'"

[7]For thus saith the Lord;
"Sing with gladness for Jacob,
And shout among the chief of the nations:
Publish ye, praise ye, and say,
'O Lord, save thy people, the remnant of Israel.'
[8]Behold, I will bring them from the north country,
And gather them from the coasts of the earth,
And with them the blind and the lame,
The woman with child and her that travaileth with child together:
A great company shall return thither.
[9]They shall come with weeping,
And with supplications will I lead them:
I will cause them to walk by the rivers of waters
In a straight way, wherein they shall not stumble:
For I am a father to Israel,
And Ephraim is my firstborn.

[10]"Hear the word of the Lord, O ye nations,
And declare it in the isles afar off, and say,
'He that scattered Israel will gather him,
And keep him, as a shepherd doth his flock.'
[11]For the Lord hath redeemed Jacob,
And ransomed him from the hand of him that was stronger than he.
[12]Therefore they shall come and sing in the height of Zion,
And shall flow together to the goodness of the Lord,
For wheat, and for wine, and for oil,
And for the young of the flock and of the herd:
And their soul shall be as a watered garden;
And they shall not sorrow any more at all.
[13]Then shall the virgin rejoice in the dance,
Both young men and old together:
For I will turn their mourning into joy,
And will comfort them, and make them rejoice from their sorrow.
[14]And I will satiate the soul of the priests with fatness,
And my people shall be satisfied with my goodness,"
saith the Lord.

[15]Thus saith the Lord;
"A voice was heard in Ramah,

Chapter 31

Lamentation, and bitter weeping;
Rahel weeping for her children
Refused to be comforted for her children,
Because they were not."

[16]Thus saith the LORD;
"Refrain thy voice from weeping,
And thine eyes from tears:
For thy work shall be rewarded," saith the LORD;
And they shall come again from the land of the enemy.
[17]And there is hope in thine end", saith the LORD,
"That thy children shall come again to their own border."

THE NEW COVENANT

Chapter 31

"BEHOLD, THE DAYS COME," SAITH THE LORD,
"That I will make a new covenant
With the house of Israel,
And with the house of Judah:
[32]Not according to the covenant
That I made with their fathers
In the day that I took them by the hand
To bring them out of the land of Egypt;
Which my covenant they brake,
Although I was an husband unto them," saith the LORD:
[33]"But this shall be the covenant that I will make with the house of Israel;
After those days," saith the LORD,
"I will put my law in their inward parts,
And write it in their hearts;
And will be their God,
And they shall be my people.
[34]And they shall teach no more every man his neighbour,
And every man his brother, saying, 'Know the LORD':
For they shall all know me,
From the least of them unto the greatest of them," saith the LORD:
"For I will forgive their iniquity,
And I will remember their sin no more."

LAMENTATIONS

The Prophet's Affliction and Hope

Chapter 3

I AM THE MAN THAT HATH SEEN AFFLICTION
By the rod of his wrath.
[2]He hath led me, and brought me
Into darkness, but not into light.
[3]Surely against me is he turned;
He turneth his hand against me all the day.

[4]My flesh and my skin hath he made old;
He hath broken my bones.
[5]He hath builded against me, and compassed me with gall and travail.
[6]He hath set me in dark places, as they that be dead of old.

[7]He hath hedged me about, that I cannot get out:
He hath made my chain heavy.
[8]Also when I cry and shout,
He shutteth out my prayer.
[9]He hath inclosed my ways with hewn stone,
He hath made my paths crooked.

[10]He was unto me as a bear lying in wait,
And as a lion in secret places.
[11]He hath turned aside my ways, and pulled me in pieces:
He hath made me desolate.
[12]He hath bent his bow, and set me as a mark for the arrow.
[13]He hath caused the arrows of his quiver to enter into my reins.

[14]I was a derision to all my people;
And their song all the day.
[15]He hath filled me with bitterness,
He hath made me drunken with wormwood.
[16]He hath also broken my teeth with gravel stones,
He hath covered me with ashes.
[17]And thou hast removed my soul far off from peace:
I forgat prosperity.

[18]And I said, "My strength and my hope
Is perished from the LORD":
[19]Remembering mine affliction and my misery,
The wormwood and the gall.
[20]My soul hath them still in remembrance,
And is humbled in me.

[21]This I recall to my mind, therefore have I hope.
[22]It is of the LORD's mercies that we are not consumed,
Because his compassions fail not.
[23]They are new every morning:
Great is thy faithfulness.
[24]"The LORD is my portion," saith my soul;
"Therefore will I hope in him."

[25]The LORD is good unto them that wait for him,
To the soul that seeketh him.
[26]It is good that a man should both hope and quietly wait
For the salvation of the LORD.

[27]It is good for a man that he bear the yoke in his youth.
[28]He sitteth alone and keepeth silence,
Because he hath borne it upon him.
[29]He putteth his mouth in the dust;
If so be there may be hope.
[30]He giveth his cheek to him that smiteth him:
He is filled full with reproach.

[31]For the Lord will not cast off for ever:
[32]But though he cause grief, yet will he have compassion
According to the multitude of his mercies.
[33]For he doth not afflict willingly
Nor grieve the children of men.

EZEKIEL

The Valley of Dry Bones

Chapter 37

THE HAND OF THE LORD WAS UPON ME, AND carried me out in the spirit of the LORD, and set me down in the midst of the valley which was full of bones, [2]and caused me to pass by them round about: and, behold, there were very many in the open valley; and, lo, they were very dry. [3]And he said unto me, "Son of man, can these bones live?"

And I answered, "O Lord GOD, thou knowest."

[4]Again he said unto me, "Prophesy upon these bones, and say unto them, 'O ye dry bones, hear the word of the LORD. [5]Thus saith the Lord GOD unto these bones; Behold, I will cause breath to enter into you, and ye shall live: [6]and I will lay sinews upon you, and will bring up flesh upon you, and cover you with skin, and put breath in you, and ye shall live; and ye shall know that I am the LORD.'"

[7]So I prophesied as I was commanded: and as I prophesied, there was a noise, and behold a shaking, and the bones came together, bone to his bone. [8]And when I beheld, lo, the sinews and the flesh came up upon them, and the skin covered them above: but there was no breath in them.

[9]Then said he unto me, "Prophesy unto the wind, prophesy, son of man, and say to the wind, 'Thus saith the Lord GOD; Come from the four winds, O breath, and breathe upon these slain, that they may live.'" [10]So I prophesied as he commanded me, and the breath came into them, and they lived, and stood up upon their feet, an exceeding great army.

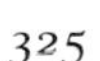

Chapter 37

THE VISION OF EZEKIEL *by Francisco Collantes*

Chapter 37

[11]Then he said unto me, "Son of man, these bones are the whole house of Israel: behold, they say, 'Our bones are dried, and our hope is lost: we are cut off for our parts.' [12]Therefore prophesy and say unto them, 'Thus saith the Lord GOD; Behold, O my people, I will open your graves, and cause you to come up out of your graves, and bring you into the land of Israel. [13]And ye shall know that I am the LORD, when I have opened your graves, O my people, and brought you up out of your graves, [14]and shall put my spirit in you, and ye shall live, and I shall place you in your own land: then shall ye know that I the LORD have spoken it, and performed it, saith the LORD.'"

Chapters & Verses
FROM
THE BOOK OF

DANIEL & JOEL AMOS & JONAH MICAH ZEPHANIAH ZECHARIAH & MALACHI

Daniel at Babylon

Chapter 1

In the third year of the reign of Jehoiakim king of Judah came Nebuchadnezzar king of Babylon unto Jerusalem, and besieged it. [2]And the Lord gave Jehoiakim king of Judah into his hand, with part of the vessels of the house of God: which he carried into the land of Shinar to the house of his god; and he brought the vessels into the treasure house of his god.

[3]And the king spake unto Ashpenaz the master of his eunuchs, that he should bring certain of the children of Israel, and of the king's seed, and of the princes; [4]children in whom was no blemish, but well favoured, and skilful in all wisdom, and cunning in knowledge, and understanding science, and such as had ability in them to stand in the king's palace, and whom they might teach the learning and the tongue of the Chaldeans. [5]And the king appointed them a daily provision of the king's meat, and of the wine which he drank: so nourishing them three years, that at the end thereof they might stand before the king.

[6]Now among these were of the children of Judah, Daniel, Hananiah, Mishael, and Azariah: [7]unto whom the prince of the eunuchs gave names: for he gave unto Daniel the name of Belteshazzar; and to Hananiah, of Shadrach; and to Mishael, of Meshach; and to Azariah, of Abednego.

[8]But Daniel purposed in his heart that he would not defile himself with the portion of the king's meat, nor with the wine which he drank: therefore he requested of the prince of the eunuchs that he might not defile himself. [9]Now God had brought Daniel into favour and tender love with the prince of the eunuchs. [10]And the prince of the eunuchs said unto Daniel, "I fear my lord the king, who hath appointed your meat and your drink: for why should he see your faces worse liking than the children which are of your sort? Then shall ye make me endanger my head to the king."

[11]Then said Daniel to Melzar, whom the prince of the eunuchs had set over Daniel, Hananiah, Mishael, and Azariah, [12]"Prove thy servants, I beseech thee, ten days;

Chapter 1

and let them give us pulse to eat, and water to drink. [13]Then let our countenances be looked upon before thee, and the countenance of the children that eat of the portion of the king's meat: and as thou seest, deal with thy servants." [14]So he consented to them in this matter, and proved them ten days.

[15]And at the end of ten days their countenances appeared fairer and fatter in flesh than all the children which did eat the portion of the king's meat. [16]Thus Melzar took away the portion of their meat, and the wine that they should drink; and gave them pulse.

[17]As for these four children, God gave them knowledge and skill in all learning and wisdom: and Daniel had understanding in all visions and dreams.

[18]Now at the end of the days that the king had said he should bring them in, then the prince of the eunuchs brought them in before Nebuchadnezzar. [19]And the king communed with them; and among them all was found none like Daniel, Hananiah, Mishael, and Azariah: therefore stood they before the king. [20]And in all matters of wisdom and understanding, that the king inquired of them, he found them ten times better than all the magicians and astrologers that were in all his realm.

Shadrach, Meshach and Abednego

Chapter 3

NEBUCHADNEZZAR THE KING MADE AN IMAGE of gold, whose height was threescore cubits, and the breadth thereof six cubits: he set it up in the plain of Dura, in the province of Babylon. [2]Then Nebuchadnezzar the king sent to gather together the princes, the governors, and the captains, the judges, the treasurers, the counsellors, the sheriffs, and all the rulers of the provinces, to come to the dedication of the image which Nebuchadnezzar the king had set up. [3]Then the princes, the governors, and captains, the judges, the treasurers, the counsellors, the sheriffs, and all the rulers of the provinces, were gathered together unto

the dedication of the image that Nebuchadnezzar the king had set up; and they stood before the image that Nebuchadnezzar had set up.

[4]Then an herald cried aloud, "To you it is commanded, O people, nations, and languages, [5]that at what time ye hear the sound of the cornet, flute, harp, sackbut, psaltery, dulcimer, and all kinds of musick, ye fall down and worship the golden image that Nebuchadnezzar the king hath set up: [6]and whoso falleth not down and worshippeth shall the same hour be cast into the midst of a burning fiery furnace."

[7]Therefore at that time, when all the people heard the sound of the cornet, flute, harp, sackbut, psaltery, and all kinds of musick, all the people, the nations, and the languages, fell down and worshipped the golden image that Nebuchadnezzar the king had set up.

[8]Wherefore at that time certain Chaldeans came near, and accused the Jews. [9]They spake and said to the king "Nebuchadnezzar, O king, live for ever. [10]Thou, O king, hast made a decree, that every man that shall hear the sound of the cornet, flute, harp, sackbut, psaltery, and dulcimer, and all kinds of musick, shall fall down and worship the golden image: [11]and whoso falleth not down and worshippeth, that he should be cast into the midst of a burning fiery furnace. [12]There are certain Jews whom thou hast set over the affairs of the province of Babylon, Shadrach, Meshach, and Abednego; these men, O king, have not regarded thee: they serve not thy gods, nor worship the golden image which thou hast set up."

[13]Then Nebuchadnezzar in his rage and fury commanded to bring Shadrach, Meshach, and Abednego. Then they brought these men before the king. [14]Nebuchadnezzar spake and said unto them, "Is it true, O Shadrach, Meshach, and Abednego, do not ye serve my gods, nor worship the golden image which I have set up? [15]Now if ye be ready that at what time ye hear the sound of the cornet, flute, harp, sackbut, psaltery, and dulcimer, and all kinds of musick, ye fall down and worship the image which I have made; well: but if ye worship not, ye shall be cast the same hour into the midst of a burning fiery furnace; and who is that God that shall deliver you out of my hands?"

[16]Shadrach, Meshach, and Abednego, answered and said to the king, "O Nebuchadnezzar, we are not careful to

SHADRACH, MICHAK AND ABEDNEGO *by Jacopo Bassano*

answer thee in this matter. [17]If it be so, our God whom we serve is able to deliver us from the burning fiery furnace, and he will deliver us out of thine hand, O king. [18]But if not, be it known unto thee, O king, that we will not serve thy gods, nor worship the golden image which thou hast set up."

[19]Then was Nebuchadnezzar full of fury, and the form of his visage was changed against Shadrach, Meshach, and Abednego: therefore he spake, and commanded that they should heat the furnace one seven times more than it was wont to be heated. [20]And he commanded the most mighty men that were in his army to bind Shadrach, Meshach, and Abednego, and to cast them into the burning fiery furnace. [21]Then these men were bound in their coats, their hosen, and their hats, and their other garments, and were cast into the midst of the burning fiery furnace. [22]Therefore because the king's commandment was urgent, and the furnace exceeding hot, the flame of the fire slew those men that took up Shadrach, Meshach, and Abednego. [23]And these three men, Shadrach, Meshach, and Abednego, fell down bound into the midst of the burning fiery furnace.

[24]Then Nebuchadnezzar the king was astonied, and rose up in haste, and spake, and said unto his counsellors, "Did not we cast three men bound into the midst of the fire?"

Chapter 3

They answered and said unto the king, "True, O king."
[25]He answered and said, "Lo, I see four men loose, walking in the midst of the fire, and they have no hurt; and the form of the fourth is like the Son of God."

[26]Then Nebuchadnezzar came near to the mouth of the burning fiery furnace, and spake, and said, "Shadrach, Meshach, and Abednego, ye servants of the most high God, come forth, and come hither."

Then Shadrach, Meshach, and Abednego, came forth of the midst of the fire. [27]And the princes, governors, and captains, and the king's counsellors, being gathered together, saw these men, upon whose bodies the fire had no power, nor was an hair of their head singed, neither were their coats changed, nor the smell of fire had passed on them.

[28]Then Nebuchadnezzar spake, and said, "Blessed be the God of Shadrach, Meshach, and Abednego, who hath sent his angel, and delivered his servants that trusted in him, and have changed the king's word, and yielded their bodies, that they might not serve nor worship any god, except their own God. [29]Therefore I make a decree, That every people, nation, and language, which speak any thing amiss against the God of Shadrach, Meshach, and Abednego, shall be cut in pieces, and their houses shall be made a dunghill: because there is no other God that can deliver after this sort."

[30]Then the king promoted Shadrach, Meshach, and Abednego, in the province of Babylon.

Belshazzar's Feast

Chapter 5

BELSHAZZAR THE KING MADE A GREAT FEAST TO A thousand of his lords, and drank wine before the thousand. [2]Belshazzar, whiles he tasted the wine, commanded to bring the golden and silver vessels which his father Nebuchadnezzar had taken out of the temple which was in Jerusalem; that the king, and his princes, his wives, and his concubines, might drink therein. [3]Then they brought the golden vessels that were taken out of the temple of the house of God which was at Jerusalem; and the king, and his princes, his wives, and his concubines, drank in them. [4]They drank wine, and praised the gods of gold, and of silver, of brass, of iron, of wood, and of stone.

[5]In the same hour came forth fingers of a man's hand, and wrote over against the candlestick upon the plaster of the wall of the king's palace: and the king saw the part of the hand that wrote. [6]Then the king's countenance was changed, and his thoughts troubled him, so that the joints of his loins were loosed, and his knees smote one against another.

[7]The king cried aloud to bring in the astrologers, the Chaldeans, and the soothsayers. And the king spake, and said to the wise men of Babylon, "Whosoever shall read this writing, and shew me the interpretation thereof, shall be clothed with scarlet, and have a chain of gold about his neck, and shall be the third ruler in the kingdom."

[8]Then came in all the king's wise men: but they could not read the writing, nor make known to the king the interpretation thereof. [9]Then was king Belshazzar greatly troubled, and his countenance was changed in him, and his lords were astonied.

[10]Now the queen, by reason of the words of the king and his lords, came into the banquet house: and the queen spake and said, "O king, live for ever: let not thy thoughts trouble thee, nor let thy countenance be changed: [11]there is a man in thy kingdom, in whom is the spirit of the holy gods; and in the days of thy father light and understanding and wisdom, like the wisdom of the gods, was found in him; whom the king Nebuchadnezzar thy father, the king, I say, thy father, made master of the magicians, astrologers, Chaldeans, and soothsayers; [12]forasmuch as an excellent spirit, and knowledge, and understanding, interpreting of dreams, and shewing of hard sentences, and dissolving of doubts, were found in the same Daniel, whom the king named Belteshazzar: now let Daniel be called, and he will shew the interpretation."

[13]Then was Daniel brought in before the king. And the king spake and said unto Daniel, "Art thou that Daniel, which art of the children of the captivity of Judah, whom the king my father brought out of Jewry? [14]I have even

BELSHAZZAR'S FEAST, *circle of Andrea Michieli*

heard of thee, that the spirit of the gods is in thee, and that light and understanding and excellent wisdom is found in thee. [15]And now the wise men, the astrologers, have been brought in before me, that they should read this writing, and make known unto me the interpretation thereof: but they could not shew the interpretation of the thing: [16]and I have heard of thee, that thou canst make interpretations, and dissolve doubts: now if thou canst read the writing, and make known to me the interpretation thereof, thou shalt be clothed with scarlet, and have a chain of gold about thy neck, and shalt be the third ruler in the kingdom."

[17]Then Daniel answered and said before the king, "Let thy gifts be to thyself, and give thy rewards to another; yet I will read the writing unto the king, and make known to him the interpretation.

[18]"O thou king, the most high God gave Nebuchadnezzar thy father a kingdom, and majesty, and glory, and honour: [19]and for the majesty that he gave him, all people, nations, and languages, trembled and feared before him: whom he would he slew; and whom he would he kept alive; and whom he would he set up; and whom he would he put down. [20]But when his heart was lifted up, and his mind

Chapter 5

hardened in pride, he was deposed from his kingly throne, and they took his glory from him: [21]and he was driven from the sons of men; and his heart was made like the beasts, and his dwelling was with the wild asses: they fed him with grass like oxen, and his body was wet with the dew of heaven; till he knew that the most high God ruled in the kingdom of men, and that he appointeth over it whomsoever he will.

[22]"And thou his son, O Belshazzar, hast not humbled thine heart, though thou knewest all this; [23]but hast lifted up thyself against the LORD of heaven; and they have brought the vessels of his house before thee, and thou, and thy lords, thy wives, and thy concubines, have drunk wine in them; and thou hast praised the gods of silver, and gold, of brass, iron, wood, and stone, which see not, nor hear, nor know: and the God in whose hand thy breath is, and whose are all thy ways, hast thou not glorified: [24]then was the part of the hand sent from him; and this writing was written.

[25]"And this is the writing that was written, MENE, MENE, TEKEL, UPHARSIN. [26]This is the interpretation of the thing: MENE; God hath numbered thy kingdom, and finished it. [27]TEKEL; Thou art weighed in the balances, and art found wanting. [28]PERES; Thy kingdom is divided, and given to the Medes and Persians."

[29]Then commanded Belshazzar, and they clothed Daniel with scarlet, and put a chain of gold about his neck, and made a proclamation concerning him, that he should be the third ruler in the kingdom.

[30]In that night was Belshazzar the king of the Chaldeans slain. [31]And Darius the Median took the kingdom, being about three score and two years old.

Daniel in the Den of Lions

Chapter 6

IT PLEASED DARIUS TO SET OVER THE KINGDOM AN hundred and twenty princes, which should be over the whole kingdom; [2]and over these three presidents; of whom Daniel was first: that the princes might give accounts unto them, and the king should have no damage. [3]Then this Daniel was preferred above the presidents and princes, because an excellent spirit was in him; and the king thought to set him over the whole realm. [4]Then the presidents and princes sought to find occasion against Daniel concerning the kingdom; but they could find none occasion nor fault; forasmuch as he was faithful, neither was there any error or fault found in him. [5]Then said these men, "We shall not find any occasion against this Daniel, except we find it against him concerning the law of his God."

[6]Then these presidents and princes assembled together to the king, and said thus unto him, "King Darius, live for ever. [7]All the presidents of the kingdom, the governors, and the princes, the counsellors, and the captains, have consulted together to establish a royal statute, and to make a firm decree, that whosoever shall ask a petition of any God or man for thirty days, save of thee, O king, he shall be cast into the den of lions. [8]Now, O king, establish the decree, and sign the writing, that it be not changed, according to the law of the Medes and Persians, which altereth not." [9]Wherefore king Darius signed the writing and the decree.

[10]Now when Daniel knew that the writing was signed, he went into his house; and his windows being open in his chamber toward Jerusalem, he kneeled upon his knees three times a day, and prayed, and gave thanks before his God, as he did aforetime. [11]Then these men assembled, and found Daniel praying and making supplication before his God. [12]Then they came near, and spake before the king concerning the king's decree; "Hast thou not signed a decree, that every man that shall ask a petition of any God or man within thirty days, save of thee, O king, shall be cast into the den of lions?"

The king answered and said, "The thing is true, according to the law of the Medes and Persians, which altereth not."

[13]Then answered they and said before the king, "That Daniel, which is of the children of the captivity of Judah, regardeth not thee, O king, nor the decree that thou hast signed, but maketh his petition three times a day." [14]Then the king, when he heard these words, was sore displeased with himself, and set his heart on Daniel to deliver him:

and he laboured till the going down of the sun to deliver him.

[15]Then these men assembled unto the king, and said unto the king, "Know, O king, that the law of the Medes and Persians is, that no decree nor statute which the king establisheth may be changed."

[16]Then the king commanded, and they brought Daniel, and cast him into the den of lions. Now the king spake and said unto Daniel, "Thy God whom thou servest continually, he will deliver thee."

[17]And a stone was brought, and laid upon the mouth of the den; and the king sealed it with his own signet, and with the signet of his lords; that the purpose might not be changed concerning Daniel. [18]Then the king went to his palace, and passed the night fasting: neither were instruments of musick brought before him: and his sleep went from him.

[19]Then the king arose very early in the morning, and went in haste unto the den of lions. [20]And when he came to the den, he cried with a lamentable voice unto Daniel: and the king spake and said to Daniel, "O Daniel, servant of the living God, is thy God, whom thou servest continually, able to deliver thee from the lions?"

[21]Then said Daniel unto the king, "O king, live for ever. [22]My God hath sent his angel, and hath shut the lions' mouths, that they have not hurt me: forasmuch as before him innocency was found in me; and also before thee, O king, have I done no hurt."

[23]Then was the king exceeding glad for him, and commanded that they should take Daniel up out of the den. So Daniel was taken up out of the den, and no manner of hurt was found upon him, because he believed in his God.

[24]And the king commanded, and they brought those men which had accused Daniel, and they cast them into the den of lions, them, their children, and their wives; and the lions had the mastery of them, and brake all their bones in pieces or ever they came at the bottom of the den.

[25]Then king Darius wrote unto all people, nations, and languages, that dwell in all the earth; "Peace be multiplied unto you. [26]I make a decree, that in every dominion of my kingdom men tremble and fear before the God of Daniel: for he is the living God, and stedfast for ever, and

Chapter 6

Daniel in the Lions' Den, *Illuminated manuscript*

Chapter 6

his kingdom that which shall not be destroyed, and his dominion shall be even unto the end. [27]He delivereth and rescueth, and he worketh signs and wonders in heaven and in earth, who hath delivered Daniel from the power of the lions."

[28]So this Daniel prospered in the reign of Darius, and in the reign of Cyrus the Persian.

JOEL

The Day of the Lord

Chapter 2

Fear not, O land;
Be glad and rejoice:
For the Lord will do great things.
[22]Be not afraid, ye beasts of the field:
For the pastures of the wilderness do spring,

For the tree beareth her fruit,
The fig tree and the vine do yield their strength.
[23]Be glad then, ye children of Zion,
And rejoice in the LORD your God:
For he hath given you the former rain moderately,
And he will cause to come down for you the rain,
The former rain, and the latter rain in the first month.
[24]And the floors shall be full of wheat,
And the vats shall overflow with wine and oil.

[25]And I will restore to you the years that the locust hath eaten,
The cankerworm, and the caterpillar, and the palmerworm,
My great army which I sent among you.
[26]And ye shall eat in plenty, and be satisfied,
And praise the name of the LORD your God,
That hath dealt wondrously with you:
And my people shall never be ashamed.
[27]And ye shall know that I am in the midst of Israel,
And that I am the LORD your God, and none else:
And my people shall never be ashamed.

[28]And it shall come to pass afterward,
That I will pour out my spirit upon all flesh;
And your sons and your daughters shall prophesy,
Your old men shall dream dreams,
Your young men shall see visions:
[29]And also upon the servants and upon the handmaids
In those days will I pour out my spirit.
[30]And I will shew wonders in the heavens and in the earth,
Blood, and fire, and pillars of smoke.
[31]The sun shall be turned into darkness,
And the moon into blood,
Before the great and the terrible day of the LORD come.
[32]And it shall come to pass,
That whosoever shall call on the name of the LORD shall be delivered:
For in mount Zion and in Jerusalem
Shall be deliverance, as the LORD hath said,
And in the remnant whom the LORD shall call.

AMOS

Justice, Not Sacrifice

Chapter 5

SEEK GOOD, AND NOT EVIL, THAT YE MAY LIVE:
And so the LORD, the God of hosts, shall be with you, as ye have spoken.
[15]Hate the evil, and love the good,
And establish judgment in the gate:
It may be that the LORD God of hosts will be gracious
Unto the remnant of Joseph.

[16]Therefore the LORD, the God of hosts, the Lord, saith thus;
"Wailing shall be in all the streets;
And they shall say in all the highways, 'Alas! alas!'
And they shall call the husbandman to mourning,
And such as are skilful of lamentation to wailing.
[17]And in all vineyards shall be wailing:
For I will pass through thee," saith the LORD.

[18]Woe unto you that desire the day of the LORD!
To what end is it for you?
The day of the LORD is darkness, and not light.
[19]As if a man did flee from a lion,
And a bear met him;
Or went into the house, and leaned his hand on the wall,
And a serpent bit him.
[20]Shall not the day of the LORD be darkness, and not light?
Even very dark, and no brightness in it?

[21]"I hate, I despise your feast days,
And I will not smell in your solemn assemblies.

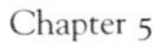
Chapter 5

[22]Though ye offer me burnt offerings and your meat offerings,
I will not accept them:
Neither will I regard
The peace offerings of your fat beasts.
[23]Take thou away from me the noise of thy songs;
For I will not hear the melody of thy viols.
[24]But let judgment run down as waters,
And righteousness as a mighty stream."

JONAH

Jonah

Chapter 1

Now the word of the Lord came unto Jonah the son of Amittai, saying, [2]"Arise, go to Nineveh, that great city, and cry against it; for their wickedness is come up before me."

[3]But Jonah rose up to flee unto Tarshish from the presence of the Lord, and went down to Joppa; and he found a ship going to Tarshish: so he paid the fare thereof, and went down into it, to go with them unto Tarshish from the presence of the Lord.

[4]But the Lord sent out a great wind into the sea, and there was a mighty tempest in the sea, so that the ship was like to be broken. [5]Then the mariners were afraid, and cried every man unto his god, and cast forth the wares that were in the ship into the sea, to lighten it of them.

But Jonah was gone down into the sides of the ship; and he lay and was fast asleep. [6]So the shipmaster came to him, and said unto him, "What meanest thou, O sleeper? Arise, call upon thy God, if so be that God will think upon us, that we perish not."

Chapter 1

[7]And they said every one to his fellow, "Come, and let us cast lots, that we may know for whose cause this evil is upon us." So they cast lots, and the lot fell upon Jonah.

[8]Then said they unto him, "Tell us, we pray thee, for whose cause this evil is upon us; What is thine occupation? and whence comest thou? What is thy country? and of what people art thou?"

[9]And he said unto them, "I am an Hebrew; and I fear the LORD, the God of heaven, which hath made the sea and the dry land."

[10]Then were the men exceedingly afraid, and said unto him, "Why hast thou done this?" For the men knew that he fled from the presence of the LORD, because he had told them.

[11]Then said they unto him, "What shall we do unto thee, that the sea may be calm unto us?" For the sea wrought, and was tempestuous.

[12]And he said unto them, "Take me up, and cast me forth into the sea; so shall the sea be calm unto you: for I know that for my sake this great tempest is upon you."

[13]Nevertheless the men rowed hard to bring it to the land; but they could not: for the sea wrought, and was tempestuous against them. [14]Wherefore they cried unto the LORD, and said, "We beseech thee, O LORD, we beseech thee, let us not perish for this man's life, and lay not upon us innocent blood: for thou, O LORD, hast done as it pleased thee." [15]So they took up Jonah, and cast him forth into the sea: and the sea ceased from her raging. [16]Then the men feared the LORD exceedingly, and offered a sacrifice unto the LORD, and made vows.

[17]Now the LORD had prepared a great fish to swallow up Jonah. And Jonah was in the belly of the fish three days and three nights.

Chapter 2

THEN JONAH PRAYED UNTO THE LORD HIS GOD OUT OF THE fish's belly, [2]and said.

"I cried by reason of mine affliction unto the LORD,
And he heard me;

JONAH BEFORE NINEVEH, *circle of Jan de Cock*

Chapter 2

Out of the belly of hell cried I,
And thou heardest my voice.
[3]For thou hadst cast me into the deep,
In the midst of the seas;
And the floods compassed me about:
All thy billows and thy waves passed over me.
[4]Then I said, 'I am cast out of thy sight;
Yet I will look again toward thy holy temple.'
[5]The waters compassed me about, even to the soul:
The depth closed me round about,
The weeds were wrapped about my head.
[6]I went down to the bottoms of the mountains;
The earth with her bars was about me for ever:
Yet hast thou brought up my life from corruption,
O LORD my God.

[7]"When my soul fainted within me I remembered the LORD:
And my prayer came in unto thee, into thine holy temple.
[8]They that observe lying vanities
Forsake their own mercy.

Chapter 2

[9]But I will sacrifice unto thee
With the voice of thanksgiving;
I will pay that that I have vowed.
Salvation is of the LORD."

[10]And the LORD spake unto the fish, and it vomited out Jonah upon the dry land.

Chapter 3

AND THE WORD OF THE LORD CAME UNTO JONAH THE second time, saying, [2]"Arise, go unto Nineveh, that great city, and preach unto it the preaching that I bid thee."

[3]So Jonah arose, and went unto Nineveh, according to the word of the LORD. Now Nineveh was an exceeding great city of three days' journey. [4]And Jonah began to enter into the city a day's journey, and he cried, and said, "Yet forty days, and Nineveh shall be overthrown." [5]So the people of Nineveh believed God, and proclaimed a fast, and put on sackcloth, from the greatest of them even to the least of them.

[6]For word came unto the king of Nineveh, and he arose from his throne, and he laid his robe from him, and covered him with sackcloth, and sat in ashes. [7]And he caused it to be proclaimed and published through Nineveh by the decree of the king and his nobles, saying, "Let neither man nor beast, herd nor flock, taste any thing: let them not feed, nor drink water: [8]but let man and beast be covered with sackcloth, and cry mightily unto God: yea, let them turn every one from his evil way, and from the violence that is in their hands. [9]Who can tell if God will turn and repent, and turn away from his fierce anger, that we perish not?"

[10]And God saw their works, that they turned from their evil way; and God repented of the evil, that he had said that he would do unto them; and he did it not.

MICAH

The Mountain of the Lord

Chapter 3

HEAR THIS, I PRAY YOU, YE HEADS OF THE
house of Jacob,
And princes of the house of Israel,
That abhor judgment,
And pervert all equity.
[10]They build up Zion with blood,
And Jerusalem with iniquity.
[11]The heads thereof judge for reward,
And the priests thereof teach for hire,
And the prophets thereof divine for money:
Yet will they lean upon the LORD, and say,
"Is not the LORD among us? None evil can come upon
us."
[12]Therefore shall Zion for your sake be plowed as a field,
And Jerusalem shall become heaps,
And the mountain of the house as the high places of the
forest.

Chapter 4

BUT IN THE LAST DAYS IT SHALL COME TO PASS,
That the mountain of the house of the LORD
Shall be established in the top of the mountains,
And it shall be exalted above the hills;
And people shall flow unto it.
[2]And many nations shall come, and say,
"Come, and let us go up to the mountain of the LORD,
And to the house of the God of Jacob;

Chapter 4

And he will teach us of his ways,
And we will walk in his paths":
For the law shall go forth of Zion,
And the word of the LORD from Jerusalem.
[3]And he shall judge among many people,
And rebuke strong nations afar off;
And they shall beat their swords into plowshares,
And their spears into pruninghooks:
Nation shall not lift up a sword against nation,
Neither shall they learn war any more.
[4]But they shall sit every man under his vine
And under his fig tree;
And none shall make them afraid:
For the mouth of the LORD of hosts hath spoken it.

[5]For all people will walk every one in the name of his god,
And we will walk in the name of the LORD our God for ever and ever.

A Promised Ruler from Bethlehem

Chapter 5

BUT THOU, BETHLEHEM EPHRATAH,
Though thou be little among the thousands of Judah,
Yet out of thee shall he come forth unto me
That is to be ruler in Israel;
Whose goings forth have been from of old,
From everlasting.
[3]Therefore will he give them up,
Until the time that she which travaileth hath brought forth:
Then the remnant of his brethren shall return
Unto the children of Israel.
[4]And he shall stand and feed in the strength of the LORD,
In the majesty of the name of the LORD his God;
And they shall abide: for now shall he be great
Unto the ends of the earth.

Chapter 5

THE ADORATION OF THE CHILD *by Fra Filippo Lippi*

A CALL FOR JUSTICE AND MERCY

Chapter 6

WHEREWITH SHALL I COME BEFORE THE LORD,
And bow myself before the high God?
Shall I come before him with burnt offerings,
With calves of a year old?
[7]Will the LORD be pleased with thousands of rams,
Or with ten thousands of rivers of oil?
Shall I give my firstborn for my transgression,
The fruit of my body for the sin of my soul?
[8]He hath shewed thee, O man, what is good;
And what doth the LORD require of thee,
But to do justly, and to love mercy,
And to walk humbly with thy God?

ZEPHANIAH

Jerusalem's Deliverance

Chapter 3

SING, O DAUGHTER OF ZION; SHOUT, O ISRAEL;
Be glad and rejoice with all the heart,
O daughter of Jerusalem.
15The Lord hath taken away thy judgments,
He hath cast out thine enemy:
The king of Israel, even the Lord, is in the midst of thee:
Thou shalt not see evil any more.
16In that day it shall be said to Jerusalem, "Fear thou not":
And to Zion, "Let not thine hands be slack.
17The Lord thy God in the midst of thee is mighty;
He will save, he will rejoice over thee with joy;
He will rest in his love,
He will joy over thee with singing."

18"I will gather them that are sorrowful for the solemn assembly,
Who are of thee, to whom the reproach of it was a burden.
19Behold, at that time I will undo all that afflict thee:
And I will save her that halteth,
And gather her that was driven out;
And I will get them praise and fame
In every land where they have been put to shame.
20At that time will I bring you again,
Even in the time that I gather you:
For I will make you a name and a praise
Among all people of the earth,
When I turn back your captivity
Before your eyes," saith the Lord.

ZECHARIAH

The Man Among the Myrtle Trees

Chapter 1

UPON THE FOUR AND TWENTIETH DAY OF THE eleventh month, which is the month Sebat, in the second year of Darius, came the word of the LORD unto Zechariah, the son of Berechiah, the son of Iddo the prophet, saying, [8]"I saw by night, and behold a man riding upon a red horse, and he stood among the myrtle trees that were in the bottom; and behind him were there red horses, speckled, and white.

[9]"Then said I, 'O my lord, what are these?'

"And the angel that talked with me said unto me, 'I will shew thee what these be.'

[10]"And the man that stood among the myrtle trees answered and said, 'These are they whom the LORD hath sent to walk to and fro through the earth.'

[11]"And they answered the angel of the LORD that stood among the myrtle trees, and said, 'We have walked to and fro through the earth, and, behold, all the earth sitteth still, and is at rest.'

[12]"Then the angel of the LORD answered and said, 'O LORD of hosts, how long wilt thou not have mercy on Jerusalem and on the cities of Judah, against which thou hast had indignation these threescore and ten years?' [13]And the LORD answered the angel that talked with me with good words and comfortable words.

[14]"So the angel that communed with me said unto me, 'Cry thou, saying, Thus saith the LORD of hosts; "I am jealous for Jerusalem and for Zion with a great jealousy.

Chapter 1

[15]And I am very sore displeased with the heathen that are at ease: for I was but a little displeased, and they helped forward the affliction."

[16]"'Therefore thus saith the LORD; "I am returned to Jerusalem with mercies: my house shall be built in it," saith the LORD of hosts, "and a line shall be stretched forth upon Jerusalem."

[17]"'Cry yet, saying, Thus saith the LORD of hosts; "My cities through prosperity shall yet be spread abroad; and the LORD shall yet comfort Zion, and shall yet choose Jerusalem."'"

THE COMING OF ZION'S KING

Chapter 9

REJOICE GREATLY, O DAUGHTER OF ZION;
Shout, O daughter of Jerusalem:
Behold, thy king cometh unto thee:
He is just, and having salvation;
Lowly, and riding upon an ass,
And upon a colt the foal of an ass.
[10]And I will cut off the chariot from Ephraim,
And the horse from Jerusalem,
And the battle bow shall be cut off:
And he shall speak peace unto the heathen:
And his dominion shall be from sea even to sea,
And from the river even to the ends of the earth.

A DAY OF MOURNING

Chapter 12

AND I WILL POUR UPON THE HOUSE OF DAVID, and upon the inhabitants of Jerusalem, the spirit of grace and of supplications: and they shall look upon me whom they have pierced, and they shall mourn for him, as one mourneth for his only son, and shall be in bitterness for him, as one that is in bitterness for his firstborn. [11]In

Chapter 12

that day shall there be a great mourning in Jerusalem, as the mourning of Hadadrimmon in the valley of Megiddon. [12]And the land shall mourn, every family apart; the family of the house of David apart, and their wives apart; the family of the house of Nathan apart, and their wives apart; [13]the family of the house of Levi apart, and their wives apart; the family of Shimei apart, and their wives apart; [14]all the families that remain, every family apart, and their wives apart.

Chapter 13

In that day there shall be a fountain opened to the house of David and to the inhabitants of Jerusalem for sin and for uncleanness.

MALACHI

The Day of Judgment

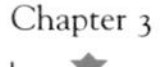

Chapter 3

"Behold, I will send my messenger, and he shall prepare the way before me: and the Lord, whom ye seek, shall suddenly come to his temple, even the messenger of the covenant, whom ye delight in: behold, he shall come," saith the Lord of hosts.

[2]But who may abide the day of his coming? And who shall stand when he appeareth? For he is like a refiner's fire, and like fuller's soap: [3]and he shall sit as a refiner and purifier of silver: and he shall purify the sons of Levi, and purge them as gold and silver, that they may offer unto the Lord

Chapter 3

an offering in righteousness. [4]Then shall the offering of Judah and Jerusalem be pleasant unto the Lord, as in the days of old, and as in former years . . .

Chapter 4

"For, behold, the day cometh, that shall burn as an oven; and all the proud, yea, and all that do wickedly, shall be stubble: and the day that cometh shall burn them up," saith the Lord of hosts, "that it shall leave them neither root nor branch. [2]But unto you that fear my name shall the Sun of righteousness arise with healing in his wings; and ye shall go forth, and grow up as calves of the stall. [3]And ye shall tread down the wicked; for they shall be ashes under the soles of your feet in the day that I shall do this," saith the Lord of hosts.

[4]"Remember ye the law of Moses my servant, which I commanded unto him in Horeb for all Israel, with the statutes and judgments.

[5]"Behold, I will send you Elijah the prophet before the coming of the great and dreadful day of the Lord: [6]and he shall turn the heart of the fathers to the children, and the heart of the children to their fathers, lest I come and smite the earth with a curse."

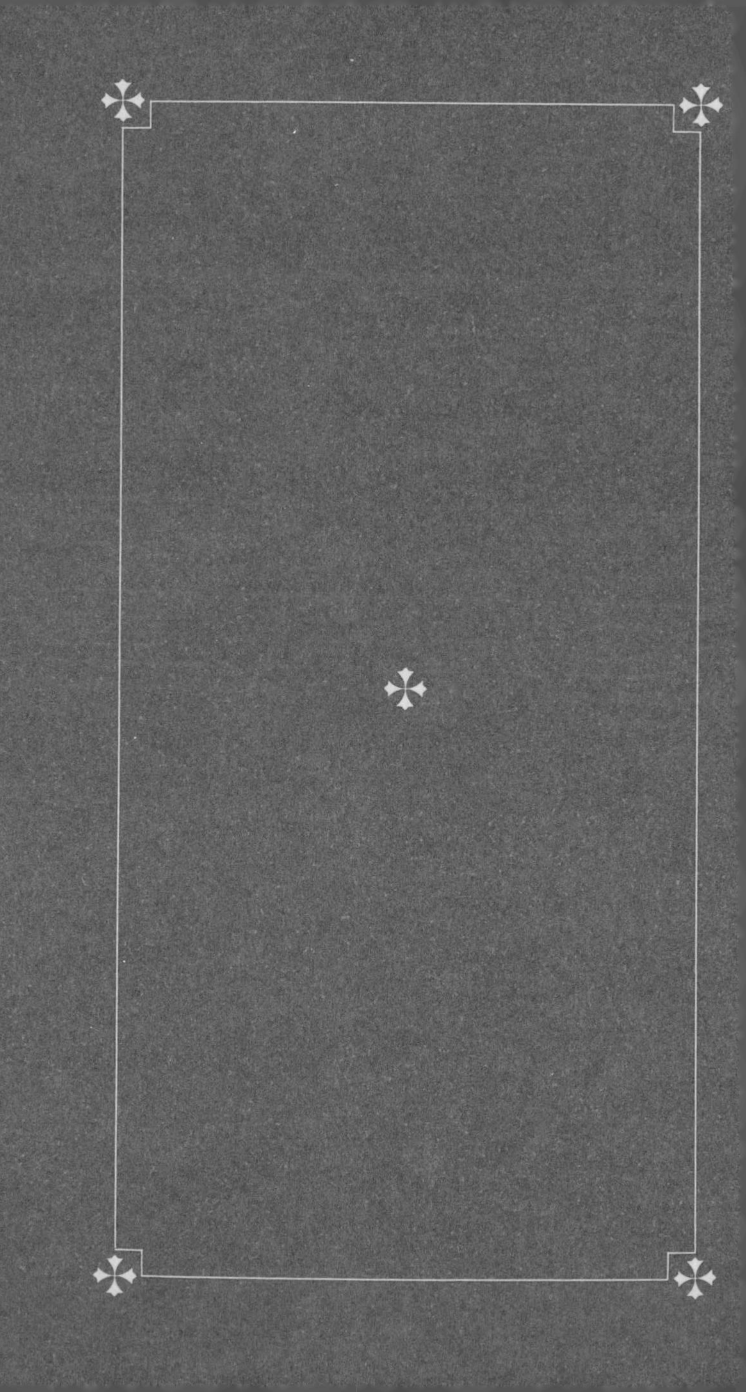